CULTURES
IN CONFLICT
THE ARAB-ISRAELI
CONFLICT

**Recent Titles in
The Greenwood Press Cultures in Conflict Series**

Cultures in Conflict—The American Civil War
Steven E. Woodworth

CULTURES IN CONFLICT
THE ARAB-ISRAELI CONFLICT

Calvin Goldscheider

The Greenwood Press Cultures in Conflict Series

GREENWOOD PRESS
Westport, Connecticut • London

Library of Congress Cataloging-in-Publication Data

Goldscheider, Calvin.
    Cultures in conflict : the Arab-Israeli conflict / Calvin Goldscheider.
      p. cm.—(The Greenwood Press Cultures in Conflict
    series, ISSN 1526-0690)
    Includes bibliographical references (p.) and index.
    ISBN 0-313-30722-9 (alk. paper)
    1. Arab-Israeli conflict. 2. Israel—Emigration and immigration. 3. Israel—
Ethnic relations. 4. Palestinian Arabs—Israel. 5. Refugees, Arab. I. Title.
DS119.7G642 2002
305.8'0095694—dc21   00-064052

British Library Cataloguing in Publication Data is available.

Copyright © 2002 Calvin Goldscheider

All rights reserved. No portion of this book may be
reproduced, by any process or technique, without
the express written consent of the publisher.

Library of Congress Catalog Card Number: 00-064052
ISBN: 0-313-30722-9
ISSN: 1526-0690

First published in 2002

Greenwood Press, 88 Post Road West, Westport, CT 06881
An imprint of Greenwood Publishing Group, Inc.
www.greenwood.com

Printed in the United States of America

The paper used in this book complies with the
Permanent Paper Standard issued by the National
Information Standards Organization (Z39.48-1984).

10 9 8 7 6 5 4 3 2

Copyright Acknowledgments

The author and publisher gratefully acknowledge permission for use of the following material:

From REQUIEM FOR NA'AMAN by Benjamin Tammuz, translated by Mildred Budny & Yehuda Saffran, copyright © 1982 by Benjamin Tammuz. Used by permission of Dutton Signet, a division of Penguin Putnam Inc.

Excerpts from Illana Sugbaker Messika, "Memories of an Indian Upbringing" in Ammiel Alcalay, *Keys to the Garden* (New Israel Writing, 1999). Courtesy of City Lights Bookstore.

From THE STRUGGLE FOR PEACE: ISRAELIS AND PALESTINIANS edited by Elizabeth Warnock Fernea and Mary Evelyn Hocking, Copyright © 1992. By permission of the University of Texas Press.

Excerpts from Mamdouh Nofal, "Reflections on al-Nakba." © by Institute for Palestine Studies. Reprinted from *Journal of Palestine Studies* vol. 28, no. 1, Issue Autumn 1998, pp. 5–35, by permission.

Reprinted with the permission of The Free Press, a Division of Simon & Schuster, Inc., from EXILE'S RETURN: The Making of a Palestinian-American by Fawaz Turki. Copyright © 1994 by Fawaz Turki.

From *Homeland: Oral Histories of Palestine and Palestinians*, published by Interlink Books, an imprint of Interlink Publishing Group, Inc. copyright © Staughton Lynd, Sam Bahour and Alice Lynd 1994.

Excerpt from STILL SMALL VOICES, copyright © 1989 by John and Janet Wallach, reprinted by permission of Harcourt, Inc.

Every reasonable effort has been made to trace the owners of copyright materials in this book, but in some instances this has proven impossible. The author and publisher will be glad to receive information leading to more complete acknowledgments in subsequent printings of the book and in the meantime extend their apologies for any omissions.

To
Atalya
(born July 23, 2000)
and her parents
Avigaiyil and Peter

Contents

Preface	xi
Acknowledgments	xv
An Arab-Israeli Timeline	xvii

Part I Historical and Sociological Contexts

Chapter 1	Historical Overview	3
Chapter 2	The State of Israel and the Arab-Israeli Conflict	13
Chapter 3	Arab Israelis: Dependency and Distinctiveness	59
Chapter 4	The Palestinian and Jewish Diasporas	87

Part II Documents

Chapter 5	Ethnic Clashes among Jewish Immigrants	123
Chapter 6	Voices of Israeli Jews	139
Chapter 7	Voices of the Palestinians	147
Chapter 8	Issues of Identity	163

Part III Reflecting

Chapter 9　Ideas for Exploration　195

　　　　　　Appendix: Official Documents　199

　　　　　　Annotated Bibliography　219

　　　　　　Index　225

Preface

The conflicts between the State of Israel and the Arabs are deeply embedded in history, politics, economic conditions, and culture. The details of the conflict are radically different at the beginning of the twenty-first century than was the case a century earlier. The areas now referred to as the states of Israel and Jordan were then called Palestine, and included as well the territory in the nascent Palestinian state. In 1900 fewer than 50,000 Jews were living in Palestine, a rather unattractive territory under the control of the Ottoman Empire. The Jewish population was a small minority with rich cultural and historical roots from Biblical times but little demographic or political presence in the area. Agriculture was the dominant economic activity in this part of the world; sickness and death at young ages were the dominant concerns of families and clans. Poor roads and a low level of technology prevented extensive communication outside of small neighborhoods and regions.

The major events of the twentieth century transformed the lives of everyone in the region. Among the most important of these were the devastation of the Jewish population of Eastern and Western Europe during the Holocaust, the mass immigration of Jews to British-controlled Palestine and subsequently to the newly established state of Israel, and the exodus of hundreds of thousands of Arab residents of Palestine during Israel's struggle for independence. The Arab-Israeli conflict has manifested itself directly and most conspicuously in the several wars fought between the State of Israel and the Arab countries, the internal terrorists activities carried out against Israel, the Israeli military presence in Palestinian territories controlled by Israel, and the residential segregation of the Israeli-Arab population. The conflict penetrates to the very core of Arab and Israeli hopes and dreams, their culture and ideology, and their daily lives.

Clearly much has changed over the last century, but some of the fundamental issues associated with the Arab-Israeli conflict have remained the same. This book outlines both the changes and the continuities. To understand the cultural conflicts between Arabs and Israelis it is necessary to examine how people reacted to these radical transformations. How have Arabs and Jews, the current and former residents of the country called Israel, reacted to the events of the last century? How do these communities interpret these events and their lives within the context of these radical changes? How do these different interpretations influence the conflicts between the communities and shape their political and social discourse?

This book addresses these questions by focusing on several key themes that have shaped the conflict. These include the changing perspectives on nation building of these communities, the critical population and economic development issues, and the ethnic clashes that have been shaped by these broad development changes. Underlying these themes are the giant issues of politics, power, and control. The primary focus of the analysis presented in this volume is how the conflict is reflected in the lives of the people living in the area. What do they think about themselves and each other? How do they interpret the grand events and the larger context? In the final judgment, it is the people who must overcome the history and the generations of conflict to get on with their lives. It is my view that Jews and Arabs share the fundamental goals of improving their economic conditions and those of their children and living their lives in harmony with the emerging society. Most people everywhere want the same thing for themselves and their families: a good home, a reasonable income, safety, and peaceful relations with family and neighbors. How they define these things will vary enormously. That is both the challenge and the hope of the future. While ideology and culture play a role in shaping these elementary goals, they always operate in the context of social, political, and economic relationships. If history is any guide, ideology and culture will change in the emerging contexts of societies and family life. Martyrs and extremists are nurtured by ideology and fueled by poverty, desperation, and hopelessness.

Preface

The complexity of the Arab-Israeli conflict and the relationships between these communities are outlined by means of a brief overview of the historical context. It is first necessary to get straight the complex outline of the events and characters involved before proceeding to an understanding of the social side of group conflict. Several basic themes are reviewed to help us understand the emergence of the conflict and where the potential seeds of its resolution lie. This requires that we review the patterns of immigration, Zionism, and ethnic differences within the Jewish population and the differences between Arabs living in the State of Israel and the Palestinians who live outside of the state but under the administrative control of the state. Internal issues within the State of Israel are then placed in the contexts of both the Jewish and Palestinian diasporas.

I have focused on Jewish immigration and ethnic conflict as rays of the prism through which we can better view the conflict. Jews and Arabs inside and outside of the State of Israel have viewed the conflict in these terms. These are not the only themes that one can use, and other parts of the picture can be seen through other rays of the prism. I think that the peopling of Palestine/Israel and ethnic differences are critical, but some may regard politics and power, religion and ideology, and global events as the basis. I have incorporated some of that thinking in the analysis. I am convinced that there are multiple paths to understanding the issues and, when taken together, they all lead to the same sets of understanding in our complex and multifaceted world.

Throughout, I use some human vignettes to illustrate how people feel and shed light on their values, goals, and concerns to illuminate how these grand political processes are articulated in the daily lives of people. These vignettes and the selections that follow the analysis in the book give voice to the players in the Arab-Israeli conflict. It is my hope that the reader can hear the voices of the participants directly and can thereby appreciate the depths of their feeling and learn from them. In these selections, the powerful impact of the transition of Arabs from majority to minority group in Israel and to refugee status outside of Israel is evident. The transition of Jews from minority to majority group is also highlighted, as are the changes among Jews from first-generation immigrants to native-born Israelis of different ethnic origins.

Two sets of conflicts emerge from these selections: (1) the Jewish Israeli experiences of immigration and the relationships between the generations and among diverse ethnic groups and (2) the displacement and powerlessness of Palestinians living in and outside of the Jewish state. The voices of the Jewish Israelis and the Palestinians are clear and distinctive especially when they reflect on the same events and similar experiences in radically different ways. Often the voices sound angry and frustrated. Reading these selections should remind us of the fundamental principle of social science: *the first step to resolve conflict is to understand the position of the other by placing yourself in that role*. As the analysis and the selections suggest, this is an extraordinarily difficult but essential step if the conflict is to move toward resolution.

The book ends with a series of ideas for further exploration and some official documents that provide the formal context of the Arab-Israeli conflict. The materials were selected from a very wide range of available documents. They are intended to be both provocative and interesting so that the reader can reflect on the issues, appreciate the view of the other, and find ways to pursue the study of additional materials.

Acknowledgments

Barbara Rader, executive editor at Greenwood Press, suggested the idea behind this book. She encouraged me to write directly about the Arab-Israeli conflict for a wider audience. I am grateful for her support and for her critical and helpful comments on earlier drafts of the book. I have built on the research that I have carried out over the last three decades focusing on Israeli society as a Professor of Demography and Sociology at the Hebrew University in Jerusalem and as Professor of Sociology and Judaic Studies at Brown University. In my research and teaching, I have studied and taught about the emergence of Israeli society in its historical and cultural contexts, always by necessity touching on the central issues of the Arab-Israeli conflict. I have learned much from the hundreds of students who have studied with me and the wonderful colleagues I have had in Israel and in the United States. They are the invisible contributors to this book. I am grateful to all of them for enhancing my understanding of the Arab-Israeli conflict. I cannot imagine that they would all agree with my interpretations and analysis—I know that I have not always agreed with them—but they have made me sharpen my views so at least I can be clear and systematic.

As are others, I am biased in my views of the conflict by the commitments and understandings that have shaped my own life and experiences, academically and personally. As an Israeli and an American citizen, having lived and taught in Jerusalem for fifteen years, I know something of the daily lives of Israelis. My understandings reflect my perspective as a social scientist even more than they do my personal experiences. They guide the selection of what themes I focus on and how I have organized the materials. I am committed, passionately and ideologically, to work toward the resolution of the conflict that has resulted in the pain and deaths to thousands of friends and neighbors on both sides. A final bias: I am committed also to the principle that education, understanding, and reason will bring about conflict resolution. It is a naïve position but it sustains me.

I am indebted beyond words to Fran Goldscheider who shares my life and my dreams, and who knows how to resolve conflict. I dedicate this book to my granddaughter, Atalya, and her parents, Avigaiyil and Peter, who teach me every day the meanings of culture and commitment. May Atalya grow up in a world of greater harmony and tolerance.

My daughter Avigaiyil took the photographs included in this book marked 1991 and together with her husband Peter took those marked 1999. I am grateful that they shared a few with me and permitted me to share them with others. I have not burdened the reader with extensive footnotes to document the specific sources used. They are available on request; most are contained in the annotated bibliography. All of the statistical data have been abstracted from official publications of the Central Bureau of Statistics, Israel.

An Arab-Israeli Timeline

1882–1903
First wave of modern Jewish immigration to Palestine (first Aliya); 25,000 Eastern European immigrants arrive.

1897
First Zionist Congress held in Basel, Switzerland, and organized by Theodor Herzl, formally declares aim of establishing national Jewish homeland in the Land of Israel.

1899–1902
Tensions between Arabs and Jews in Palestine follow large Jewish land purchases in the Tiberias region.

1904–1914
Second Aliya: 40–50,000 Jewish immigrants arrive from Eastern Europe and Russia; Jews demand exclusive use of Jewish labor in Jewish colonies and in Zionist-funded enterprises.

1908
First Palestinian newspaper appears in Haifa, *al-Karmil*, with a major aim of fighting against land transfers from Arab to Jewish ownership; tensions between Arabs and Jews continue.

1915–1916
Correspondence between the British high commissioner in Egypt (Henry McMahon) and Sharif Hussein of Mecca leads to an agreement between the British government and the Arabs to establish an Arab kingdom in exchange for an Arab military revolt against the Ottomans; Arabs believe the kingdom includes Palestine.

1917
Balfour Declaration is presented to the Jewish community and Zionist organization, declaring that Great Britain supports the creation of a "national home" for the Jews in Palestine; Ottoman forces in Jerusalem surrender to British military forces (see chapter 3).

1918
All of Palestine is occupied by British forces. Arabs reject the Balfour Declaration at the General Arab Congress in Damascus and consider Palestine part of southern Syria.

1919–1923
Third Aliya: 35,000 Jewish immigrants arrive, mostly from Poland and Russia.

1920
San Remo Peace Conference assigns Britain the mandate over Palestine; first Palestinian National Congress meets in Haifa and establishes the Arab Executive Committee which is recognized by Britain as representing the Arab community in Palestine (until 1935); Arabs demand recognition of Palestinian independence and an immediate halt to Jewish immigration and land acquisition.

1921
Riots occur in Jaffa; Arabs kill forty-six Jews; British attribute the disturbance to Arab concern over Jewish immigration.

1922
A British white paper emphasizes that only part of Palestine is considered the Jewish national home; excludes eastern Palestine (Transjordan) from the mandate.

1923
League of Nations internationally legitimates the British mandate over Palestine and directs Britain to encourage "close settlement of Jews upon the land."

1924–1928
Fourth Aliya: 67,000 immigrants arrive, half of them middle-class Jews from Poland.

1929
Countrywide Arab riots occur against Jews, including the massacre of members of the old non-Zionist community of Hebron.

1929–1939
Fifth Aliya: 250,000 Jews immigrate to Palestine, one quarter of them refugees from Nazi Germany—first major segment of immigrants from Central Europe.

1933
Some Palestinian leaders meet with David Ben-Gurion, chair of the Jewish Agency (the Jewish governing body in Palestine) in an attempt to find a solution to the contrasting demands of the Zionist and Arab nationalist movements; Arab Executive Committee declares a general strike and mass demonstrations against British rule, demanding independence and a halt to Jewish immigration and land acquisition.

1936
Arab political parties and organizations merge into the Arab Higher Committee; commercial strikes and waves of violence follow.

1937
The Peel Commission, established by Britain, publishes its report recommending the partition of Palestine into a Jewish state and an Arab state incorporated into Transjordan. Both parties reject the proposal. More disturbances occur, and the conflict escalates.

1938
Peel Commission partition proposal is declared impractical by new commission set up by Great Britain.

1939
Great Britain issues a new white paper that curtails Jewish immigration and land purchases in Palestine after a ten-year period, proposes an independent unitary Arab-ruled Palestinian state and annual Jewish immigration of 15,000; de facto withdrawal of Britain from the Balfour Declaration. New policy is approved by British House of Commons.

1945
World War II ends; hundreds of thousands of Jewish survivors of the Nazi Holocaust are stateless refugees.

1945–1948
75,000 mostly illegal Jewish immigrants arrive in Palestine; organized Jewish underground operations are conducted against British targets.

1947
United Nations adopts Resolution 181, which recommends the partition of Palestine into an Arab state (Golan Heights to Syria, West Bank and eastern Jerusalem to Jordan, Gaza Strip to Egypt) and a Jewish state in the remainder, along with the internationalization of Jerusalem. Palestinians and Arab states reject partition; Zionists accept.

1948
Major fighting occurs within Palestine; British mandate ends in May; Jewish state is established on May 14. War of Independence begins on May 15 with invasion of Israel by Egypt, Jordan, Syria, and Lebanon. Most Arab villages are evacuated, Arab refugee camps are formed in May and June

in Gaza and Lebanon; other military action results in Palestinians fleeing to territories held by Arab legion.

1949
Israel, Transjordan, Lebanon, and Syria sign armistice agreements. Israel holds about 80 percent of the total territories of western Palestine; the West Bank is under Transjordan rule; the Gaza Strip is under Egyptian occupation. First Knesset, the parliament of Israel, convenes with David Ben Gurion as prime minister; armistice is signed with neighboring Arab countries; Jerusalem is divided with western half to Israel and eastern half to Jordan. First census of the State of Israel counts a total Jewish population of 650,000 and 150,000 Arab residents in the new state. Arabs in Israel are in the minority.

1948–1951
Mass immigration occurs in the new State of Israel; 650,000 Jews arrive, first from Europe, then from Jewish communities in Asia and North Africa.

1950
Knesset passes Law of Return granting all Jews in the world the right to immigrate to Israel; Israel imposes military government on most Israeli Arabs after residential displacement and community reorganization; West Bank is formally annexed to Jordan.

1956
Suez crises; Egypt nationalizes Suez Canal, closing it to Israeli shipping. Israel invades Gaza Strip and most of the Sinai Desert, then withdraws under American pressure.

1964
The first Palestinian National Council convenes and adopts Palestine National Charter as the basic constitution of the Palestine Liberation Organization (PLO).

1966
The Israeli military government, which had ruled Israeli Arabs since 1948, is abolished.

1967
Six-Day War is fought. Israel launches preemptive strike against Egypt, Syria, and Jordan and gains control over the Sinai Peninsula, the Gaza Strip, the Golan Heights, and the West Bank including Jerusalem. Jerusalem is united under Israeli jurisdiction. The entire territory of the former Palestine mandate comes under Israeli control, including 650,000 Palestinians of the West Bank and eastern Jerusalem and 356,000 in the Gaza Strip. Eastern Jerusalem is annexed to Israel, and the rest of the captured territories, including the Golan Heights and the Sinai Desert, are put under

military administration. UN resolution 242 passes, calling for Israeli withdrawal from territories.

1968

First Israeli Jewish settlement is established on the West Bank. It is supported by the Labor-led government of Israel.

1969

Yassar Arafat is nominated as the chair of the ruling executive committee of the Palestine National Council.

1973

October (Yom Kippur) War is fought. Syria and Egypt attack Israeli forces on the Golan Heights and along the Suez Canal. After initial losses, Israel closes in on Damascus and crosses the Suez Canal. Gush Emunim, a Jewish settler movement, is formed on the West Bank.

1974

Disengagement agreements occur between Israel and Egypt and Syria after intense American intervention; Arab summit recognizes PLO as the sole legitimate representative of the Palestinian people; Yassar Arafat addresses the United Nations General Assembly in New York City.

1976

Municipal elections in the West Bank lead to PLO supporters being swept into office; first Land Day includes a general strike and protests of Israeli Arabs against land appropriations (declared a national holiday in 1992).

1977

Nationalist, right-wing Likud party comes to power in Israel; Likud-led coalition takes over Knesset for first time under Prime Minister Menachem Begin, ending Labor party dominance. Jewish settlements on West Bank accelerate. Egyptian President Anwar Sadat visits Jerusalem and speaks in the Knesset.

1978

Israel invades Southern Lebanon to root out Palestinian guerillas and occupies a strip constructed as a buffer zone held by locally supported militia. A United Nations buffer zone is created. At Camp David, under the auspices of U.S. President Jimmy Carter, President Anwar Sadat and Prime Minister Menachem Begin agree to conclude a peace treaty within three months. Israel recognizes "the legitimate rights of the Palestinians" and commits to grant Palestinians full autonomy after a transitional period of five years. The proposal is rejected by Palestinians. Israel commits to withdraw from the Sinai Desert in exchange for peace with Egypt.

1979

Israel Knesset approves Israel-Egypt peace treaty.

1980
Israel begins to conduct a phased withdrawal from Sinai, but invades Lebanon a second time after a series of terrorist attacks are made on northern Israel.

1981
The Knesset votes for the annexation of the Golan Heights.

1982
Israel invades Lebanon again.

1983
Menachem Begin resigns as prime minister. Israeli troops are entrenched in Southern Lebanon.

1984
The number of Jewish settlers on the West Bank reaches 30,000.

1987
A general Palestinian popular uprising, the *intifada*, breaks out in Gaza and spreads to the West Bank.

1991
Massive Jewish immigration from the Soviet Union to Israel begins and culminates in 800,000 Russian immigrants arriving in Israel in the following eight years.

1992
Labor party returns to power in Israel and promises to implement Palestinian autonomy within a year.

1993
Mutual recognition by Israel and the PLO follows negotiations in Norway. Yassar Arafat, chairman of the PLO, and Yitzhak Rabin, prime minister of Israel, shake hands publicly on the lawn of the White House in Washington, D.C.

1995
Yitzhak Rabin, the Labor party leader and prime minister, is assassinated by a Jewish extreme nationalist.

1996
Benjamin Netanyahu of the Likud party is elected prime minister. The Likud regains power.

1999
Ehud Barak (of the Labor party) is elected prime minister of Israel, defeating Benjamin Netanyahu. The Labor party again organizes the coalition government of Israel.

2000
Ehud Barak, the prime minister of Israel, and Farouk al-Shara, the foreign

minister of Syria, meet in Washington under the auspices of U.S. President Bill Clinton to discuss the future of the Golan Heights and related issues in the Syria-Israel conflict. Israel withdraws its troops from its self-defined security zone in Southern Lebanon.

Intensive peace negotiations between Ehud Barak and Yasser Arafat take place at Camp David under the auspices of U.S. President Bill Clinton. Issues associated with the control of Jerusalem are discussed openly for the first time. The talks fail to bring about a peace agreement. Tensions and skirmishes increase in October, with serious threats of continued fighting between Palestinians and Israelis. The peace talks are put on hold until the fighting is controlled.

2001

Ariel Sharon, head of the Likud (right wing nationalist) party decisively defeated Ehud Barak (of the Labor party) in direct elections for the Prime Minister position in Israel. The cycle of violence between Israelis and Palestinians continues on an almost daily basis as the death toll mounts; prospects for peace and negotiations about peace have become more remote. The American government, with the support of President George W. Bush, proposes a cease-fire plan (not a peace settlement) between the combatants. Many issues continue to divide the parties. The primary arenas of the immediate conflict remain the presence of settlers and the Israeli military in the areas of the West Bank and Gaza populated by Palestinians, and the continued attacks by Palestinians within Israel and on Jewish settlers and the military in the territories occupied and administered by Israel. Fundamental questions of control over territories and people remain unresolved between Palestinians and Israelis. There are also unresolved disagreements about the political and administrative status of Jerusalem and the potential rights of return of Palestinian refugees, former residents of pre-state Israel and their children. Both parties have postponed discussions over the larger principled issues until there is an agreed adherence to a cease-fire. The rhetoric of violence, defense, anger, frustration, revenge and hostility on all sides have replaced attempts to discuss areas of mutual interests, compromise and trust.

PART I

HISTORICAL AND SOCIOLOGICAL CONTEXTS

Chapter 1

Historical Overview

A historical overview of the Arab-Israeli conflict can be divided into two time periods. The first relates to events that were the foundation and origins of the conflict. This period extends from the end of the nineteenth century through the end of the British mandate period in Palestine in 1948. The second period relates to events in the post-1948 period when the State of Israel was established and began to develop as a Jewish state. The conflict was transformed as wars and policies changed the relationships between Jewish and Arab Israelis and between the State of Israel and the Palestinians living outside of the state.

What events triggered the conflict and hostilities between these two peoples? At the end of the nineteenth century, in 1880, fewer than 25,000 Jews resided in Palestine and owned less than twenty-five square kilometers of land. In the decades before this period, Jewish immigration and settlement in Palestine consisted of small groups, families, and individuals who moved to the Holy Land, mainly for religious reasons. Most Jews were concentrated in the four "holy cities" of Jerusalem, Hebron, Tiberias, and Safed. These settlements were, in turn, divided into subcommunities according to country of origin. Moneys collected from Jewish communities in their home countries generally sustained these Jewish settlers. They interacted infrequently with Christian and Muslim communities, did not diversify occupationally and economically, and tended to be isolated politically and culturally. In large part, they represented the transplanted cultures and social institutions of their communities of origin. They were not the foundation for the socioeconomic and political development of the emergent Jewish community in Palestine; nor were they the source of the Arab-Jewish conflict.

Toward the end of the nineteenth century, there was a dramatic shift in the volume and composition of Jewish immigration to Palestine. Organized groups of Jewish revolutionary immigrants appeared. These new Jewish immigrants were secular nationalists. They were not responding to the "pull" of religious values, economic opportunities, or the political environment of the territory administered as part of the Ottoman Empire. The social, political, and economic conditions of Palestine at the time were clearly not attractive for immigration. The immigrants were a select, small group of pioneers among the hundreds of thousands of Jews who were leaving Eastern Europe at the end of the nineteenth century. Most were going west to the United States, but a small minority of those on the move immigrated to Palestine. Relatively well educated, secular, urban residents, they were entering a different type of community, with the goal of working in agriculture to transform barren wastelands into new types of communities. Their dream was to create the basis for a new Jewish society.

Between 1880 and 1903, an estimated 25,000 Jewish immigrants arrived, doubling the size of the small Jewish settlements in Palestine. They did not join the religious communities of Jews already there but established new communities in unsettled areas of Palestine. These revolutionary immigrants lacked funds and had little or no agricultural skills. They faced the hostility of the religious Jewish settlements in urban areas, which viewed them as religious offenders and potential competitors for the limited charity moneys available. The real enemy of these pioneers, however, was their naiveté and lack of agricultural experience. They faced extremely harsh economic and ecological conditions. Many left Palestine. Those who remained were rescued economically by outside capital, particularly from Jewish investors. Over time, these first pioneers hired Arab laborers, and many of the Jewish immigrants became administrators. On the surface, the new settlers appeared similar to European colonialists, exploiting cheap labor for the benefit of colonialists. Some of the consequences of a colonial relationship between Jews and Arabs emerged during this early period.

There was little conflict with the local Arab population, since the Jewish community was small and economically helpful as employers of Arab workers. An interesting view of Arabs in Palestine at the turn of the century emerges from a novel published by Theodor Herzl, one of the founders of Zionism, in 1902. In *Altneuland* (or *Oldnewland*), Herzl writes about a new utopian society where all human potential is fulfilled and all needs are satisfied. When the novel's Jewish and Christian characters first visit Palestine, their impressions are all negative, but, on their return, twenty-one years later, they find a new and thriving society. The Arab in the story is a Berlin-educated doctor of chemistry whose family has resided in Palestine for generations. The Christian asks whether the Arab residents have not been ruined by immigration. The Arab responds, "On the contrary, Jewish immigration has been a blessing for us." Land sales have brought profits, and Arab workers have benefited from schools and Jewish welfare institutions. According to the Arab character in the story,

> We Mohammedans have always been better friends with the Jews than you Christians. Even in those early years, when the first Jewish settlers came here, we were always good neighbors, and it often happened that in a quarrel between Arabs my people went to the nearest Jewish village and begged the Jewish mayor to arbitrate, often enough, too, we asked for instruction or help from the Jews, which was always freely given. (1902, 100)

Obviously this is a romanticized version of the relationship between Arabs and Jews in the early twentieth century. And it was the vision and literary construction of Jews living outside of Palestine. Nevertheless, there was a kernel of truth involved since the Jewish community was small and more educated than the Arabs and was not threatening or living in conflict with the Arabs in their settlements.

Jointly with their sponsors, the surviving settlers of this first wave of immigration initiated more modern agricultural settlements in Palestine, overcame some ecological hardships, and laid the foundation for further Jewish immigration. By the turn of the twentieth century, almost 100,000 acres of land in Palestine had been purchased. Agriculturally productive and self-supporting Jews settled in new villages. Doubling in population size as a result of immigration, the *Yishuv* (as the settlement of the Jewish community in Palestine was known) continued to be dependent economically and politically on European Jewish communities.

A second wave of Jewish immigrants entered Palestine in the decade beginning in 1904. Many were part of organized Zionist organizations responding to political upheavals in Russia. They combined socialist and nationalist themes and rejected the possibility of improving the conditions of Jews in Russia or settling in America. Between 40,000 and 50,000 immigrants came to Palestine determined to build a new social order based on socialist principles and a Jewish national ideology. They expanded existing farms and developed new communally based agricultural communities. They were educated, politically articulate, and organizationally skillful. They transferred their political orientations from Russia to Palestine and thereby laid the foundation for the Jewish labor movement, collective settlements (kibbutzim), and secular Jewish cultural activities. By the outbreak of World War I, 85,000 Jewish settlers lived in Palestine.

There was some opposition to the growing Jewish presence in Palestine. Most of the concern came from formal Ottoman policy against Jewish immigration. Some of the opposition was anti-European rather than anti-Jewish. Apprehension among the Turkish political leaders also resulted from the exaggerated claims of Zionist leaders about the large number of potential Jewish immigrants to Palestine. There was however, no organized system of immigration control, regulation, and enforcement in Palestine. The small size of the Jewish population, the lack of effective Ottoman opposition to Jewish immigration, and the absence of organized local Arab organizations meant the absence of open and organized protest to the Jewish presence in Palestine from the Arab side.

The end of World War I altered the power distribution in the Middle East. The Ottoman control over Palestine was replaced by the British military command and subsequently by the British mandate in 1922. Earlier, the British had made formal commitments to Jewish nationalism and settlement in Palestine through the Balfour Declaration in 1917. The declaration supported the rights of Jews to a Jewish national homeland but in the context of protecting the rights of the local Arab population. Initially, such a double commitment presented no problem for the British authorities. The Jewish community was relatively small, and the Arab population seemed to be positively affected by the presence of Jewish settlements. While the local Jewish community was expanding, and Jewish nationalism was the inspiration for further Jewish immigration, Arab nationalism was developing. Just as Jewish nationalism emphasized the need for political control and authority, and an increase in the Jewish presence in Palestine through immigration and the acquisition of land, so Arab nationalism emphasized the need for increasing their political control and restricting the expansion of Jewish communities. The battle between Arabs and Jews in Palestine began when the Jewish presence became more conspicuous. Arab workers were being replaced by Jewish immigrants to work the land that Jews had purchased, and new "pushes" for Jewish immigration to Palestine from Europe intensified.

The Arabs totally rejected the idea of a national Jewish homeland embodied in the Balfour Declaration and the British commitment to immigration. Arab pressures to stop immigration and land purchases and Jewish pressures for the continuation of both activities became the conspicuous issue around which British policies in Palestine revolved for three decades. At first, the formal British policy regarding immigration was to limit Jewish immigration on economic grounds. The argument the British made was that new Jewish immigrants could be absorbed economically within Jewish enterprises and would therefore present little economic competition for the local Arab population.

Economic and political changes were occurring within Europe that directly affected the Jewish communities there. Changes in Poland eliminated many of the job opportunities for the large Jewish population living there, and there was a general deterioration of the economic and political conditions in Europe during the 1930s. By the 1920s, the United States had set quotas for the entrance of immigrants from Eastern Europe. These changes resulted in an increase in Jewish immigration to Palestine. By the early 1930s, there were 175,000 Jews in Palestine and 859,000 Arabs. The Arab population was now better organized and reacted negatively to the growing number and presence of Jews in Palestine. Widespread economic difficulties, particularly unemployment associated with Jewish immigration and a downturn in the local economy, occasioned Arab protests. Arab reaction and the Jewish response to these events were often couched in political and ideological language, but economic competition and political control were at the heart of the intensifying Arab-Jewish conflict.

Beginning in the 1930s, there were new sources of immigration to Palestine, neither motivated by Jewish nationalism nor attracted to better economic opportunities. These Jewish immigrants were directly influenced by the deteriorating political situation in Europe, in particular the rise of Adolf Hitler and Nazism in the 1930s. Over

200,000 Jewish immigrants entered Palestine between 1932 and 1936, doubling the Jewish population and increasing the percentage of Jewish population from 17 percent in 1931 to 30 percent in 1936. As in earlier periods, increases in the volume of Jewish immigration generated negative reactions among the Arabs and led to strikes, demonstrations, and attacks. Clearly, the British regulation of immigration based on economic considerations could not limit the number of Jewish immigrants.

Jews pressured for increased immigration, and Arabs counterpressured to stop the flow of Jewish immigrants. The British were caught with vague commitments to both nationalisms and an unenforceable immigration policy. Acceding to Arab pressure, British policy changed after 1937 to restrict the total number of Jewish immigrants based on political, not economic, criteria. Numerical quotas were set based on this new British policy. Numerous commissions and policy conferences surrounded the clash of politics and ideology within Palestine. External events in Europe were engulfing all of Europe, in general, and Jews within Europe, in particular, and these events overwhelmed local concerns in Palestine.

British policy was designed to regulate the size of the Jewish population in Palestine relative to the Arabs in Palestine, and thereby make the Jewish population a permanent minority. It was an impossible policy for nationalistic Jews to accept, having escaped the painful minority status of Jews in their countries of origin. The British policy to limit Zionist control over their own Jewish community was clearly contrary to the fundamental goals of Jewish nationalism. Subsequently, British policy evolved to grant control over Jewish immigration to the Arab government, relinquishing British control of Palestine to the majority Arab population and ending British commitments to the idea of a Jewish national homeland. These proposals were not acceptable to Jews in Palestine or elsewhere. Conflicts among the British, Arabs, and Jews intensified in Palestine.

As soon as political controls on immigration were instituted, Zionists in Palestine sought illegal channels of bringing immigrants from Europe to Palestine. The symbolic importance of the immigration to Palestine of European refugees was enormous. Illegal immigration became a rallying point for Jewish political activities in Europe, America, and Palestine. It became the most dramatic political weapon for the establishment of the Jewish state. Deporting illegal immigrants back to Europe or imprisoning them in Cyprus added tensions and tragedy to an already volatile conflict. These British activities exerted enormous political pressure on their mandate in Palestine and dominated the Arab-Jewish conflict during World War II.

The postwar pressure mounted for the immigration of a large number of Jewish refugees, survivors of the European holocaust. The British proposed to give up their mandate and divide Palestine into Jewish and Arab sectors. As the British were packing their colonial bags, the Arab armies of neighboring countries were preparing to invade Palestine, and the Jews gathered their military forces. Less than two years after the last commission struggled with the triangle of British political control, Arab nationalism, and Zionism, the State of Israel was declared in May 1948. When the dust of battle had settled, and international recognition from the United Nations was obtained, the new country covered part of mandate Palestine and included 650,000 Jews and 150,000 Arabs.

The establishment of the Jewish state created new sources of conflict with the Arab minority within its borders. It also generated an increasing problem with Palestinian Arab residents who were not included in the state and who had left the state, hoping to return after the military conflict ended. These Palestinian refugees, who were dispersed in several countries, most under Arab or international auspices, became a critical source of the Arab-Israeli conflict after Israeli statehood.

The State of Israel was established on the basis of an urban, industrial, and European Jewish population. Jewish immigration in the first period after statehood altered the size and ethnic composition of the state. World War II and the Holocaust left hundreds of thousands of Jewish refugees scattered throughout Europe. Almost three quarters of a million Jewish refugees and immigrants from Europe and Arab countries came to the State of Israel between 1948 and 1951. Immigration, socioeconomic development, and political legitimacy created the basis for a viable, stable Jewish community in its homeland. While the Jewish national polity was formed as one response to the threats of assimilation and Holocaust, the survival of Israel as a state was based on the outcome of the conflict over territory and population with the Arabs. The Arab-Israeli conflict shifted dramatically with the establishment of state when the majority Israeli Jewish population had to consider the Arab minority population within Israel and the role of Palestinians outside the state.

The highest priority when the State of Israel was established was to secure the borders of the state and to control the conflict with neighboring Arab countries. Together, these objectives would gain the political legitimacy of Israel in the international arena. The historical period after the establishment of the state may be roughly subdivided into two segments that shaped the conflicts between Israeli Jews and Arabs. The first period was from the establishment of the state in 1948 until 1967. This was a period of major nation building for Israel. During this period, population growth through immigration was extensive, increasing the size of the state from 800,000 to 2.8 million, and incorporating over 1.25 million Jewish immigrants.

Jewish immigrants came from diverse countries of origin, but significant proportions arrived from Middle Eastern countries. Emerging during this period was a clear ethnic division among Jews, between those of western or Ashkenazic background and those of Middle East of Sephardic background. This ethnic difference was significant because it was associated with economic and cultural differences between the two groups and resulted in social class divisions. High levels of economic development and significant improvements in the level of living and in industrial development occurred despite increases in ethnic inequalities among Jews. The Labor political party in Israel retained political control from the founding of the state and throughout this first period.

The Arab population that had remained within the borders of Israel was in large part consolidated within restricted areas after the establishment of the state. The Arabs who were not refugees from Palestine living outside the state viewed themselves as internal refugees within the state. The Israeli Arabs, who lived under a military administration of the state, were residentially concentrated and economically and educationally disadvantaged. While Israeli Arabs worked in the Jewish controlled economy, and increased their levels of education, the gap increased between their socioeconomic circumstances and those of Israeli Jews, including those from the Middle Eastern countries. The major forms of conflict were between Israel and the Arab countries; there was little direct confrontation with Israeli Arabs or with Palestinians. In 1966 the Israeli Military Administration of Arab Israelis was lifted.

Part of the conflict between Israel and the Arab states was over the legitimacy of the State of Israel as a political entity of Jews in the region. For most purposes, the question of legitimacy and viability was answered by the Six-Day War of 1967. Israel defeated the Arab countries and retained control over the areas of Sinai (from Egypt), the West Bank and Jerusalem (from Jordan), and the Golan Heights (from Syria). In turn, the administration of these occupied territories brought into sharper focus the Palestinian refugee problem. Over one million Arab Palestinians were living in the areas administered by Israel. The retention of these territories highlighted the Palestinian question in political as well as in population terms.

This period involved more intense confrontation between Israel and the Palestinians in these administered territories. The conflict was often direct and bloody, with an Israeli military presence in the territories and some terrorist activities of the Palestinians within the State of Israel. There were other forms of conflict during this period, including the October 1973 war with Egypt and Syria, the emergence of new political organizations among the Palestinians and among Israeli Arabs, and conflicts on the northern border with Lebanon.

There were also moves toward peace and normalization with Arab neighbors and with Palestinians. A breakthrough peace treaty with Egypt emerged in the late 1970s, and Israel withdrew from occupying the Sinai area. Meetings with Palestinian leadership and the setting up of Palestinian Autonomous areas in Gaza and Jericho heralded a new process of selectively returning administered territory to the control of Palestinians. At the same time, there were popular uprisings (the *intifada*) among the Palestinians demanding total political control of a homeland for the Palestinian people.

During this second phase, the Israeli economy shifted toward much greater emphasis on service and technology, and a general increase in economic development occurred. A new phase of immigration from Russia and other areas of the former Soviet Union to Israel enhanced the Israeli economy. Almost 800,000 Russian Jewish immigrants arrived in Israel, many with modern, urban, and technological skills. These new immigrants have been integrated economically and politically. The political landscape changed from the dominance of the Labor party to the Likud party in 1977, a more nationalistic, right-wing political coalition. Political control changed back to the Labor Party during the 1990s with a broad coalition from religious political parties and new Russian immigrant parties. The Arab-Israeli conflict shifted toward a Palestinian-Israeli conflict during this period. One of the emergent elements in the conflict is the increasing presence of Jewish settlers in the areas administered by Israel. With political and economic support from the government of Israel, the Jewish settlers and their communities have become a conspicuous presence on the West Bank and a source of direct confrontation between Israel and the Palestinians.

This historical picture is a sketch and an outline. The details of the changing story of the Arab-Israeli conflict follow.

Chapter 2

The State of Israel and the Arab-Israeli Conflict

The core of the Arab-Israeli conflict focuses on the State of Israel: its formation, development, legitimacy, and place in the Middle East. The rapid changes that have characterized Israeli society over more than half a century have reinforced the Jewish character of the state and have had profound implications for how Jews in Israel and Arabs in and outside of Israel interpret their lives. To assess the unfolding Arab-Israeli conflict requires an extended look at the emergence of Israeli society and the relative power of ethnic communities within Israel. Against the background of the changes that have characterized the society, and the interpretations offered by different sides of the conflict to account for these changes, the impact of the conflict on the daily lives of families emerges. An overview of the formation of the state will provide a context for a contemporary social portrait of its communities.

NATION BUILDING: DIFFERENT PERSPECTIVES

The central features of Israeli society, and the Jewish and Arab communities of Palestine before the establishment of the state in 1948, have been interpreted differently by Israeli Jews and by Arabs. How have these communities perceived the events surrounding the emergence of Israeli society and its development? How have the leaders and the elite, as well as the communities and the people within them, characterized the lifestyle and conflicts of Jews and Arabs in

Israel? Different perceptions of Israel are grounded in the different experiences of these communities, in the cultural orientations of Israeli and Arab communities and their conflicting goals and values.

The State of Israel is one of the oldest new societies to have been established in the post–World War II era. Its roots are embedded in the very distant past of the Hebrew Bible and in centuries of minority status and anti-Semitism in Christian and Muslim societies. Emerging politically out of the ashes of a destroyed European Jewry in the Holocaust, Israel was carved out of the nineteenth-century Ottoman Empire and was based on European ideologies of nationalism and ethnic politics. Built on Western foundations of justice, independence, and democracy, it has struggled continuously for political legitimacy among its neighbors. The members of the Israeli society have battled over its boundaries and territory, the distribution of its resources, and the treatment of its minorities. Committed to peace, Israel has been involved in several wars and ceaseless conflict. Although Israel defines itself as a secular state, religion has played an integral part in Israeli politics. The political culture of Israel is dedicated to being an open, pluralistic, and egalitarian society, yet Israel is divided by ethnicity and religion, gender, and social class. Fiercely independent as a state, it remains the major recipient of economic and military aid from the United States and from Jews around the world. Designed as a haven for the remnants of world Jewry, it contains less than 40 percent of the Jewish population of the world after more than five decades of statehood, immigration, and population growth.

Israeli society has integrated millions of Jewish immigrants from an enormous range of diverse countries. Culturally, Israel has invigorated an ancient language to form a common basis of modern communication and has developed a rich repertoire of literature, theater, film, and scholarship. It has become one of the leaders in agricultural innovation and rural communal experiments, while, at the same time, it is one of the most urban of contemporary societies. The deserts have bloomed and modern technologies have flourished in Israel. Over time, Israelis have experienced a shift from large to small family size, from extended to nuclear families, and from marriage at an early age to cohabitation and marriage at a later age. Nevertheless, family ties retain their importance in the lives of the younger generation. Extensive health care institutions have been organized, and infant and child care in Israel have become among the most developed in the world. General welfare policies have been extended to cover diverse groups in Israel—new immigrants as well as the native born, Arabs and Jews, and those in cities as well as those in rural areas. Israel has become a model state for many Third World nations of Africa and Asia and a major source of identity for Jewish communities around the world. Characterized by heterogeneity and by intense and continuous change, Israel is a small state occupying a disproportionate share of the headlines and stories in the Western press. Indeed, contradictions and paradoxes seem to be some of the defining features of Israeli society, as well as complexity.

At the same time, the State of Israel is at the core of the broader Arab-Israeli conflict. In the past, Arabs have challenged the establishment of Israel as a Jewish state. There has been continuous conflict over the implications of Israel as a state with a majority Jewish population. A dominant Arab view is that the Jewish community in Palestine was the colonial creation of a European colonial regime, Great Britain. In this view, the State of Israel continues to be a colonial presence in the Middle East. The imagery of colonialism implies the importation of foreigners as residents and workers. It suggests that political leaders are not indigenous to the region but nevertheless control the state. This is one Arab view of Jewish immigration and settlement in Israel. Furthermore, the argument has been made that, as a colonial state, Israel has exploited the local native-born population. This exploitation involves both the minority Arab-Israeli community and the Palestinians who were exiled when the state was established. At times, the argument is extended to include the exploitation of Jews from Middle East origins living in Israel by the European-origin population. Most important, this colonial perspective views the political regime in Israel as oppressive, discriminatory, and illegitimate. Hence, this Arab view (and its variants) perceives the accomplishments of Israeli society as negative and unjust, resulting in inequality and oppression. This view contrasts sharply with the Jewish view of Israel as a modern state based on democratic principles, committed to equality of opportunity, and as refuge for the oppressed Jewish populations around the world.

It is not surprising that Arabs and Palestinians consider in negative terms some specific features of Israeli society that are viewed positively by its Jewish leadership and its majority Jewish population. Arabs view economic growth in Israel as the basis of increased social inequality. Social and political modernization is interpreted as the further basis of exploitation of the Arab population and the extension of Jewish control and power. The integration of Jewish immigrants within Israel is perceived by Arabs as a symbol of exclusionary and racist population policies. Educational advances even among the Arab population of Israel are interpreted as Jewish control over resources and over access to upward social mobility. The renaissance of Hebrew language and Jewish culture and the rejuvenation of Judaism are symbols for Arab Israelis of the suppression of their own cultural developments in the Israeli state. Military victories against Arab states can hardly be considered celebrations as "national" holidays for Israeli Arabs who are citizens of the state. Nor can Israeli Jews empathize with the Arab Israeli celebration of Land Day, which marks the protest against the dispossession by the Israeli government of Arab land. How can Arab citizens of the State of Israel relate to Israel's Independence Day; or the "national" spring festival of Passover, which celebrates the origins of Jewish peoplehood; or annual memorial days to commemorate those who fought in various wars with Arabs?

In the last several decades, the Arab-Israeli conflict has focused more on the territory and the people controlled and administered by Israel and less on questions of the political legitimacy of the Jewish state. Arabs have increasingly viewed the establishment of their own state as essential, given the increased international recognition of the legitimacy of the Jewish State of Israel. In the first decade of the twenty-first century, the Arab perspective has become less an anti–State of Israel position than a pro–Palestinian state argument. Fewer have challenged whether a Jewish state has a right to exist, and more have raised the question of the territories that such a state should encompass and who should be counted among its citizens. The core of the conflict has focused on the specific boundaries of the state—how much of the West Bank should be under Israeli control, and what kind of political unit should define Palestinian territory? These issues are joined by the question about the "rights" of former residents of Palestine within the Jewish State of Israel and in the emergent political unit that has been defined as Palestine.

The fundamental goal for most Arabs and Palestinians is the establishment of their own political autonomy to be able to have control over their own lives. Living under the control of others is a form of powerlessness. In human terms, the establishment of a Palestinian state would represent the power of cultural symbols and ethnic and national pride. It is the basis of the day-to-day organization of the education of the young, the welfare of the needy, self-regulation, and policies regarding the quality of life and the distribution of resources. Statehood and the political control that it implies is more than symbolic, as Israeli Jews know so well from their own recent history. Although symbols are powerful, establishing a state is a basis for political, economic, cultural, and social development. Palestinians interpret the political independence celebrated by Israeli Jews in their state as their disaster as a people. In Arab literature, the establishment of the State of Israel is referred to as *al-Nakba*—the catastrophic shattering of the Palestinian community in the 1948 war with the Jews.

There is a considerable diversity of views within the Israeli Jewish population and among the Palestinians. Views expressed by extremists on both sides of the Arab-Israeli conflict should not be taken as representative of the vast majority of either Palestinians or Jews. A small minority of Israeli Jews argues that Palestinians have no legitimate stake in the control of the greater Land of Israel and that only Jews have a historic right to live there. They argue that other Arab states can accommodate the national aspirations of the Palestinian population. Israel is the only Jewish state in the world and therefore requires broad political support. A minority of Palestinian Arabs argues that Israel has no legitimacy as a Jewish state and that most Jews have no right to live in an Arab-controlled greater Palestine. Most of the parties to the Arab-Israeli conflict take intermediate positions about the politics of Jews and the rights of Arabs. To characterize "Israeli Jews" or "Israeli Arabs" and to specify their views and perceptions is to gloss over some of the complexities and the internal divisions within their communities. Internal diversity within these communities is often as great as the differences between communities. Thus, both the overall character of these communities and the heterogeneity within each must be considered, as each set of views changes over time.

These complex themes are important components in understanding the changing Arab-Israeli conflict. The identification of the changes that Israel has experienced provides clues about the sources of these changes and their consequences. The major point of departure is an examination of the linkages between nation building and population growth. This requires an investigation into the assimilation of Jewish immigrants from diverse societies and their mobilization into a coherent, pluralistic polity. How do immigrants become Israelis? How are economic and educational resources allocated within the state? How do external dependencies on other countries affect ethnic and other inequalities within Israel? How are internal divisions within Israel linked to these international contexts? Answers to these questions are located in the everyday life of its citizens, the normal, recurrent events of the life course—birth, marriage and family formation, sickness and death. Clues are located in the types of communities in which people live, the jobs they have, the children they love, their schooling, and their resources. The common themes of national development in Israel revolve around culture, politics, and religion; the retention of minority inequalities and their differential access to opportunities; the significance of gender roles and the sources of family values; the relationship of others to Israelis and their society—Jews and Arab Palestinians in their diasporas. These themes provide a rich portrait of contemporary Israeli society and an assessment of the historical roots of current conflicts.

An overall context is necessary to understand Israeli society and to serve as a basic orientation for understanding the Arab-Israeli conflict. Three major themes continue to shape the Arab-Israeli conflict and the diversity within each community.

Population Issues

The "peopling" of Palestine/Israel has been, and continues to be, critical for the evolution of the Arab-Israeli conflict. Immigration patterns over the last century reveal how Jews and Arabs have differed sharply over the meaning and implications of Jewish immigration. More important, immigration has been a powerful symbol of controversy throughout the conflict. For Jews, the need for immigration was the raison d'être of establishing a Jewish state. For Arabs, Jewish immigration to Palestine and Israel meant disenfranchisement, the entry of foreigners into their land, and their own displacement. Immigration and population growth indicated power, and each community interpreted that power differently. Immigration is linked directly to concerns about the land areas that have been incorporated as part of the state, and it has been connected to conflicts over differences between Jews and Arabs in economic development.

Political Issues

Differences in political orientations of Arabs and Jews are of obvious importance in the Arab-Israeli conflict. Each group defines its national goals as exercising political control over its own community and its development. The political claims of each group are in direct conflict with those of the other. While many features of Zionist and Arab nationalisms are shared, they are in sharp conflict over the specifics of territory, political control, and the details of culture. External political events have also shaped events within the State of Israel. These issues include broad themes of globalization in the most recent period, the economic interdependence of countries around the world, and the political interrelationships that are implied by that set of relationships. Specific issues include the role of Great Britain in the mandate period (1919–1948), the role of the United States as an active partner in political agreements between Arabs and Israel, and the role of events in the Middle East and in Europe in shaping attitudes toward Israel and the Arabs and toward statehood and power. Political cultural issues and political ideology are also important in an assessment of the political basis of the Arab-Israeli conflict.

Economic Development Issues

The growth of the Israeli economy and the distribution of resources among the diverse groups within Israel are major parts of the economic development issue. In broad terms, ethnic inequality is how economic development issues are translated into policies of resource allocations within the Jewish and Arab communities of Israel. Inequalities characterize economic differences between the Jewish and Arab communities as well as within both communities. Included are questions about whether resources are available, who has access to the opportunities that are open, and how welfare and entitlements are distributed. What have been the economic consequences of the administration and control exercised by Israel over Palestinians? How does the quality of life of Arabs and Jews in Israel differ? What are their educational levels and the future prospects of their children in the labor market? Inequalities focus on current economic differences and how contemporary patterns are likely to influence the generational continuation of inequalities.

These three themes of population, politics, and economic development are complex because they involve diverse indicators and because they are interrelated. Resources and their allocation connect directly to issues of population size and political power; population growth has been part of the changing power relationships between

Jews and Arabs. Population, politics, and economy are the core patterns of nation building in Israel as well as the sources of the conflicts among communities. They are linked to issues of culture and lifestyle, of religion and family. Changes in immigration, health and family, the ethnic identity of people and where they live, their children and their lifestyles have been critical in shaping nation building and economic development in Israeli society. Since population, political, and economic issues have changed over time, it is not surprising that social and economic inequalities within Israel have changed as well and new divisions among Jews and between Jews and Arabs have emerged. These inequalities have become the manifestation of the Arab-Israeli conflict in the lives of people and their communities.

Some population, political, and economic patterns in Israel are similar to those in other developing, small countries dependent on large and powerful nations for socioeconomic resources and political support. Other processes reflect the specifics of the Jewish and Arabic conditions in recent history and the relationships between Israeli and non-Israeli Jews. Still other patterns in Israel can be understood only in the light of Israel's particular history, its economic and political developments and its role in the Middle East. Israel is unique in the forces that have shaped its history and, at the same time, it is also a microcosm of population, development, and ethnic relationships. It is one country comprising many communities—a political entity unified and organized, with official boundaries and administrative networks. Israel is an example of a country that is economically dependent yet fiercely values its independence. The State of Israel is illustrative of countries with a history of colonial relationships, internal ethnic diversity, and a commitment to cultural pluralism. Israel is at the crossroads of East and West, where Western democracy, European socialism, Western capitalism, and Jewish and Muslim fundamentalisms blend with Middle Eastern culture and society.

CHANGING POPULATION SNAPSHOTS

Changes in population size is a helpful entry point since size is a core component of a community, shaping the development of institutions and culture, the distribution of resources, and the allocation of rewards. Population factors have played a powerful role in the formation of Israeli society and the changes that it has experienced over time. The key population factors are (1) the role of immigration in

Israel's population growth, (2) the links between increases in Jewish population size and economic development, (3) the geographic distribution of Israelis and the borders that define the political legitimacy of the state, and (4) the residential patterns that have created ethnic networks and ethnic exclusion within a pluralistic society. Changes in the relative size of the Jewish and Arab populations have been of central political importance since the turn of the twentieth century. Therefore, no understanding of the Arab-Israeli conflict can proceed without a clear appreciation of the changing demographic balance of Arabs and Jews in Israel.

Before 1967 the State of Israel included the recognized international boundaries following the 1948 War of Independence. After the 1967 war, the State of Israel included the eastern part of Jerusalem. The territories added after 1967—the West Bank and Gaza—are defined as administered territories or those occupied by the State of Israel. In 1994 Gaza and Jericho on the West Bank were placed under Palestinian control. These recent political changes will undoubtedly alter the future demography of the State of Israel.

With minor exceptions, the Biblical names Judea and Samaria are not used for these administered territories, and data are not included for them unless explicitly noted. Thus, *Jewish Israelis* are Jews living in the State of Israel, including those living in settlements on the West Bank and Gaza area. *Arab Israelis* are Arabs living within the State of Israel who have the option of Israeli citizenship. *Palestinians* are those who were resident in the area included within the State of Israel but were no longer resident after 1948. They include former Arab residents of Palestine who live in the West Bank, Gaza, and in Arab countries in the region. Not included within the Palestinian population are former residents of Palestine who live in Western or other countries. The Jewish population, former residents of Palestine who no longer live in the State of Israel, are not included. All designations of these areas and groups carry with them political significance. These categories of groups of persons need to be made clear so that there can be shared communication. They are the social constructions of territories and people and do not convey a political statement or imply any judgment. The first demographic focus is on the State of Israel and its population. A subsequent section will deal explicitly with the population in the territories administered by Israel and the Palestinians, as well as their relationships to Jewish and Arab Israelis within the State of Israel.

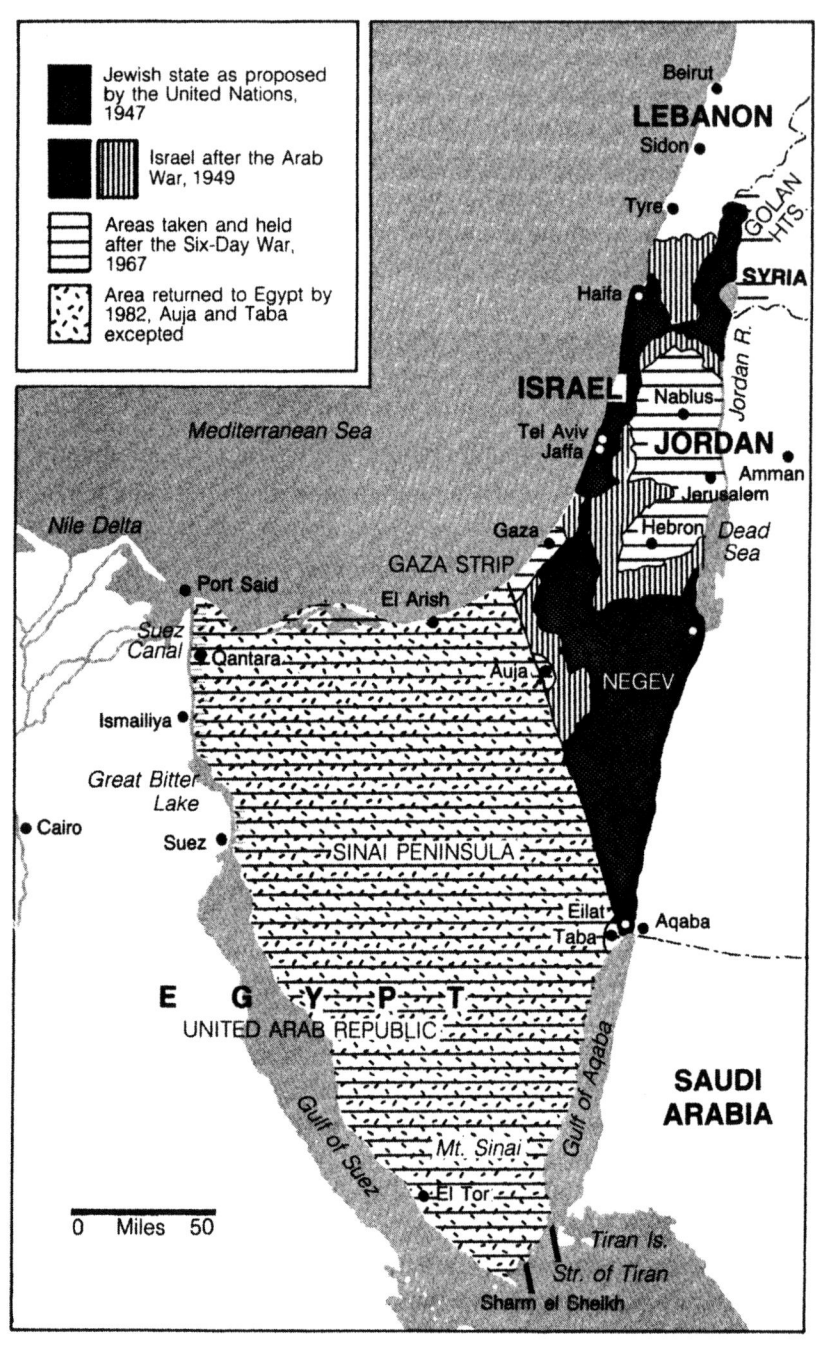

Source: Charles D. Smith, *Palestine and the Arab-Israeli Conflict*, 2nd ed. (New York: Bedford/St. Martin's, 1992), p. 207. Copyright © 1992 Bedford/St. Martin's. Reprinted with permission of Bedford/St. Martin's.

A simple population profile of contemporary Israel is a snapshot, cross-sectional view of the demographic contours of the society and the diverse groups within it. The total population size in Israel at the end of the twentieth century was six million persons with a rate of population growth of 2.5 percent per year, over a fifteen-year period, from 1983 to 1999. Israel is an overwhelmingly urban society; close to 90 percent of the population lives in areas designated as urban. About three out of ten Israelis are below the age of fifteen, and 9 percent are above the age of sixty-five. Between 1990 and 1999, over 800,000 immigrants arrived in Israel, mainly from the former Soviet Union. Birthrates in the State of Israel were higher than in most industrialized Western countries but lower than in Third World countries. The birthrate at the end of the twentieth century was 22 per 1,000 population, and the total fertility rate was just under three children per woman. Death rates were among the lowest in the world (6 deaths per 1,000 population, an infant mortality rate of 6.2 per 1,000 births, and life expectancy of 79 years). The dominant ethnic-religious population in the state is Jewish (82 percent of the total), with a rather even split between those of European (Western) origins (sometimes referred to as Ashkenazim) and those of Asian and African (Middle Eastern) origins (sometimes referred to as Sephardim). Six out of ten Jews were born in Israel, and one-quarter of the Jewish population in 1997 were third-generation Israelis, or Israelis born of Israeli-born parents. Three-fourths of the Arab population in Israel is Muslim. Arab Israelis are concentrated in the northern district of the country (40 percent of the Muslims, 60 percent of the Christians, and 80 percent of the Druze). The Jewish population, in contrast, is more evenly distributed throughout the regions of the country (10 percent in the northern district, 10 percent in the Jerusalem district, 13 percent in the Haifa district, 15 percent in the southern district, about 25 percent in the central district, and 25 percent in the Tel Aviv district).

Contemporary snapshots convey some information, but "moving" pictures begin to capture the dynamics. Changes in the demographic portrait of Israeli society can be sketched in a preliminary way by examining these same elements about five decades earlier when the State of Israel was first established. At the end of 1948, 872,700 persons were living in approximately the same land area in Israel: 82 percent were Jews, and 85 percent were of European origin. There was a low rate of natural growth. During the first several months subsequent to statehood, there were very high rates of immigration and a potential for continuous Jewish immigration from a wide range of countries. At the same time, there was an exodus of Arab residents as war raged between Israel and neighboring Arab countries. This exodus is a major source of controversy, because many Arabs became refugees in the hope of returning to their homes. They became the basis of the Palestinian population in exile. It is somewhat unclear historically whether the Arabs left the new State of Israel because the Israeli military forced them out, because the Arab leadership encouraged them to go, or because they wanted to avoid the battles between Israeli and Arab armies. It is likely that all three elements were involved; in any event, they became a displaced refugee population. Their fate and their future constitute one of the core elements of the Arab-Israeli conflict.

Israel was established in part of the area of Palestine when territorial control switched from the British mandate to an emerging Jewish administration. When the State of Israel was declared in 1948, there was a low level of industrial activity but a high level of urban concentration. Israel was a country without a secure future; war and political and economic uncertainty marked its birth. In 1948 it was unclear whether Israel had the territorial and economic resources economically and socially to integrate large numbers of Jewish immigrants. With the establishment of the state and the shifts in population and territory, the Jews became the majority, and the Arab population remaining within the state became a demographic, political, and social minority. The Arab population had been a clear majority of British mandate Palestine, constituting two-thirds of the total population at the end of the mandate period in 1948.

The demographic snapshots begin to sharpen when detailed patterns of population growth are reviewed. The path of demographic growth in Israel has been rather uneven over the last several decades, even as the rate has been high. The increases in population size and the fluctuations since 1948 for both the Jewish and Arab populations have been dramatic. Starting with a base population of 650,000 in mid-1948, the total population of the state surpassed its first million within the first year and doubled to two million within the subsequent decade. By the end of 1970, the population had increased to over three million; another million persons were added by 1982. About six million people were living in Israel at the end of 1990s—a ninefold population increase in fifty years.

Much obviously has happened over this five-decade period which has transformed the fundamental character of the society. Questions of war and economic uncertainty remain, but they are totally different from those of earlier times. The integration of Israel's Jewish immigrant populations continues to be of concern at the beginning of the twenty-first century, but the dimensions of the issue have radically changed. Israel's status as an independent state is largely unquestioned internationally, and it is increasingly accepted by its Arab neighbors, even as the boundaries that mark its political borders remain tentative and contested. The two snapshots sketching formal beginnings and the current demographic profile only hint at the sources of underlying change. The dynamics need to be examined directly in order to understand the society and fit Israel into a comparative context.

ISRAEL'S DEMOGRAPHY: UNIQUE OR ILLUSTRATIVE

The high rates of population growth for both the Jewish and Arab populations of Israel reflect different combinations of demographic sources. Over the last fifty years, the Jewish population of Israel has increased primarily as a result of immigration. In contrast, natural increase (the rate of births minus the rate of deaths) has accounted for most of the Arab population growth since 1948. Key features of these patterns for the entire society are as follows:

- Mortality levels have declined with improvements in public health services and have been extended to all sectors of the population.
- There has been a transition from a more extended family system to a nuclear family structure, an increasing use of efficient contraception, and the emergence of small family size. Together, reductions in mortality and the shift from high to low fertility have resulted in a period of rapid population growth followed by a slowing of the population growth rate.
- The population has become increasingly urban in concentration, and metropolitan areas have expanded as populations have moved to suburban areas surrounding cities.
- Immigration and ethnic residential concentration have characterized the society over time, along with the economic integration of Jewish immigrants from diverse countries of origin.

- The population of Israel has become older—relatively and absolutely—as a result of the reduction of fertility and the extension of life. Welfare and health services have expanded to meet the changing needs of a growing and aging population.
- The state has become more involved in the formulation and implementation of a broad range of population and welfare policies.

These demographic changes in Israel have been linked to the expansion of health services and economic opportunities, the changing roles of women, the spread of Western technology to developing nations, and the increasing political and economic dependencies of small nations on a select number of large, powerful, core countries. Israel shares these features with many other countries. Nevertheless, the specific contexts of Israel have shaped these processes.

Population pyramids of Israel (pictoral views of the distribution of age and sex) in the 1950s, when the state was first growing rapidly through the immigration of high-fertility populations, closely resembled those of other Third World countries, with a broad base to the pyramid and a slowly narrowing apex as age increases. In the early 1990s, the population pyramid was becoming more like the European-American structure. Some subpopulations in Israel retain the triangular structure of a Third World population (e.g., the Israeli Muslim population), but others have an inverted age structure (very narrow base and aging apex) because they are a disappearing segment (e.g., first-generation Jewish immigrants). Detailed pyramids of subpopulations illustrate the range of these age/sex population structures.

What about the geographic distribution of Israel's population? The urban centers of Tel Aviv, Jerusalem, and Haifa are the major areas of residential density in Israel. Since its founding as a state, Israel has been an urban society, more similar to the European, more economically developed country model than the more heavily rural areas of Third World countries. Israel is small in population size and geographic spread, and it conveys a sense of being a local community. In part, Israel's small geographic space and population size resemble a large, extended community in which each event has significance because of the connections among persons and families throughout the country. Modern technology, radio, television, and telephone are ubiquitous throughout all sectors of the society and reinforce this interconnectedness.

Figure 2.1
Age-Sex Pyramid, Israeli Jews, 1992

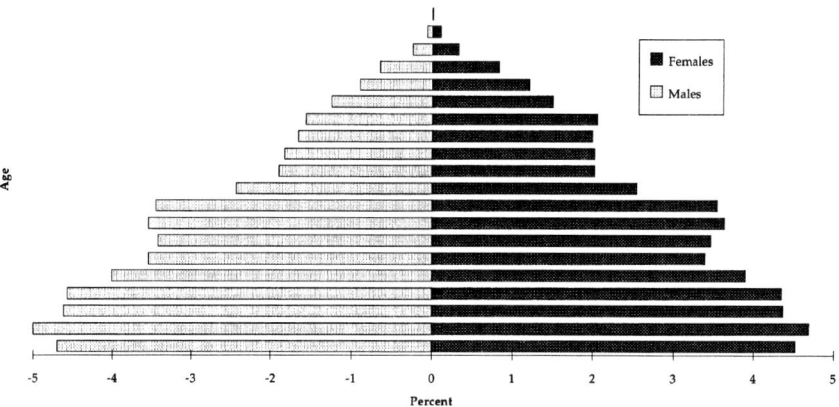

Population processes are also associated with social inequalities based on ethnic origins, religion, and gender. Immigration brought Jews to Israel from diverse communities of origin, which were characterized by differences in economic background, religious culture, and relationships between men and women. Thus, when people of different origins immigrated to Israel, there were initial differences in their economic experiences, in the intensity of their religious observances and customs, and in the relative equality of men and women within the family. Some of these features of immigrant origins have changed over the generations as the Israeli born have grown up in Israeli society. Family values and gender roles are also linked to the changing size of families, as those with larger families may have different values and different economic constraints. Moreover, women who have large families are also less likely to work full-time outside the home. Often they have less than egalitarian relationships with their husbands. In similar ways, differences in the extent of and quality of health care and in rates of death are connected to the resources of people.

Demographic issues have been in the forefront of Zionism, the national ideology of Israel. In particular, Zionism has long been concerned with increasing the presence of Jews in the Jewish state. Jewish nationalism and self-government have been viewed as the solution to the disadvantaged consequences of Jewish minority status of diaspora

Figure 2.2
Age-Sex Pyramid, Moslem Israelis, 1992

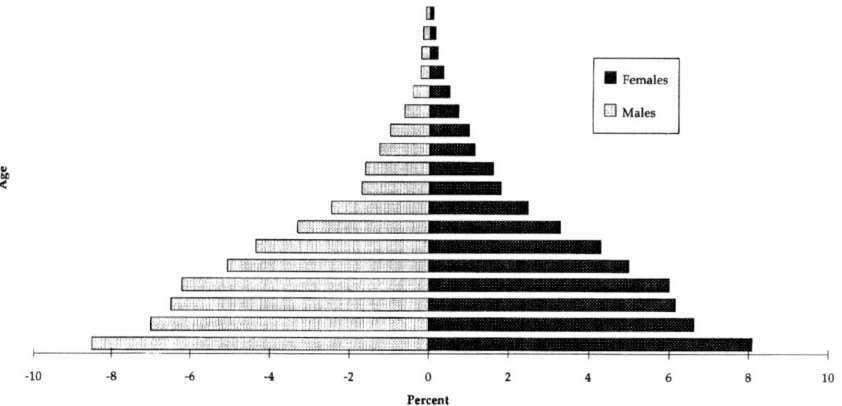

Jewish communities. Hence, the relative ratio of Jewish and Arab populations has been of concern to Jewish nationalists. Zionism and its organizational structure emphasize bringing together large numbers of Jews to the Jewish state. These include Jews who have been oppressed or stateless in their places of origin and those who are committed to the Zionist nation-building ideals.

Marriage and the formation of families are key arenas of population, since these processes bind families together and link the generations to each other in a web of relationships. A community is defined as a pattern of interrelated networks sharing a common culture; the tighter the family networks, the greater the community cohesion, and the larger the number of linkages between families through marriage, residence, jobs, and places of origin, the stronger the identification with the community. Population factors shape the set of shared intensities of interactions within and between generations. Networks build on connections to family; shared neighborhoods and residence sustain and transform culture collectively among extended kin. To the extent that Israeli society is a family-oriented community, the networks that inform the lives of people are powerful. These ideological, social, and political dimensions of population processes are therefore at the core of nation building, development, and national political integration in Israel's changing society. They are at the core of the distinctiveness of Jewish and Arab Israeli communities. Jewish and Arab Israelis are distinguished not only by their

A view of modern western Jerusalem. The continuous presence of housing construction and the density of apartments and official offices are evident. (1999)

national ideologies and politics but also by their families and social values, their residences and work places, their resources, and their schools and religious institutions.

ECONOMIC DEVELOPMENT AND NATION BUILDING

There is an economic cost to high levels of continuous population growth if the economy does not expand. Israel could not sustain population growth rates and continue to attract new immigrants without extensive economic growth. Indeed, the growth of Israel's economy has widened the opportunities and generated increases in the standard of living for its population. In part, economic changes were brought about through immigration (the human capital and resources brought by the immigrants and their contributions to production and consumption) and the increased economic investments made in Israel from outside the country. Often, increases in immigration followed periods of economic growth, as Israel developed new economic opportunities and provided an expanded job market. Whether population growth generated economic changes or whether immigrants responded to the job opportunities created by an expanded economy, both population growth and economic production have increased over time.

A view of the multi-layers of religious and secular life and history in Jerusalem. Central and most dramatic is the Mosque of Omar with its beautiful dome. There is a Muslim minaret and the top of the Church of the Holy Sepulchre. The photo was taken from the back of an Arab house in the old city of Jerusalem looking toward the Western Wall, an area of special significance and holy to Jews. In the background, to the left are the buildings of the Hebrew University on Mount Scopus and to the right on the hill is the Mount of Olives cemetery and the top of a UN building and Protestant church. The multiple cultural contrasts between the major religions and their juxtaposition in the Old City of Jerusalem and in east Jerusalem are evident. (1999)

The demographic transitions in Israel outlined above occurred in the contexts of economic growth and national politics. Immigrants and their families were responsive to economic opportunities and affected economic change, as they developed a new national political system after the establishment of the state in 1948. The unequal distribution of resources among the immigrants and between them and their children and grandchildren has become the basis of ethnic inequalities among Jews and changing inequalities between Jews and Arabs within Israel.

While economic conditions in the country as a whole have improved, several questions remain about the sources of Israel's economic development. How much of the growth was the result of internal economic changes versus external investments? Which industries and economic sectors have expanded? What has been the distribution of economic activities over time among ethnic and social class groups? Has economic growth been the same for Arab and Jewish

The David Inter-continental hotel built around a Muslim minaret. Note the billboard advertisement in front of the minaret. (1999)

Israelis? Answers to these questions will allow us to understand the connections between ethnic origins and emerging social-class inequalities. Associated with economic growth are the transformations in the labor force and markets as the population becomes more educated, technology develop, and new sectors of the economy expand in a postindustrial, world economy. These economic developments translate into lifestyles and resources that are distributed unequally among groups.

Overall Economic Measures

By using a range of economic indicators at the national level, it is clear that Israel's economy has grown in terms of domestic production, technological developments, and labor force improvements. (Unless otherwise noted, all the data reported in this and subsequent sections are taken from the *Statistical Yearbook of Israel*.) From 1950 through the mid-1970s, economic growth was quite high, apart from recessions in 1953 and in 1966–1967 and stagnation in the mid-

Table 2.1
Selected Socioeconomic Indicators in Israel, 1960–1990

	GDP per Capita (constant prices)		Years of Schooling (age 15 and over)				Percent of Food in Consumption Expenditure
			Jews		Arabs		
Year	NIS*	Index	None	13+	None	13+	
1950	2,736	1					39
1960	4,513	1.65	13	10	50	2	34
1970	7,474	2.73	9	13	36	2	31
1980	9,612	3.51	6	21	19	8	29
1990	11,045	4.04	4	29	13	9	26

Note: Dates are approximate and are within one year.
*National Israeli Shekels.

Source: *Statistical Abstract of Israel*, various issues.

1970s. During the quarter of a century from 1950 to 1975, the national product rose nine times, an average of 9 percent per year; per capita national product grew at an annual rate of 4.5 percent. The sharp rise reflected an increase in capital stock (11 percent per year) and the number of employed (4 percent per year). Hence, capital per employed increased 7 percent per year. The quality of the labor force increased dramatically after an initial decline (which reflected the socioeconomic background of immigrants). Educational capital per employed declined by 7 percent in the first half of the 1950s, rose 22 percent in the period from 1961 to 1972, and continued to increase in the 1970s through the 1990s. Gross domestic product (GDP) per capita at constant prices doubled between 1950 and 1965 and doubled again between 1965 and 1990.

The share of agriculture in the domestic product rose in the first years of the state, then declined steadily with a modest rise in the share of industry. The share of trade, finance, and personal services declined, and the share of public services rose indicating an increased share in social services. The biggest rise in capital stock occurred in the shares of public services, transport, and communications, revealing the expansion of the infrastructure.

In 1950 Israel's annual growth of per capita income was about one fourth the level of the United States and similar to the richer Latin America countries and Italy, well above Japan, but only half the level of Western Europe. From 1950 to 1970, per capita income grew more than 5 percent annually in Israel, similar to the high rates in

Europe, Taiwan, and Korea. The growth of per capita income had slowed considerably in Israel by the 1970s. The growth after 1950 led to an increase in Israel's relative real income to over half that of the United States by 1980 and to about 75 percent of the average level in Western Europe.

Economic growth is directly related to changes in the population of Israel. In the quarter century before 1948, the Jewish population increased eight-fold with the population doubling on average each decade. The total product of the Jewish economy in Palestine in the same period increased twenty-five-fold at an average annual rate of 13.7 percent; the total stock of capital increased fifteen-fold. Immigration affected the economy by expanding the supply of labor and the working age population, increased the supply of capital, and changed the demand as well.

Economic and Occupational Shifts

Economic shifts over time can be observed in the changing structure of branches of the economy and in occupational patterns. The most striking overall feature of the forty years from 1955 to 1995 is the stability of the employment distribution among various sectors. The industrial branch of the economy has remained relatively steady (at about 25 percent of the employed) as has commerce, transportation, and personal services. The major shifts in employment have been in agriculture, declining from 18 percent to 4 percent, and in construction, declining from 9 percent to 5 or 6 percent. At the same time, there have been increases in employment in the finance sector (doubling to 10 percent in the two decades to 1990) and in public and community services (from 21 percent to 30 percent of the employed in forty years).

A similar picture emerges from an examination of shifting occupational distribution over time in Israel. There has been a clear and sharp decline in the proportion engaged in agriculture from the mid 1950s to the mid-1990s (17 percent to 3 percent), modest declines in skilled laborers (from around 30 percent of the employed in the 1950s through the 1970s to 25 percent in the 1980s and 1990s), and slow declines in the level of unskilled laborers. Service and sales workers have remained at around the same level over time. The most conspicuous overall occupational shift has been in the increases in the

Table 2.2
Economic Branch and Occupation, 1955–1990, Israel: Employed Population

Economic Branch (%)

Year	Agr	Ind	Con	Com	Tran	Fin	Pub	Per	Total
1955	18	24	9	13	6	*	22	8	100
1960	17	25	9	12	6	*	22	8	100
1970	9	26	8	13	8	5	24	8	100
1975	6	26	8	12	7	7	27	6	100
1980	6	25	6	12	7	8	30	6	100
1985	6	24	5	13	6	10	30	7	100
1990	4	23	5	15	6	10	30	7	100
1995	3	22	7	17	6	13	26	6	100

Occupation (%)

Year	Sci	Pro	Mgr	Cle	Sal	Ser	Agr	Ski	Unsk	Total
1955		10	16		11	10	17	29	6	100
1960		11	14		9	13	17	31	5	100
1965		13	17		8	11	13	33	5	100
1970		16	17		8	12	8	32	5	100
1975	7	13	3	17	8	12	6	28	6	100
1980	8	15	4	19	8	11	6	26	4	100
1985	9	15	6	18	8	13	5	24	4	100
1990	9	17	5	17	9	13	4	24	3	100
1995	12	14	5	17		17	2	25	9	100

Note: Agr: Agriculture, forestry, fishing; Ind: industry (mining, manufacturing; electricity and water); Con: construction (building and public works); Com: commerce, restaurants, and hotels (includes banking in 1955); Tran: transport, storage, and communication; Fin: financing and business services; Pub: public and community services; Per: personal and other services.

Note: Sci: scientific and academic workers; Pro: professional and other technical workers; Mgr: managers and administrators; Cle: clerical and related workers; Sal: sales workers; Ser: service workers; Agr: agricultural workers; Ski: skilled workers in industry and elsewhere; Unsk: unskilled workers.

Note: The occupational categories for 1955, 1961, and 1995 are somewhat different.

Source: *Statistical Abstract of Israel*, Various Issues.

professional, scientific, and academic category (from 10 percent of the employed in 1955 to 25 percent in the 1990s).

Educational Changes

Along with these broad economic changes have been improvements in the educational levels of the population. The median years of schooling for the total population in 1961 was eight years; 9 percent of the population had thirteen or more years of schooling. The median had increased two-and-a-half years by 1980, and the proportion with higher education doubled to 19 percent. Average education

Table 2.3
Educational Level of Employed persons, 1963–1990, by Gender

Years of Schooling	Employed Persons (%)			
	1963	1971	1979	1990
Men				
0–8	58	50	34	20
9–12	30	35	43	50
13+	11	15	23	30
Total	100	100	100	100
Women				
0–8	45	34	21	11
9–12	40	43	46	48
13+	15	23	34	40
Total	100	100	100	100

Source: Statistical Abstract of Israel, various issues.

in Israel in the beginning of the 1990s was twelve years, and fully one-third of the population has thirteen or more years of schooling. These increases are even more impressive when the educational levels of Jews and Arabs are examined separately. Fully half of the Arab population age fifteen and over in 1961 had no formal education and only 1.5 percent had thirteen or more years. By the end of the 1990s, 87 percent of the Arab population had some formal education, and 16 percent had more than a high school education. Among Jews, there was a sharp decrease at the lower level of education from the early 1960s to the 1990s, and the proportion at the higher educational level tripled during the same period to close to 37 percent having at least some college education.

These educational shifts have transformed the employed population in Israel and their educational background. In the early 1960s, about six out of ten of the employed men in Israel had less than eight years of education, and only about one in ten had more than a high school education. By the 1990s, only two out of ten men had less than eight years of education, and three out of ten had thirteen or more years of education. The same pattern applies to women. In the 1990s, about one out of ten women employed in Israel had a low level of education, but four out of ten had thirteen or more years of education. This distribution is almost the reverse of the patterns in the 1960s when almost half of the employed women had less than eight years of schooling and only 15 percent had thirteen or more years of schooling.

Standard of Living

Other economic indicators reveal an increased standard of living and an improved quality of life among Israelis. For example, examining how much of annual family expenditure is spent on food (rather than on nonfood items) shows that the percent declined continuously from 39 percent in 1950 to less than 20 percent in the 1990s. Increasing possession of consumer goods also indicates improvements in the standard of living and the quality of life among Israelis. Only 2 percent of the Israeli households in 1950 had electric refrigerators; half the households had them in 1960 and virtually all had them by 1975. In the mid-1950s, 7 percent of the households had washing machines, increasing to 43 percent in 1970 and to 80 percent in 1980. Only 4 percent of Israeli families owned a private car in 1960; 15 percent owned cars in 1970 and 34 percent in 1980. Indicators of housing and crowding reveal an increase in the amount of household space available. In 1967, 85 percent of the Jewish population lived in households where there was more than one person per room; by 1990, it had dropped to 58 percent. The proportion of households that had two persons or more per room declined from 31 percent to 8 percent. These and related data reveal the overall increase in the standard of living, access to modern consumption items, and the diffusion of these items to major sectors of the population.

Economic Dependency

These economic and industrial indicators reveal improvements over time in the overall economy, in the expansion of consumption, and in the educational quality of the labor force. Many of these internal dynamics reflect the growing economic dependency of Israel on external resources. In part, this is a direct result of the military burden experienced by Israel and the economic cost of building a modern defense system. Israel has devoted a considerable part of its economic capacity to defense, a much higher level per capita than in Western countries. Since World War II, the average rate of defense expenditures of Western countries has been below 10 percent; defense outlays in Israel averaged 25 percent per year from 1969 to 1981. In 1970 total U.S. assistance to Israel was less than $100 million, and 85 percent was in the form of loans. A decade later, the assistance had increased to over $2 billion, with half in loans. In 1985 Israel received

$3.3 billion of military and economic assistance from the United States; all of it was in the form of grants.

Israel has also received increasing support from the American Jewish community (as well as other Jewish communities around the world) and annual restitution payments from Germany as a result of the Nazi Holocaust. Estimates of this external private and public support add up to over $8 billion annually according to some and considerably less according to others. The important point is that Israel has increasingly become economically dependent on other states and on Jews living outside of the state for its continued economic growth. This is the case even though Israel's economy has increased substantially and the standard of living among its residents has grown. Israel's financial obligations abroad increased over threefold to $3 billion during the 1970s and jumped to $21 billion in the 1980s. By the beginning of the 1990s, these foreign obligations fluctuated at around $33 billion. While the net export of goods from Israel increased from $211 million in 1960 to $5.3 billion in 1980 and to over $11 billion in 1990s, net imports have increased even more sharply.

Overall economic, occupational, and educational shifts raise a number of questions about the distribution of these economic improvements among Jews and Arabs, among Jews of different ethnic origins and generations from the immigration experience, and between women and men. These themes will be revisited when we examine these Israeli groups.

ZIONISM, POPULATION, AND DEVELOPMENT

Zionism is the nationalistic ideology of the Jews. The primary theme of the several variants of Zionism revolves around the establishment of a political unit in which Jews are in control of their lives and develop all the institutions associated with statehood. The ideas underlying Zionism and the political movement were developed in the context of European society in the nineteenth century as Europe was undergoing its own nationalist agenda. Zionism is connected to the very long tradition, after the destruction of the Jewish Temple in Jerusalem in the year 70, of yearning to return to Jerusalem and the land of Israel as a people. Its secular, national tone and its formal institutions developed in the late nineteenth and early twentieth centuries, prior to the establishment of the state. All the variants of Zionism have emphasized the centrality of Jewish immigration to the State of Israel and the importance of building an autonomous Jewish community in an independent political unit. Zionism has influenced economic growth and political representation among Jews and, as a result, has been a key factor in the Arab-Israeli conflict.

At various points in time, Zionism has shaped the rate and sources of immigration, the development and support of institutions that encourage maternal and child care, and the formation of the welfare system that provides benefits to children and families. Zionist institutions and the ideologies underlying Zionism were instrumental in the development of agricultural enterprises and in subsidizing agricultural communities and new towns. Zionist institutions mobilized financial support for Israel among the Jewish communities outside of Israel, linking Jews together in supporting the State of Israel as a national Jewish homeland.

There are diverse ideologies of Zionism and a variety of activities under the rubric of Zionism. Economic, social, cultural, or religious developments are not the direct outcomes of Zionist ideological movements. While immigration to the state is consistent with and often sponsored by Zionist organizations, many other factors influencing immigration are not the direct consequence of Israeli nationalism. Similarly, ethnic inequalities among Jews and between Jews and Arabs are not traceable to Zionist ideology. As a combination of ideology, social movement, and a set of organizations, Zionism has been both a legitimating ideology and a source of financial support for the development of Israeli society.

As the national ideology of the Jews, Zionism defined the *Yishuv* (the Jewish community in British mandate Palestine) and the State of Israel as the homeland of the Jews. Zionism placed priority therefore on an increase in the Jewish population in the state and its distribution throughout all the areas under Israeli control. The goal of this emphasis within Zionism was to enhance political and economic development, as well as the cultural renaissance of the Jewish people. In the emphasis on Jewish nationalism, Zionism recognized the non-Jewish inhabitants living in the areas under its political control. While extending rights to that population as a minority, the clear policy priority of the state was the development of the Jewish community.

The Arab Israeli reaction to becoming a minority group when Israel became a Jewish state and loss of political control was directed against the state's institutions as well as against the ideological priorities of Zionism. The Palestinian population, former residents of British mandate Palestine, was even more enraged over its loss of political control and its refugee status. The hostility of Arabs in and outside of Israel toward Zionism focuses on Zionist policies and its cultural symbols.

Israel has emerged as a national state, has developed and expanded its population and economy, and has articulated its commitment to national goals, institutions, symbols, and culture. Israelis who have immigrated from dozens of countries have become integrated politically and economically into the emerging nation-state. At the same time that the national society developed, signs of internal divisions within the society have occurred. Some of these divisions are not specific or unique to Israel's development. There are differences in the economic opportunities of men and women, for example, that characterize all countries. There are also diverse levels of religious commitments and different types of regions of residence that are typical of many countries. However, there are particular divisions within Israel that are clearly a manifestation of local-regional contexts and specific historical circumstances. Two are obvious—divisions between Jews and Arabs and divisions among Jews by ethnic origins and generational status. These ethnic and religious divisions, their sources and their intensities, are key to understanding the basis of the Arab-Israeli conflict.

IMMIGRATION AND THE NATIONAL-ETHNIC CONNECTION

More than in most countries, Israeli society has been shaped by immigration. Almost three million immigrants arrived in Israel between 1948 and the end of the twentieth century. This is an extremely large number in absolute terms and relative to the native-born Jewish population of Israel (there were 717,000 Jews at the end of 1948 in Israel, of whom 65 percent were foreign born). These Jewish immigrants have come from diverse national origins over the last hundred years. Two-thirds of the immigrants to the State of Israel have come from European countries (or from Western origins), and one-third have come from Asian or African countries (or from Middle Eastern origins).

There are powerful ideological, Zionist underpinnings of Israel's immigration policies that are unique in a comparative context. Immigration has had a major impact on the Arab-Israeli conflict because of the large number of conspicuous foreign persons in Israel who do not fit into Middle Eastern culture. Immigration has had an indirect impact on the Arab-Israeli conflict through the formation of Jewish ethnic groups who have competed with the Israeli Arab community for government resources. Regional developments and social inequalities within Israel have been influenced by immigration. Immigration has resulted in cultural diversity and ethnic pluralism and in new forms of Westernization and capitalistic economic development.

Immigration has been a major strategy of nation building and national integration in the State of Israel. The Zionist movement since the nineteenth century and the state from its establishment in 1948 have sought to gather together in one country those around the world who consider themselves Jewish by religion or ancestry. Several obvious external circumstances have influenced the immigration of Jews from a wide range of countries to Israel. These include the conditions preceding and following the Holocaust and World War II in Europe, the emerging nationalism among Jews around the world, the conditions of Jews in Arab-Muslim countries, and the radical changes in the 1990s in Eastern Europe with the breakup of the Soviet Union. The emergence of a large and integrated American Jewish community, which has not immigrated in substantial numbers to Israel, is another factor in understanding the selectivity of immigration to Israel.

Specific circumstances internal to Israel have also influenced the pace and selectivity of immigration over time. The expansion of the Jewish population over a larger geographic area, the attractions of economic opportunities and Jewish political control, and Israel's cultural development and religious activities have all been important factors in the decisions of many to immigrate. War and military conflicts and general internal tensions have often generated national commitments and euphoria (as in the immediate post-1948 and post-1967 war periods), but they have also caused fear and anxiety about living in dangerous and uncertain circumstances.

Many Jews who have immigrated to Israel are likely to come under some broad definition of refugee movement in the sense of having been stateless, or of having been forced to move out of some country, or having been on the move with few other destination options. Throughout most of Israel's short history, the absence of alternatives for those with reduced options to stay where they were living has been the major force encouraging periodic large-scale Jewish immigration to Israel. Two peaks mark the figure on immigration to the State of Israel: (1) the period of mass immigration immediately following the establishment of the state in 1948 and (2) the more recent immigration from the former Soviet Union in the 1980s and 1990s. These immigration streams can be understood in the context of major factors in places of origin when there were few if any options for Jews to immigrate elsewhere Those strong push factors, combined with the ideological and policy commitments among Zionist organizations to subsidize Jewish immigration, explain much of the history of immigration to the State of Israel.

Immigration to Israel symbolizes the renewal of Jewish control over national development, and it is an important value shared by Jewish communities around the world. At the same time, immigration is, and has been, one of the core arenas of conflict between Jews and Arabs in the Middle East. Even before the establishment of the state, Jews and Arab populations perceived Jewish immigration in radically different terms. The overwhelming majority of Israeli Jews are committed to the continuation of immigration as an implementation of the Zionist agenda and a justification of their own national commitments. The Israeli Arab population (and the Palestinians) view Jewish immigration to Israel as part of the asymmetry between Jews and Palestinians, as a further diminution of their political power, and as a dilution of national economic resources. In short, past and future immigration is viewed as a national raison d'être among Jews—a basis of strength, national renewal, and unity—the building blocks of national identity and the cement of nationalism. Arabs view immigration as a perpetuation of their political subjugation in a "foreign" regional state, a basis for discrimination against their interests and continued inequality, a source of political and economic deprivation, an excuse for second-class citizenship, and a distorted allocation of limited national resources. As in the past, the powerful symbols of Jewish nationalism and renewal are sources of exclusion and conflict with the Palestinian people and Arab nationalism.

Despite its unique features, immigration to Israel shares many common features with other countries. Many countries have used the strategy of nation building through immigration. Third World countries and industrialized nations have used immigration incentives to reinstate residents of other countries who share their identity. Many have courted their former country persons to return home, particularly those with special skills, and have invested resources to lure back

Figure 2.3
Jewish Immigrants by Year of Immigration to Israel, 1948–1998

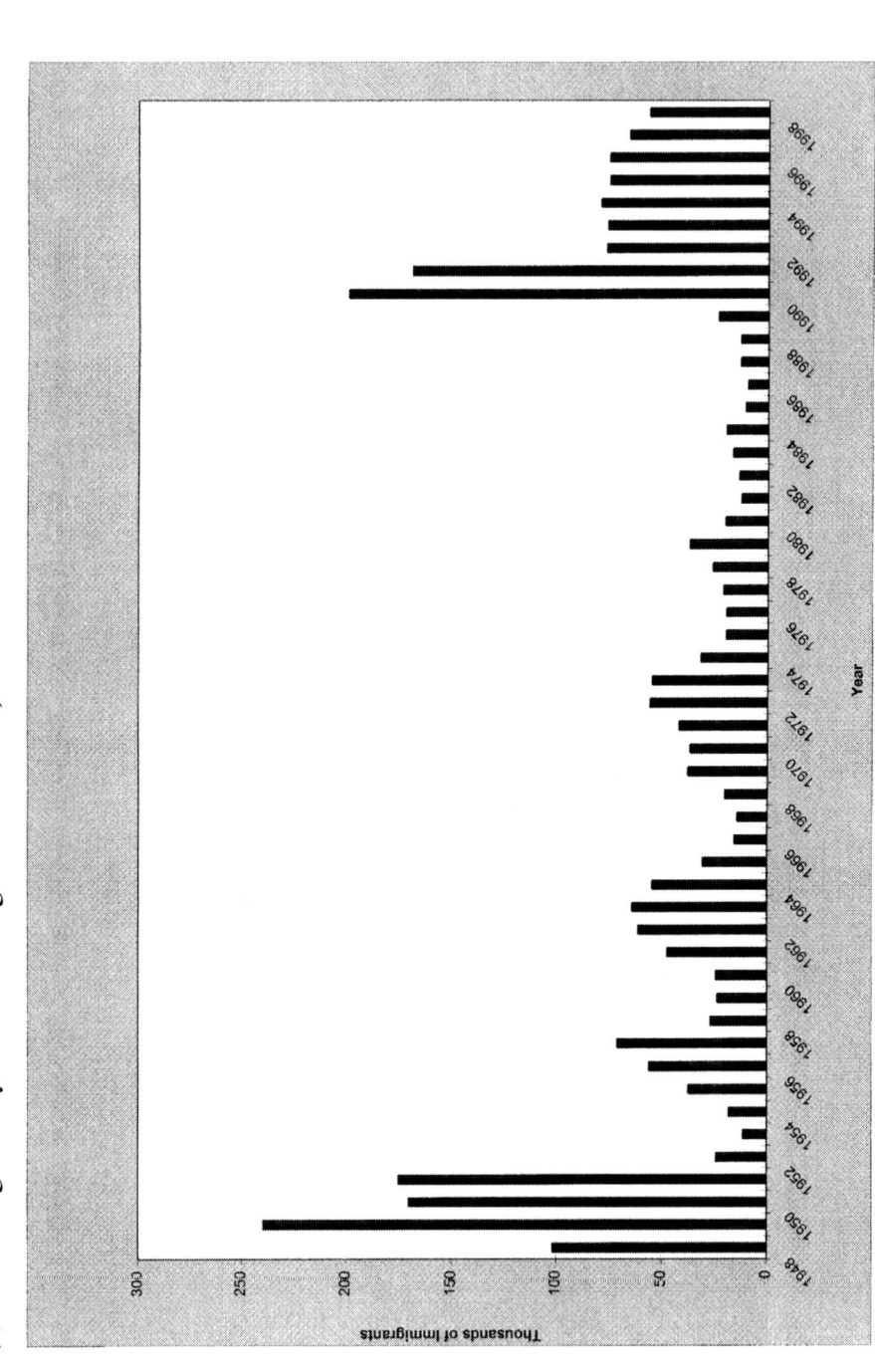

those living elsewhere who have obtained higher levels of education and commercial success. But perhaps in no other country is immigration so central a policy and an ideological doctrine. For no other country has immigration been of overwhelming importance in the composition and diversity of its population. And the "return" of Jews to their homeland from every corner of the globe has occurred after an interval of 2,000 years when Jewish people were exiled from their land and became a landless, wandering people in countries around the world.

LOOKING BACKWARD AND ASSESSING IMMIGRATION

About two-thirds of all immigrants to Israel from 1948 to 1997 have been of European or Western origins; the rest have come from Asian and African countries, mainly from the Middle East region. These Jewish immigrants entered the newly established state that was characterized by a large foreign-born population (two-thirds), and 90 percent were either European born or children of European immigrants. Just as the immigrants were not evenly spread over the last half century, so the particular national origins of the immigrants have shifted significantly over time. The proportion from Asian and African countries has shifted from 70 percent in the period from 1952 to 1957 to less than 10 percent in the 1970s and in the 1990s. While the immigration in the first period after the establishment of the state was from a very wide range of countries, the recent movement in the 1990s was dominated (over 90 percent) by those with Eastern European origins, largely from the former Soviet Union.

The formal context of Israel's immigration policy is contained in the Declaration of Independence (passed on May 14, 1948), which states, "The State of Israel is open to Jewish immigration and the Ingathering of Exiles" (see appendix). This policy statement was combined with the first order enacted by the provisional government to abolish the British-imposed restrictions on immigration to Palestine and retroactively to define those who had entered illegally as legal residents of the new state. These two elements formed Israel's immigration policy during the first two years of statehood. The Law of Return, enacted on July 5, 1950, granted to every Jew in the world the right to immigrate and settle in Israel, with minor exceptions related to health and security. These formal regulations do not convey the main thrust of immigration policy in Israel, which is to encourage and subsidize Jewish immigration actively and to facilitate the early stages of the immigrant settlement processes.

THE FOUR IMMIGRATION STREAMS

Since the establishment of Israel, there have been four major waves of immigration—each with its unique character, building on the experience of a previous wave. Immigrants of these four waves entered a changing Israeli society characterized by emerging, new political, economic, and cultural contexts.

Mass Immigration, 1948–1951

The first and most dramatic immigrant stream, referred to as the period of "mass" immigration, occurred immediately after the establishment of the state. A very high volume and rate of Jewish immigration from diverse origins arrived in Israel in the contexts of the 1948 War of Independence and in the transition to national control and integration. The immigrants doubled the size of the Jewish population in three years—350,000 immigrants arrived in the first eighteen months after statehood, and an additional 350,000 arrived during the following year and a half. It was a massive undertaking to provide basic housing, jobs, schooling, and health services. The problems were exacerbated by the fact that many of the immigrants were not able to speak or write the national language (Hebrew) and often arrived from the depths of deprivation in postwar Europe. Israel was immersed in a war for its survival as a new nation, and its economic base was fragile and weak.

Europeans dominated the first stage of mass immigration to Israel. They were Jewish refugees from the Holocaust coming to a predominately European-origin society. Even when they did not know Hebrew, they were able to communicate with the Israeli authorities in Yiddish. In 1948, 85 percent of the Jewish population of Israel was of European origin as were the immigrants. The first immigrants therefore had cultural, language, and social connections to the Jewish population of the state. This was not the case for the Jewish immigrants who arrived from the Middle East. As Jewish immigrants from Middle East countries joined the stream of immigrants, the ethnic-origin composition changed. By 1951 over 70 percent of the immigrants to Israel were from Asian and North African countries, primarily Iraq, Iran, and Libya. They were not Western or European in culture and background, and they were unable to communicate in Hebrew or in a European language. During this early period of statehood, in conjunction with immigration, Israeli society expanded and consolidated its political, economic, and cultural institutions and developed and extended its welfare entitlement system.

North African Immigration

The second major stream of immigration occurred in the mid-1950s, when over half of the immigrants were from North African countries, particularly Morocco, Tunisia, and Egypt. The occupational skills, educational background, and exposure to urban modern society of many of these immigrants differed significantly from those of the earlier European immigrants. Many of these immigrants came from small towns, worked in crafts and small business and trades, had low levels of secular or religious education, and tended to have high levels of religious observance (in a Sephardic cultural context). They were neither the secular, socialist Zionists of earlier prestate immigrations nor Holocaust survivors of the mass immigration period.

Selective immigration quotas and regulations to control the negative economic impact of large-scale immigration were imposed in Israel during this period, primarily guided by economic considerations. The restrictions were often interpreted as a reflection of the cultural differences between these Middle Eastern and European immigrants and the discrimination of the former by the latter. Between 1955 and 1957, 165,000 immigrants arrived in Israel; between 1961 and 1964, an additional quarter of a million arrived, the majority of whom were from North African countries. The shifting ethnic-origin composition of immigrants from European to Middle Eastern countries (often Arabic-speaking countries) has also had significance for the Arab-Israeli population. Many of these Middle Eastern immigrants were relocated to development towns within Israel, on the periphery of Israeli society. Residential concentration reinforced social-class inequalities and ethnic cultural separation.

Post-1967: Soviet and Western Immigration

A fluctuating but relatively low volume of immigration in the next decade was followed by the third major wave of immigration after the 1967 Arab-Israeli war (often referred to by Israelis as the Six-Day

War). Most of these immigrants came from Eastern Europe (the Soviet Union and Romania) and from Western countries (mainly the United States). Between 1972 and 1979, over 250,000 immigrants arrived, about 50 percent from the Soviet Union and 8 percent from the United States. Of the 150,000 immigrants who arrived during the 1980s, 65 percent were from Eastern Europe (mainly the Soviet Union) or the United States; 11 percent, from Ethiopia; and 6 percent, from Iran. This immigration occurred at a time of economic growth in Israel, geographic expansion (the inclusion of Israeli settlements in areas administered by Israel after the war—the West Bank, Gaza, and the Golan Heights), and new national political and military self-confidence.

In general, the commitment of the government to the encouragement of immigration extended to providing subsidies for the early stages of immigrant adjustment. During this period, the Israeli government set higher economic standards of immigrant integration. The Ministry of Absorption established extensive financial incentives for adequate housing, jobs, and provisions for university-level education for immigrants from Europe and the United States. This contrasted sharply with the basic health care and minimum living accommodations provided to those of previous immigrant streams, particularly among those from Middle Eastern countries. In part, the immigrant subsidies reflected the increasing resources available in Israel and the occupational skills and educational backgrounds that characterized these immigrants. Nevertheless, the contrast between the subsidies offered the European and Western immigrants and those offered to immigrants of earlier periods from Middle Eastern countries was conspicuous. By the mid-1980s, half of the Israeli Jewish population was of Middle Eastern origins, largely reflecting their higher rates of natural increase. They no longer represented a demographic minority but were clearly disadvantaged in economic and social spheres. The Jewish population of Israel was characterized by a growing polarization between the "haves" and the "have nots." The economic divide was coterminous with the ethnic divide—those from Western, European countries were advantaged; those of Middle Eastern origins were disadvantaged. The economic/ethnic divide reflected the different resources (urban experience, occupational skills, educational levels) brought by European immigrants, the timing of their immigration, and the special subsidies that they received in Israel. Increasingly, social and economic gaps emerged not only among those who were foreign born but among the second generation as well. The continuing economic and educational gap between Jews of European and Middle Eastern origins among second-generation native-born Israeli children has raised troubling questions about the integration of immigrants and their children within Israeli society. The differential subsidies offered by the government to new immigrants during this period suggest that the ethnic gap in economic and cultural spheres was being reinforced for the second-generation native-born.

Russians: The New Masses

Beginning in 1989, significant numbers of Jews emigrated from the former Soviet Union. About half a million Russians entered Israel in the four years prior to 1993, and an additional 300,000 to 400,000 immigrants arrived in the final years of the twentieth century. By the close of 1999, over 800,000 Russian immigrants had arrived. By the year 2000, Russian immigrants represented one-fifth of the Jewish population of Israel. The number of immigrants (but not the rate per native-born population) was the largest since the period of mass immigration. It is the largest volume ever arriving from any single national origin during such a brief period of time. An additional number of Ethiopian Jews (about 35,000) arrived during the 1990s, adding to the 17,000 who had arrived in the 1980s. This immigration symbolized Israel's continuing commitment to be the political haven for diverse Jews and Jewish communities around the world. Most Ethiopian immigrants have had very different cultural, religious, and economic experiences from those from European and Middle Eastern countries, and they are distinct in comparison to the Israeli-born population. Their low levels of educational attainment, their specific occupational skills and experiences, and their limited exposure to modern health care systems contrast sharply with those of immigrants from the former Soviet Union who arrived in Israel during this time period.

As in the past, the immediate challenge facing the immigrants of this period was their short-term accommodation in Israel in terms of housing, jobs, and education. Government policies have been designed to address the immediate needs of the immigrants. Russian Jews are well educated, with white-collar, urban occupational skills and high socioeconomic aspirations for their children. Their numbers and their skill levels require major adjustments in the economy and society of Israel, which itself is changing. The experience of these immigrants with political democracy has been weak. Nevertheless, for the first time in Israeli political history, they formed a successful ethnic-based political party that began to be a serious political presence in Israel. In the 1996 national elections they represented a small but growing political party under Prime Minister Benjamin Netanyahu. In 1999 the Russian political party became the fourth largest party in the Knesset (the parliament) and joined the new coalition government under Prime Minister Ehud Barak. In the most recent period, starting in 1998, the proportion of Russians entering the State of Israel, who were not Jewish by religious criteria used in Israel, increased. They immigrated on the strength of their family connection (they may have had a Jewish grandfather or were married to a person who was Jewish). Their increasing numbers (estimated at over half of the immigrants) was a disturbing Zionist and Jewish dilemma for the state.

Although commitment to Jewish nationalism, or Zionism, is among the determinants of immigration to Israel, not all immigrants are Zionists. Many have immigrated to Israel as political refugees, and some have immigrated primarily for religious (often antisecular Zionist) reasons. Zionist ideology has attracted immigrants to Israel in specific social, economic, and political contexts, but the changes in the rates and sources of immigration over time cannot be accounted for by changes in Zionist ideology. Overall, Jewish nationalism has facilitated international migration to Israel when economic conditions in Israel provided better opportunities than in various places of origin. Economic factors account for most of the fluctuations in voluntary immigration to Israel. Political factors in countries of origin have been more important in refugee and nonvoluntary movements. Indeed, changes in political conditions of Jews in countries outside of Israel and the options available for migration to alternative destinations have shaped the fluctuating rates of migration to Israel and the changes in the national origins of immigrants. The political, social, and economic factors that have been critical in determining immigration to Israel are mostly beyond the control of the Jewish political organizations, in or outside of the State of Israel. As such, Israel's immigration policies are not likely to have a major impact on the sources and rates of Jewish immigration to Israel, unless the policy was to limit and exclude Jewish immigrants. The Zionist ideological foundations of the society would have to be altered radically for that change to occur.

Calls to end Jewish immigration to Palestine and subsequently to the State of Israel have been expressed by the Arab population throughout the period. From the end of the nineteenth century, when several thousand Jewish pioneers from Russia came to settle in Palestine throughout the period of the British mandate (1919–1947), and after the establishment of the state in 1948, Arabs have viewed Jewish immigration negatively. The Arab population has clearly viewed the mass immigration of Jews as threatening Arab control over Palestine. Jewish immigration would most directly have an impact on the number of Jews and Arabs living in the area and reduce the Arab population to a demographic minority in their own country. The political and economic consequences of this demographic change were obvious. After the establishment of the State of Israel, Jewish immigrants were granted Israeli citizenship upon arrival and had immediate access to government assistance. In sharp contrast, native-born Arabs in Israel had a difficult time connecting with their Palestinian relatives living outside the state, who often were in refugee centers in neighboring Arab countries. Native-born Arabs who are citizens of the State of Israel view themselves as disadvantaged second-class citizens in competition with recent immigrant foreigners in a Jewish-controlled labor market. Jewish immigration is subsidized, the education of Jewish immigrant children is guaranteed, and the health and welfare of Jewish families are comparable to those of long-term Jewish residents of Israel; Israeli Arabs, however, continue to be disadvantaged educationally and economically.

CONSPICUOUS IMMIGRATION CONSEQUENCES

The consequences of Jewish immigration have reverberated throughout the society. The most conspicuous impact of immigration has been in the increase in the size of the Jewish population. Indirectly, immigration has had a major impact on economic growth and cultural diversity, which is linked to the sources of immigration. In addition, the diverse national origins of Jewish immigrants to Israel have led to a changing ethnic mixture among Jews. In turn, the ethnic diversity and the links between ethnic origins and economic characteristics have had profound implications for national integration and inequality. The ethnic and economic divisions within Israel and the priorities attached to Jewish immigration and the integration of Jewish immigrants have reshaped the economic basis of the Arab-Israeli conflict and have redefined the cultural and social separation of Jewish and Arab populations within Israel.

Immigration has had a direct effect on the size of the Jewish population in Israel. Although immigration has been extensive and almost exclusively Jewish, the Jewish and Arab populations of Israel have increased at about the same rate since the establishment of the state. The country's population has remained over 80 percent Jewish. This Jewish-Arab demographic balance is striking, since half of the total growth of the Jewish Israeli population after 1948 is *directly* attributable to immigration while 98 percent of the Arab Israeli growth is due to natural increase. No reasonable assumption of future demographic dynamics would lead to an Arab Israeli demographic threat to the Jewish majority. Only the full incorporation of the Arab Palestinian populations currently not Israeli citizens (e.g., those living on the West Bank and in Gaza) or the mass emigration of Jewish Israelis from the country would alter the permanent minority demographic status of Arab Israelis. These are two most unlikely scenarios.

Immigration has resulted in a shift away from total European dominance to a greater demographic balance between Jews from European origins and Jews from Middle Eastern origins. Given the overlap of ethnic origin with social and economic resources, political orientations, and culture, the ethnic compositional shifts have had and will continue to have major social, economic, and political implications. These include the educational and economic disadvantage of Jews from Middle Eastern origins, the political alliances that differently characterize the European and the Middle Eastern origin populations, and the family and cultural differences of these ethnic Jewish communities. Different relationships with the Israeli Arab population are likely to characterize Jews of European and Jews of Middle Eastern origins. This primarily reflects greater social class and cultural similarities between Jews from the Middle East and Arab Israelis. Both are likely to share the Arabic language and culture. Nevertheless, their similarities often mean economic competition rather than greater cooperation. Their religious cultural differences and their politics often prevent closer relationships from emerging.

There is a strong basis for the distinctiveness of the foreign born of different national origins in Israel. Raised in different societies and cultures, they are transplanted to Israel and retain some of these distinguishing traits even as they become Israeli. The key question is: What happens to the culture of their children? Do those of the second generation become Israelis, not distinguishable on the basis of their parents' national origins? In short, is there an Israeli melting pot for the Jewish population?

These are difficult questions to answer for three reasons. First, there continues to be a large sector of the Jewish population who are foreign born, both because of the recent immigration from the former Soviet Union and also because of the older population of previous immigrant waves. There may not have been sufficient time for a melting pot to emerge. Second, all ethnic groups in Israel have changed over the last two generations relative to the immigrant generation. However, not all changes have been toward the convergence of cultural differences among ethnic groups. Indeed, some changes have resulted in the reinforcement of ethnic differences among Jews. For example, there have been major convergences among the various ethnic-origin groups in Israel in marriage, family, and health patterns. Initial differences in these areas of social life have diminished over time and have become similar among Jewish ethnic groups in the second generation. At the same time, there has been continued ethnic distinctiveness in residential location, educational attainment, occupational concentration, and political behavior. Ethnic residential concentration has been retained in some local areas and in some regions of the country (e.g., development areas and border towns). The residential concentration of ethnic groups is linked to access to educational institutions and job opportunities, to marriage markets and interethnic marriages, and to a reinforced sense of ethnic pride, connecting ethnic origins, families, and networks. Ethnic segregated residential patterns characterize significant segments of the Jewish population and are almost total between Jews and Arabs in Israel. By the second and third generation, real ethnic differences characterize where ethnic groups live, their level of school achievement, and the jobs they have. These differences result in the greater advantage to those Israeli Jews of European or Western origins and the disadvantage to those of Middle Eastern background.

What are the sources of these ethnic differences among Jews? The timing of marriage and the family size of ethnic groups, as well as their health characteristics, are carryovers from societies and cultures of origin. These tend to diminish over time among the second-generation native-born Jewish population. In contrast, ethnic differences in educational level and in jobs directly reflect Israeli policies of settlement and integration. These latter ethnic features tend to be reinforced by culture and politics and are discriminatory against those from Middle Eastern origins. Ethnic communities have surely moved away from specific countries of origin (e.g., Iraq, Tunisia, Yemen, Morocco, or France, Russia, Germany) toward an amalgamation of broader ethnic groups that represent new forms of ethnic differentiation. These new forms (such as "Middle Eastern" or "Western") are specific to Israeli society and mark Jews off from one another. Several of the documents included in the appendix illustrate the diverse ethnic and generational origins of Sephardic Jews and their struggle with the retention of the cultural distinctiveness of their specific ethnic communities.

Immigration has been the engine of ethnic group formation, the source of the transition from immigrant to ethnic group. Inherent features of Israeli society are related to what parts of the country ethnic groups were settled in, the ways in which Israeli governments have allocated resources for schools, and how they have invested in economic development that favored European-origin immigrants. Ethnic differences were therefore reinforced by where people lived, the jobs they held, and the educational attainments of their children. In turn, these differences by ethnic origin were not simply in culture and lifestyle, but they were related to economic disadvantage and the development of new ethnic communities. Often these differences resulted in ethnic conflict over the allocation of resources. These conflicts exist not simply because of immigration, but immigration reinforces and reflects the emergent internal and often regional conflicts.

Despite periodic ethnic clashes among Jews, two factors reinforce Jewish national unity. The first is that Jewish Israelis view Arab Israelis and Palestinians as the common "enemy" or at least a more deprived "minority" group within Israel. The second is that almost all native-born Jews have improved their socioeconomic circumstances, relative to their parents' generation. These gains have dampened feelings of deprivation and disadvantage, even in the face of ethnic group differences among Jews. The Jewish commitment to immigration is unlikely to waver in the future, even when there are signs of tension between recent and longer-term residents and among major ethnic

Jewish groups. The immigrant character of the society, its symbols, and its deep ideological and institutional roots balance these tensions between Jewish groups of different ethnic origins. So ingrained is the Jewish Zionist commitment to immigration that the large numbers of non-Jewish immigrants entering Israel in the late 1990s from Russia has not altered the application to them of the basic "Law of Return."

The future of immigration to Israel is linked to the political and social conditions of Jewish populations outside of the State of Israel. Given the major depletion of some of these communities through emigration to Israel and elsewhere (almost all of the Middle Eastern Jewish communities and a significant proportion of the Eastern European communities have been depleted of potential Jewish immigrants), there is a limited potential for large-scale future immigration. At least in the next generation, there is no reasonable basis for assuming any significant movement of Jews to Israel from the United States, the largest Jewish community in the world. Only the movements from Russia and areas of the former Soviet Union are potential sources of Jewish immigration to Israel.

The question of the future of ethnic pluralism in Israel is tied in to Jewish ethnic inequalities. While there is some chance of the reduction of these social inequalities, there is significant evidence of continued Jewish ethnic difference along broad social class and cultural lines. There is every reason to assume that the Jewish-Arab divide, even in the circumstance of peace between Israel and the Palestinians, will remain firm and conspicuous. All of the evidence points to continued internal divisions among Jews and between Arabs and Jews and to the continuation of Israel as a divided society at least for the next generation. Even if the Israeli-Palestinian peace process moves forward, relationships between Israel and her regional and global neighbors are likely to be different in the next generation than in the past. Immigration and ethnic issues within Israel are not likely to diminish in the future, although they will undoubtedly change with new generations and different challenges.

One of the consequences of immigration is the direct confrontation of immigrants with their short-term adjustment. The brief sketch of Vladamir, his wife Tanya, and his son Alex illustrates the initial adjustments of recent immigrants from Russia and their reflections on Jewish/Israeli identity.

A RUSSIAN JEWISH IMMIGRANT FAMILY

Vladamir is learning Hebrew. He barely gets by with some elementary Hebrew phrases that he learned in the Ulpan, the intensive language program that he took when he first arrived in Israel in 1997. He feels frustrated by his foreignness and his inability to master the language of his new country. He is mainly bitter about his job. He does gardening and some odd jobs when he can get work, although he has had several years of technical engineering training in Russia. His wife Tanya works as a medical technician in a small technical factory on the outskirts of Jerusalem run by a former resident of Russia who immigrated to Israel in the 1980s. She used to work as a lab technician in Russia in a government agency before she and several of her Jewish friends lost their job.

Vladamir and Tanya have a small two-bedroom apartment in a housing bloc built by the government on the outskirts of Jerusalem in an area that was "no-man's-land" before 1967. Most of the people who live there are also from Russia. All the notices on the apartment house bulletin board about the collective responsibility of the building, its maintenance, and classes for newcomers are in Russian. Most of their neighbors speak Russian rather than Hebrew. Neither Vladamir nor Tanya is a Zionist and had not been in Russia. Neither knows much about Judaism. In Russia, they were referred to as Jews and it was clear what that meant. They immigrated to Israel after both lost their jobs and a number of their friends had already left for Israel. They thought about going to America or to Germany but visas were only available to Israel. With economic shortages in Russia and no prospect of a decent job, immigrating to Israel looked attractive. They knew of stories of economic difficulties in Israel, housing and language problems, but they were concerned about their son's education in Russia and thought that he would have a better chance of success in Israel.

Their only child, Alex, attends a local school in Jerusalem and seems to be adapting well. His science background placed him in the best school in Jerusalem and he is doing well academically. He had made some Israeli friends but most were the children of Russian immigrants. His parents have high aspirations for him. When asked why he came to Israel, Vladamir almost always responds in terms of his son. Alex, he says, won't face the uncertainty he felt in Russia. He has friends. When pressed he says that his son can be a Jew without paying the price of discrimination. But it is not clear what being a Jew means in Israel. In Russia it was clear when the government identified him as a Jew. But in Israel, he is not sure what his Jewishness is. It is not religion, since he and his family know little of religion and are not observant of Jewish rituals. When pressed, Tanya says that Jewishness means being an Israeli, although living in Israel reveals to both of them that are not yet very Israeli in culture or ideology. They voted for the Russian political party in the last election in Israel and they read the Russian language newspaper. Their major worry is the conflict with the Arabs and the military. After two years in Israel, Vladimir has changed and his friends who have been in Israel longer have changed even more. How Israeli or how Jewish Alex will be is not a question that concerns Vladimir or Tanya as they struggle to adjust to the challenges of their new society. Finding a better job and buying some of the appliances that their friends have seem to have the highest priority for them.

OFFICIAL VIEWS OF ETHNICITY

Israel is a society that prides itself on being one Jewish nation and on integrating very large numbers of immigrants from diverse societies. Ethnic origin among Jews is viewed as transitional and largely irrelevant to the longer-term goals of Jewish national integration and nation building. Politically and officially, ethnic-origin differences are expected to disappear, and immigrants are expected to be absorbed into the national culture and polity. The goal of absorption (in Israel, *Klita*, which means absorption) has been among the nation's ideological and political objectives since its establishment. Policies to close the economic and cultural gaps among immigrants were designed in the hope of achieving the rapid integration and equalization of immigrant groups from diverse countries of origin.

Jews of the third generation are distant from their ethnic origins, socialized into national politics and culture by exposure to educational institutions and the military, and raised in families in which the parents are native-born Israelis. Indeed, the ethnic background of the Israeli born is expected to be marginal, the cultural remnant of no social or economic significance. Nation building is expected to remove the diversity of ethnic origins as new forms of state loyalty emerge focusing solely on Jewish peoplehood. Religious similarity, military service, and the collective consciousness derived from Israel's security situation operate to dilute ethnic differences. This is the official ideology within Israel. Ethnic cleavage and ethnic community organization become problems to be solved, not cultural traits or sources of inequality.

Official government publications treat ethnic origin among Jews in

Israel almost always in terms of place of birth of the person. For the Israeli born, place of birth of the parents (usually the father) is obtained. It is a simple step from these definitions to the conclusion that generational distance from foreignness or exposure to Israeli society marks the progress toward the end of ethnic identity. The question of ethnic origin and of "ancestry" of the third generation (the native born of native-born parents) has not so far been addressed officially in Israel. Indeed, to judge solely from the official government publications and statistical bureaus in Israel, the third generation in Israel has no differentiating ethnic origin of significance. They are defined simply as Israeli born of Israeli-born parents, "just" Israeli without ethnic markers. In contrast, Arab Israelis retain their "ethnic" designation indefinitely.

How are the multitudes of countries of immigration categorized among the first two generations? These countries are grouped into two broad divisions: Europe-America and Asia-Africa. Some classifications by the government are revealing. For example, Jews from South Africa are in the Europe-America category; those from Ethiopia are in the Asian-African category. This difference reflects how those of "European origins" are categorized together. This ethnic categorization is unique historically among Jewish communities of the world, and it is constructed as an internal ethnic division only among Jews in the State of Israel. It is a rejection of the historically more complex ethnic division between Sephardi and Ashkenazi Jewries that has a series of cultural linkages. Thus, despite the salience of ethnic origin in a multiethnic society, nothing beyond foreign birth, or country of origin of fathers of those who were native born, is collected in official records. Those of the first (the foreign born) and second (the native born of foreign-born parents) generations are recategorized into newly designated ethnic forms created by Israeli society.

NON-JEWISH MINORITIES

What is the official categorization of the minority populations in Israel who are not Jewish? The significant Arab minorities in Israel are citizens of the state. As constructed in government documents, the Arab-Israeli populations are not Palestinians and are often not designated as Arabs. They are grouped as Muslims, Christians, Druze, and others. The distinction is based on religious not ethnic or national divisions. Along with the question of "who is a Jew" (by religion, national identity, self-definition, or religion of the mother), the definition of Arabs in Israel lies centrally in the quagmire of whether Jews and Arabs constitute nationalities or religious groups or both. The issue of definition is at the core of political and ideological debates about the nationality of the Arab population. The treatment of Arabs in terms of religious groupings denies (symbolically) their ethnic national identity and their political relationship to Arabs elsewhere in the region. The "religious" designation of Israelis appears on Israeli identity cards and on all formal documents (nationality among Jews does not appear, but religion does).

The category "non-Jews" is regularly used in official publications to contrast with Israelis who are Jewish. Arabs are therefore the "other" group, always in contrast to Jewish Israelis. In politically comic, but revealing, documents of official statistics among Palestinians, data in tabular form and in charts are presented to document the Arab population in Israel and categorize them as the "non-Jewish" population of Israel. This was the category used in the first Current Status Report, series no. 1, of the Palestinian Bureau of Statistics, 1994. The publication, issued by the Palestinian National Authority under the signature of Chairman Yassar Arafat, was largely copied from the *Statistical Yearbook of Israel*.

The designation of Arabs as "non-Jewish" is consistent with the earliest reference in official documents. The Balfour Declaration of 1917, specifying the British commitment toward the establishment of a national homeland for the Jewish people, explicitly notes that the civil and religious rights of the "non-Jewish" communities should be safeguarded. Indeed, the "minority" issue in Israel is a religious issue within the government bureaus, and political and economic allocations come through the Ministry of Religious Affairs. The formal designation of Arabs as non-Jews and the subdivision of Jewish Israelis into Asian-African and European-American categories are embedded in the orientation of everyday Israeli life. The official classification reinforces ethnic group labeling and, hence, the ethnic divisions within the society.

Chapter 3

Arab Israelis: Dependency and Distinctiveness

Arab Israelis are Palestinian residents of prestate Israel who remained in the emerging Jewish State of Israel. They experienced the transition from being the majority population in Palestine to a minority status in the State of Israel. This transition has had major repercussions for how Arab Israelis identify themselves and how they are identified by others. The separation of Israeli Arabs from Palestinians living outside of Israel in the period from 1948 to 1967 and the reestablishment of some ties with them after 1967 have transformed their Palestinian *and* their Israeli identities.

Who are Israeli Arabs? What are their origins? What are their lifestyles? Have they been integrated as citizens of the State of Israel? How do they relate to the Palestinians living outside of the state? The answers to these questions lie in some basic historical facts about the origins of the Arab Israelis and provide important clues in unraveling the Arab-Israeli conflict.

Subsequent to the British assumption of the administrative control of Palestine after World War I, a census of Palestine was undertaken. According to the census of 1922, there were 668,000 Arabs and 84,000 Jews living in the whole of Palestine, with Arabs representing almost 90 percent of the inhabitants. The British commitments to the Jewish settlement in Palestine and to the Arab populations living there were formulated in the Balfour Declaration.

THE BALFOUR DECLARATION AND WHITE PAPERS

The Balfour Declaration was formulated as British policy in 1917 and remained the primary document of dispute between Arabs and Jews for the duration of the British mandate in Palestine. The policy commitment was presented in the form of a letter from Lord Arthur James Balfour to Lord Rothschild:

Foreign Office
November 2, 1917

Dear Lord Rothschild,

I have much pleasure in conveying to you, on behalf of His Majesty's government, the following declaration of sympathy with Jewish Zionist aspirations which has been submitted to, and approved by, the Cabinet.

"His Majesty's Government view with favour the establishment in Palestine of a national home for the Jewish people, and will use their best endeavors to facilitate the achievement of this object, it being clearly understood that nothing shall be done which may prejudice the civil and religious rights of existing non-Jewish communities in Palestine, or the rights and political status enjoyed by Jews in any other country."

I shall be grateful if you would bring this declaration to the knowledge of the Zionist Federation.

Yours sincerely,

Arthur James Balfour

The Balfour Declaration supported the development of a "national home" for the Jewish people and had a commitment to facilitate this goal through immigration. It was unclear whether this national home initially meant a Jewish state. It was unlikely that policy makers had a state in mind, since the Jewish leaders were divided over their own long-term goals and the Arabs constituted a very large majority of the population of Palestine. The British government declared that it would facilitate the goal of establishing a national home for the Jews as long as the civil and religious rights of the Arab population were protected. Thus, there is some basis for the Arab claim that when Jewish immigration to Palestine increased the ratio of Jews to Arabs, thereby altering the civil (i.e., political) rights of the Arab population, the British no longer were responsible for facilitating the development of a Jewish national home.

In addition, the Balfour Declaration reassured the Jewish communities in Western countries that their civil rights would not be affected by the development of a Jewish community in Palestine. Thus, in the initial British formulation, there was little expectation that Jews would be moving in large numbers to Palestine or that they would become a numerical threat to the local Arab population. Therefore, the Balfour Declaration in 1917 already reflected international ambiguities over Palestine and the conflicting rights of Arab and Jewish populations. The declaration also illustrates the central role played by international agencies. How Britain would facilitate the national aspirations of Jews while protecting the rights of the Arab population was unclear and symbolized the three-way political tensions existing throughout the mandate period.

During the British mandate period, formal commissions were established by the mandate authorities and policy papers, called white papers, were issued to deal with some of the key problems of administering the Jewish and Arab communities of Palestine. Often invited to prepare reports and present perspectives to the British mandate authorities, the Jewish and Arab representatives to these forums disagreed about the implications of the changing facts of their communities in Palestine.

The Jewish position was often presented by the representatives of the Jewish Agency, the authoritative Jewish governing board set up by Great Britain to represent the Jewish community of Palestine, the *Yishuv*. The Jewish Agency and its representatives focused on the need for additional immigration and the economic absorptive capacity of Palestine. They developed the argument that immigration was a right guaranteed by the Balfour Declaration. Furthermore, they argued that Great Britain had made the commitment to facilitate immigration and immigration was the core of the government's commitment to the Jewish people. Hence, the Jews were in Palestine by right, and they should be able to immigrate to Palestine by right. While immigration could not be uncontrolled, the Jewish Agency argued that economic factors should be the only basis for immigration regulation. The economic absorptive capacity of Palestine, as determined by the British authorities, was the basis of immigration regulation through the 1930s. The critical stand of the Jewish Agency in the 1930s was that political factors should not be the basis of restricting immigration. During this first period, and through the mid-1930s, the number of Jewish immigrants entering Palestine amounted to 300,000, half of whom were subsidized by the Zionist authorities. More than 90 percent came from European countries. This was an impressive number, given an estimated Jewish population in Palestine at the end of 1931 of 175,000. The number of immigrants increased the ratio of Jews to the total population from less than 17 percent to close to 30 percent in 1930.

As for the Arab population of Palestine, the Jews argued that their economic and health conditions always improved with the increasing presence of Jews in Palestine. In addition to making the political argument about rights and providing reminders of the British commitments through the Balfour Declaration and other documents and policy statements to a Jewish national homeland, the Jewish Agency argued about the potential economic and health benefits that Jews were bringing to the region. These benefits were not only to the Jewish community but also to the Arab populations that were located near Jewish settlements and that were influenced by Jewish economic developments.

Clearly the Arab populations viewed the increase of the Jewish population with great alarm. They attacked in words and in confrontations the immigrant policy of Zionism and the British authorities as the symbol of that increase. Arabs correctly saw that immigration would change Arab control over Palestine and increase the presence of Jewish immigrants from Europe in Palestine.

Often it was difficult for British authorities to persuade Arab representatives to share their views with the various commissions, since in large part they wanted their appearance to be contingent on an end to Jewish immigration. In the 1930s, the president of the Arab Higher Committee agreed to present the Arab case before one of the British commissions, the Peel Commission. The presentation centered on the goal of Arab national independence, noting that Jewish immigration was detrimental to that goal. The Arab position was directly in conflict with the Zionist position of the *Yishuv*. They argued that the aspirations of Palestinian Arabs for self-government were frustrated by the growing Jewish presence in Palestine and, in particular, by continuous Jewish immigration. The Arabs proposed the abandonment of the Balfour Declaration and the experiment of a national Jewish homeland and called for the immediate cessation of Jewish immigration. Moreover, the Arabs presented the case for the establishment of an Arab state in treaty relations with Great Britain that would allow the majority of Palestine (i.e., the Arab population) to determine the place of Jews in Palestine. The new economic realities, implying Arab prosperity resulting from Jewish immigration, did not carry much weight. One Arab witness to the Peel Commission hearings stated, "You say we are better off; you say that my house has been enriched by the strangers who have entered it. But it is *my* house, and I did not invite the strangers in, or ask them to enrich it, and I do not care how poor or bare it is if only I am master in it."

British policy changed starting in 1936 when the British initiated a new set of policies that established a political ceiling on the number of Jewish immigrants to be allowed entrance into Palestine. This policy was designed to regulate the number of Jewish immigrants in relation to the growth of the Arab population. Hence, it would establish Jews as a permanent minority in Palestine. It posited that any further immigration would be at the will of the Arab resident majority. This position was totally unacceptable to the Jewish community, whose Zionism was based on the rejection of permanent Jewish minority status. Moreover, Zionism proclaimed the need for Jewish political autonomy, which required political control. Events in Europe and the destruction of European Jewry in the Holocaust called into question this long-term policy. Over time, it became clear that some partition of Palestine would be inevitable following the withdrawal of British troops and the end of the mandate.

POPULATION

In many ways, therefore, population issues have been in the forefront of the conflict between Arabs and Jews in Palestine from the end of the nineteenth century until the establishment of the state. These population issues have continued to be important areas of controversy within Israeli society. In the prestate period, there were political conflicts over the number of Jews permitted by the British to enter Palestine. The Arab population was concerned that increasing the number of Jewish immigrants to Palestine would not only reduce their numerical majority but also change their political and economic power. Some of the restrictions on immigration during the mandate period were based on estimates of economic opportunities made by the British authorities, and some were based on rates of Arab and Jewish demographic growth. In the areas of prestate British mandate

Palestine immediately prior to the establishment of the State of Israel, Arabs constituted two-thirds of the population. They became less than 20 percent of the State of Israel's population in 1948 when large numbers of Arabs fled or were forced to leave the territory that was to become the State of Israel.

The Jewish population has increased from immigration, but the growth of the Arab population within Palestine and the State of Israel has been a result of high levels of natural increase (large families characterize Arab Israelis, not Jewish Israelis). In contrast to the importance of immigration for the Jewish population of Israel, large Arab family size has been the path to high Arab growth rates. It is not difficult to imagine the very different implications of these two alternative growth strategies in terms of the family, the role of women, and the impact on the economy. Immigration tends to be associated with high economic growth, and it results in the economic integration of Jewish immigrants into the national system. Large family size drains the economic resources of families, often stymies educational investments in the next generation, and retains a hierarchy of gender roles in which men gain status from work and women gain status from childbearing and child rearing. Immigration tends to disrupt families and family roles; large families tend to reinforce separate spheres of activities for men and women and reinforce family centrality.

The different growth rates of Arab and Jewish populations and their geographic concentrations, which are outlined below, have been conspicuous concerns of several political regimes and within different territorial configurations in Israel. Almost always the focus had been on the Arabs as a whole, whether in Palestine or in Israel, with a clear emphasis on the contrasts and comparisons between the Arab and Jewish populations. The analysis of Arab demographic patterns is best understood in the context of the Arab-Jewish conflict and as a basis for understanding Arab communities.

As for the Israeli Jewish population as a whole, the focus will be on three central issues relating to Arab Israelis: population, politics, and economy. The changing levels of inequality between Arabs and Jews in Israel will be examined as will the role of large family size in reinforcing the position of women within the Arab community. Particular attention will focus on the importance of Arab residential segregation in sustaining the dependency of Arab Israelis on Israeli Jews. These themes are central to the Arab-Israel conflict and the question of Israeli Arab identity. These issues are integral to understanding the Arab community in Israeli society and the religious, social-class, and regional diversity within the Arab-Israeli population.

The dominant religious group among Arab Israelis is Muslim, representing about three-fourths of the Arab population of Israel in the 1990s, an increase from 69 percent in 1948. Christian Arabs constitute 15 percent of the Arab population, and Druze make up a small minority (8 percent). These three religious divisions among the Arab population in Israel have significantly different social profiles. Christian Arabs are more urbanized and educated, and they are likely to have better health care and smaller families than either Muslims or Druze. Because of their numerical dominance, "Arab Israeli" or "Israeli Arab" will be treated as approximately equivalent to "Muslim Israeli" unless otherwise noted.

The "integration" of the Arab population within the Jewish-Israeli economy has resulted in their increased dependency and continuing inequality. Paradoxically, economic integration has resulted in both social mobility and the improvement of the economic conditions of the Arab minority and at the same time has resulted in increased discrimination against them. How is it that with greater minority integration there are increasing signs of social and cultural disadvantage? Part of the answer rests with the continued residential segregation of Arab Israelis. The residential restrictions and concentration of Arab Israelis in particular regions and towns within Israel has resulted in their limited access to economic opportunities. The concept of "dependency" of a minority population is used in the sense of the power exercised by the majority population (in this case, the Jews in Israel) and its control over the opportunities available to the minority population (in this case, the Arabs in Israel). Dependency does not necessarily reflect legal or political inequalities. It does imply, however, the continued distinctiveness of the Arab minority within Israel and their social and economic inequality. Dependency often involves discrimination against the minority.

Discrimination is not necessarily the result of negative attitudes, although it may be that as well. Discrimination results from the particular location of the minority within the larger community, their relative power, and their subordinate position within the economy. Hence, discrimination is structural and institutional, not necessarily the result of active prejudice and legal status. The most obvious structural sources of discrimination against Arab Israelis are indicated by the occupational returns to education (i.e., the kinds of jobs minority group members obtain when they have levels of education similar to the majority). They are also reflected in the ways in which residential segregation limits access to economic opportunities. The residential concentration of Arab Israelis limits their access to the best jobs and the better schools. Their educational achievements cannot overcome the limitation of their residence or the discrimination against them in the labor market, which is controlled by Jewish Israelis. The following case of Ahmed, an Israeli Arab, reveals some of these restrictions.

AHMED'S STORY

Ahmed wakes up every morning at dawn in his northern Israeli community of 4,500 persons. He has a strong cup of dark coffee that his wife has prepared before his four children are ready to leave for the day. Ahmed works in a community 20 kilometers away, as there have been no new jobs in this Arab town for years. He walks about a mile, picking up several of his friends along the way to go to the main road. There they take a bus crowded with other day workers and travel about half an hour. He and his friends work as skilled laborers for their Jewish boss from Morocco. They make a reasonable salary, the work is steady but not very challenging. Ahmed has been able to purchase some small appliances for his home, some tools for work around the house, and last year he bought a color television. Ahmed was born in 1955, went to the local school for a few years, is able to read and write and enjoys Arab music that he picks up from Lebanon on his small transistor radio. His life is better than his father's who did some farming and some heavy labor as a semi skilled construction worker.

He grew up with his wife Fatima in the same town. She is also from a local farming family and she has continued to work in the orange grove during the season. Twice a week she works as a domestic for a Jewish family from Tunisia, taking care of their two year old and cleaning house in a small suburban community about 15 kilometers away. She usually stays home taking care of her own children, cleaning house and preparing meals. When Fatima is away from home working, her neighbor, a second cousin, takes care of her youngest child. Ahmed, Fatima, and their children speak Arabic at home but their children have learned Hebrew in school. They are not politically involved. Both work for Jewish employers and witness the better lifestyle that Israeli Jews have in the nearby towns. These Israeli Jewish communities have a more modern school building, better roads and more decorated homes. No Israeli Arabs live there.

Their children live at home; the oldest is 17 and has become an apprentice plumber. Ibraham, the third child, is the brightest of the children and is a whiz at math in school. Fatima's and Ahmed's major worry is about their children and whether they will be able to get good jobs, marry into the right Arab families, have children and live nearby. They would like Ibraham to go to high school but there is none in their community. They could send him to the regional high school in the nearby community but they worry that after graduation he would get the same job as his friends who didn't go to high school. There isn't much available for him to do with a high school education. Maybe, they think aloud, he could go to some vocational school and learn a trade, or become an apprentice as his older brother. The regional vocational school is far away from home and they are not sure the Jewish school would accept him. "Maybe we could send him abroad," Ahmed says but Fatima frowns at the idea. Their community is home and family closeness is very important to them. Getting an education is an important value in this family, but they are concerned. "Will Ibraham get a better job if he has more education? Will he be able to marry a girl from a better family? Will he be better off than we are?" And his older brother chimes in, "Why stay in school for several more years only to get a job working for Russians or Moroccans? You will never have a chance when you are working for them!"

Ahmed and Fatima are concerned about their younger daughter who watches too much television and reads too many fashion magazines. While she might meet someone from a good family in high school, there are many distractions for young girls. They do not worry that she will be a domestic like her mother and several of her aunts. Indeed, she is bright and more educated than they are and perhaps could become a teacher in the local school, although there does not seem to be a shortage of teachers in the community. They do worry that she will learn the "wrong" things in school. She is now a devoted daughter but what will happen when she marries? Will she remain in this community and be helpful to her family or will she move away to another town and devote herself to her husband's family? Worse still, will she abandon her family and her community, become more educated and be influenced by what she reads? Where will she be when her parents get older and need her help? "Oh the difficulties of raising children!" they often say. As a teenager, most of what she wants to do is to spend evenings with her friends who go to Haifa as a group after school and just hang out. Ahmed and Fatima just can't understand the younger generation.

The story above provides some clues about the work and family lifestyles of Israeli Arabs. They are not disadvantaged relative to the older generation but relative to Israeli Jews. They do not compete well economically with Israeli Jews, particularly with those of Middle

Eastern origins. They have access to schools and health services, but these tend to be distant, of lower quality, and more difficult to access. Their primary concerns are about family and children, and the extent to which they will be pulled away from the traditional control of the Arab community through education and outside cultural influences. They are largely apolitical in the formal sense, although they feel the potential burdens of minority status in being unsure about how their children will be able to translate their education into better jobs. The better jobs are in communities away from home, so the costs of obtaining these jobs are high, even when they are accessible to them. When asked about how they identify themselves, they have no hesitation in saying they are "Israelis" but they are at the same time Arab Israelis. Increasingly, their children are attracted to a more active Arab political orientation that is less Arab Israeli than Palestinian. They worry about their children's politics and how Israeli Jews will react to a more aggressive Palestinian identity. When Ahmed and Fatima's children discuss their identity with their friends, they share a broader identification with the Palestinian struggle for political autonomy. Around their parents and their Jewish Israeli acquaintances, they remain quiet.

ARAB-ISRAELI ISSUES

One of the core points of conflict between Arabs and Israelis has been the relative proportions of Arabs and Jews in the State of Israel and in the area of Palestine before the establishment of the state. Population size has powerful political, economic, and ideological implications. This has been a continuing issue since before the establishment of the state and dramatically after the 1967 war when Palestinians, former residents of Palestine, came under Israeli administration and control.

Demographic Themes

Some have argued that the Arab demographic pattern has reached a rapid population growth stage. This growth results from increasing health care and high levels of life expectancy, on the one hand, and large family size as a result of high birthrates that began to decline slowly during the 1970s. In contrast, it is argued that the Jewish Israeli pattern has a low rate of growth that depends on immigration

Figure 3.1 Growth of Jewish and Arab Population in Israel, 1948–1992

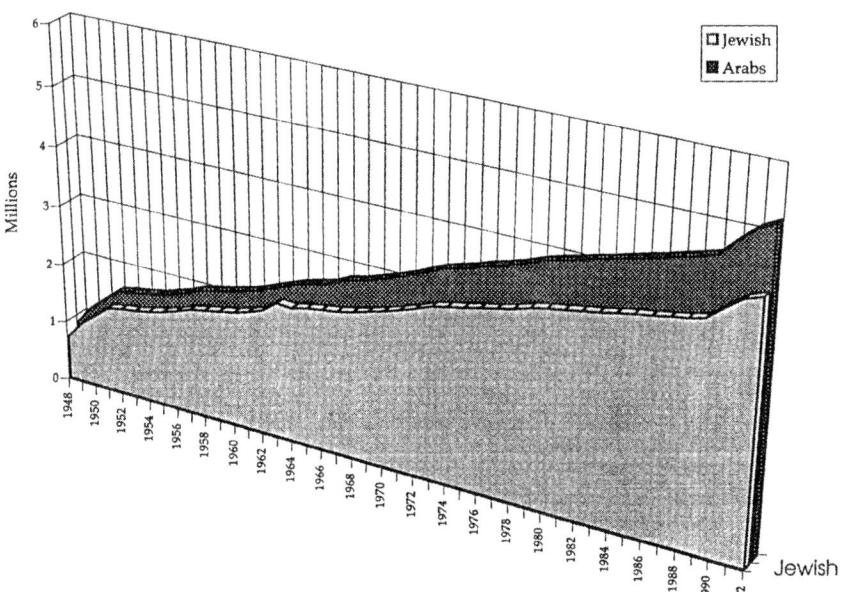

since they are characterized by small family size and good health care. Hence, Jews have a low population growth rate due to natural increase—a pattern that first characterized the European Jewish population in Israel and currently also characterizes second-generation Israeli Jews of Middle Eastern origins. In short, the younger Jewish Israelis have moved toward zero population growth, while the Arab Israeli population remains in the high-population growth stage. It does not take much imagination to exaggerate the political consequences of a rapidly growing minority population and a relatively low-growth majority population.

A careful look at the evidence suggests that this concern is unfounded. Since the establishment of Israel, the Arab proportion of the total population of the state has fluctuated around a narrow and low range, between 19 percent in 1948 and 18 percent fifty years later. Only with the political incorporation of Arab populations currently not Israeli citizens (i.e., those living on the West Bank and Gaza) or the mass exodus of Jewish Israelis from the country will Jews likely lose their majority within the state. Focusing on Israeli

Arabs, not on Palestinians living outside the state, the mass emigration of Jews from Israel or the mass movement of Arabs to the State of Israel are very unlikely events. At the national level, the Arab population is likely to remain a permanent demographic minority in the foreseeable future. The inclusion within Israel of several hundred thousand immigrant Jews from the former Soviet Union in the 1990s and the virtual stability of the Arab-Jewish population ratio over time reinforces the permanent minority status of Israeli Arabs.

At the regional or at the community level, however, the opposite is the case. There are regions within Israel that have a majority Arab population and areas within regions that have high levels of Arab population concentration and segregation. For example, in the Akko subdistrict there was a total population of 365,900 in 1991, of which 229,500 (63 percent) were not Jewish. In contrast, among the over one million inhabitants of the Tel Aviv subdistrict only 19,000 were not Jewish. It is at the local level that changes in Arab population size shape the labor supply and demand in an economic market. Local Arab population size sets up the potential for local market expansion as well as the retention of some specialized skilled labor and professionals. The importance of the region and the local community of Arab Israelis emerges from a systematic view of their relative growth rates. The national Jewish-Arab population ratio is simply not a demographic threat to the Jewish majority status.

One can speculate why this situation has been perceived as a threat among some Israeli Jews and viewed as a strategy among some Israeli Arabs. Perhaps the issue is a carryover from the British mandate period when the numbers of Jews entering Palestine were restricted. Added to this is the devastating demographic impact of the European Holocaust on the Jewish population of Europe. Taken together, the concern over Jewish population size in Israel becomes more understandable. There may be more complex reasons behind the view of Israeli leaders of the Arab challenge to Jewish quantitative power. Ironically, it may reflect the internal political divisions among Israelis over many other cultural and political issues. Perhaps only with regard to a "neutral" demographic issue (laden to be sure with emotional, historical, and cultural significance) can consensus be sustained among Israel's diverse Jewish population.

In sum, both Jewish and Arab populations have increased in size at the national level and have remained in approximately the same ratio to each other through their different demographic paths—Jews through immigration, Arabs through natural increase. There are demographic consequences of the distribution of the Arab population in smaller communities and regions of the country.

From the Arab perspective, several additional considerations are needed to understand their population growth. The first relates to the *selectivity* of poststate Arab populations relative to prestate Palestine. The Arab population remaining in the newly established State of Israel was different in size and of lower socioeconomic status when compared to the prestate Arab population. This residual Arab population (from the larger number of Arab Palestinians who were living in Palestine before the establishment of the state) had a subsequent demographic trajectory different from Palestinians who were living outside of the state. Some of the Arab demographic changes within Israel are the result of the transformation from a majority population to a demographic minority. Other changes resulted from the shift from an autonomous and somewhat diverse economic sectoral structure to a more homogeneous, agricultural, and dependent sector under military administration within the larger Jewish economy. The economic dependency of the Israeli Arab population emerges from the selectivity issue, as does its demographic minority status.

The improvement in mortality conditions among Arabs began before the establishment of the state and preceded the decline in fertility. The mortality decline was slower among Arabs than among Jewish Israelis, and their rate of infant mortality remains almost twice as high. Of every 1,000 births in the late 1990s, about 10 Israeli Muslim children do not survive to celebrate their first birthday. Among Jewish Israelis, the infant mortality rate is about 5 per 1,000 births. The significance of the mortality decline lies in the retention of a mortality gap between Arab and Jewish Israelis despite improvements in both populations. Differences in infant mortality between Arabs and Jews living in the same society reflect the inequality between these groups. The improvement in Arab health conditions has often been viewed as an indicator of the extent of Israeli welfare largess—what the Jewish State of Israel has done to take care of its minority groups, despite the fact that Israel has been at war with surrounding Arab states. From an Arab perspective, the continuing relative inequality of Arabs and Jews in Israel and the disadvantaged status of Arab Israelis becomes apparent when one examines the persistent mortality gap between populations in the same country.

Fertility, Family, and Gender

Since the 1970s, declines in fertility levels among Muslim Israelis have been recorded. The decline in family size occurred earlier among Christian than among Muslim or Druze Israelis. Muslim women who were married immediately before the establishment of the state (1944–1948) bore more than nine children over thirty years of marriage. The total fertility rate in the late 1990s (an estimate of average family size) was less than five children, similar to the "ideal" family size expressed by those married in the 1970s. Christian Arab women who were married before 1955 had an ideal family size of around six children; the younger women who married in the post-1967 period had an average ideal family size of four children. The estimated family size of Jewish Israelis in the late 1990s was 2.6, similar to the level among Christian Arabs.

The importance of the higher Arab than Jewish fertility for Arab population growth is unmistakable. Largely neglected, however, are the implications of high fertility for the role of Arab women within their communities and families. Large family size also has costs to the socioeconomic opportunities available for the next generation of Arab Israelis. In large part, the traditional role of Arab women has almost always been treated as one of the reasons underlying sustained high fertility. This position is consistent with the argument that unless the status of women changes to include non-childbearing roles, there is little likelihood of a significant reduction in family size. Indeed, the traditional role of a Muslim woman as the bearer of large number of children has been part of the explanation of the resistance of Arab Israeli women to change their fertility patterns with the first indications of economic modernization. The traditional family roles of Arab Israelis were reinforced by the absence of internal migration and by state welfare policies. Arab women remained in their local communities under the control of their husbands and the system of patriarchy. Welfare policies in Israel indirectly reinforced high Muslim fertility by providing financial supports for families with large numbers of children.

In addition, large family size sustains the family-oriented roles of Muslim women, and high Arab fertility reinforces the subordinate role of women within the family. High fertility and large family size have clear disadvantages from the point of view of the role of women and their empowerment. Nevertheless, sustained high Arab fertility

An Arab woman preparing flat bread using traditional methods, in the Carmel market of Tel Aviv. She is seated below an election poster of Benjamin Netanyahu, the former Prime Minister of Israel, which reads "a strong leader for the future of Israel." (1999)

can be appreciated from both a demographic-national Arab perspective (as a balance to the high rates of Jewish immigration) and the point of view of Arab males. The larger family size of Muslim women has been viewed by some Arabs as an indicator of the frailty of the Jewish demographic superiority. Large family size may be the last vestige of competition between Arabs and Jews in which Arabs can control their own lives. As one Arab Israeli said, "We can't win when we fight them, but we can outbreed them."

According to some Israelis, there is an Arab "mentality" or "culture" that reinforces the "backwardness" of Arab women that results in their higher fertility. This view has at times been a condescending, ethnocentric Jewish view of the Muslim population.

Improvements in mortality rates were the result of the extension of health care and public health facilities within Arab communities. The decline in Muslim fertility since the 1970s followed the continuing declines in mortality and the declining low rates of infant mortality. Equally important, there has been a continuing increase in the educational attainment of Muslim women. Muslim women who benefited from the mandatory education act of Israel reached their childbearing period in the 1970s. Less than 10 percent of the Arab women who were married in the mid-1960s had any formal education after the ninth grade compared to about 50 percent of those who married in the early 1980s. There have also been increases in the participation of Arab women in the formal and informal labor force and the exceptional growth in the labor force participation of educated Arab women. These factors have all had an impact on reducing the level of Arab fertility over time.

There has been a continuous process of Arab men leaving agriculture to commute to jobs within the Jewish sector. Increases in the standard of living and education, along with benefits from the welfare state and an increase in its opportunities, suggest that the economic futures of younger couples have become more independent of their extended family. The decline in family size among Muslim Israelis is likely to have major social and cultural repercussions for the younger generation in the twenty first century. Thus, from the point of view of the Arab community, fertility levels are important not because they are linked to population growth in Israel but because fertility is part of families and the roles of men and women. Hence, fertility trends reveal critical aspects of the social organization of Arab communities and families.

Large family size continues to bind Arab women to their households and places them in the control of their husbands, their extended family, and neighbors. Arab women and young adults have increased their dependency on Arab men, and Arab men generally have increased their dependency on Israeli Jews. Having a large family therefore reinforces the segregated roles of men and women in the Muslim culture. There is an implied hierarchy in these roles where women are less powerful than men and are subordinate to husbands and fathers. This hierarchy and power within the household connects to the circular movement of Arab laborers in the Jewish sector of Israel and their return to Arab residential areas after work. Since Arab men work for Jews in the Jewish sector of the economy, some of the Arab women have become unpaid laborers in family agriculture, substituting for the roles of Arab men.

The dependency role of young adults, but particularly of young women, is further illustrated by their pattern of living arrangements. Muslim young adults live with their families until they marry. Only when young adults marry do they move from one family role (as child) to another (as spouse). There are indeed few unmarried Muslim Israelis who live alone or in any independent relationship apart from their parents or their family's supervision. This pattern of dependency among young Muslims contrasts with the increasing proportions of Jewish Israeli adults who tend to leave home to establish some independent residence before they marry. Older widowed Arab women are most likely to be incorporated into their daughter's household rather than live alone or in some collective institutionalized care. Middle-age persons are often caught in the twin obligations to their widowed parent and their unmarried adult child living at home.

Therefore, Arab dependencies in Israeli society are manifest at a variety of levels: the level of economic activities (the economic dependencies of Arabs on Israeli Jews for work outside of their communities of residence), gender dependencies (of Arab women on Arab male control), the dependencies of young adults on their parents and extended families (through their living arrangements until they marry), and the dependency of older persons on their children. These dependencies may change as educational levels increase, as family size is reduced, and as new economic opportunities within the Arab sector open. But the multiple dependencies among Arab Israelis contrast sharply with patterns of independence among Jewish Israelis at all the stages of the life course.

These dependencies have important implications for the Arab-Israeli conflict. Clearly the economic dependency of Arab Israelis on the Jewish controlled economic sectors results in inequalities, as Arab Israelis are not in control of their jobs or their economic activities. The gender dependencies reinforce the gap between Arab and Jewish women as the trajectories of change within these communities are moving in different directions at different velocities. Jewish women are moving in the direction of greater gender equalities with Jewish men, and young Jewish adults are moving toward greater independence from their parents. Arab Israeli women continue to be in subordinate positions relative to their husbands and fathers, and young Arabs do not have the option of becoming more independent from their parents. Hence, the changes that both communities have experienced have moved them farther apart from each other, Arab women from Jewish women and young Arab adults from young Jewish adults. The asymmetry and inequalities between Israeli Arabs and Israeli Jews in the economic sphere parallel the gap between the increasingly independent Jewish Israeli women and the dependent Arab women. To the extent that conflict resolutions are enhanced by the reduction of differences between groups, the increasing gap between these communities in Israel sustains and reinforces the conflict between them.

URBANIZATION AND RESIDENTIAL CONCENTRATION

The basis for understanding these dependencies begins with a description of where Arab Israelis live, their interactions with Jewish Israelis, and the forms of residential segregation that have emerged. From the establishment of the state in 1948 through the mid-1960s, the Israeli government exercised direct control over the internal movement of Arabs in Israel. They were confined to particular villages and towns, and their movements within Israel were regulated. Significant Arab property and agricultural lands were confiscated, and residential and housing restrictions were imposed. These formal government regulations were part of the administration of a minority population who were defined as a security risk. Since the mid-1960s, the constraints on Israeli Arabs have become more informal but continue to limit the internal migration of Arabs. Hence, Arab Israelis cannot move to new neighborhoods or to new areas or decide to integrate residentially with the Jewish population.

In order to secure jobs, the Arab Israeli population has had to seek opportunities within reasonable daily commuting from their homes. There is extensive daily commuting of Arabs to work in Jewish areas. The absence of large-scale permanent internal migration directly reinforces the dependency status of Arab women on Arab men, since women return to their communities and the social control of males, even when they are exposed to Israeli society. The absence of eco-

A former Arab house (below) in local stones and a wooden shack on top built by a squatter in Achziv, Northern Israel. The local Jewish resident and his family use both houses. (1999)

nomic opportunities in the areas where Arab Israelis reside reinforces their economic dependencies on Israeli Jews. The regional concentration of the Arab Israeli population and the development of commuting as a substitute for internal migration exacerbate their dependencies on the Israeli Jewish population. The absence of new housing for young, single Arab adults makes leaving the parental home before marriage all the more difficult.

Almost all Arab and Jewish communities are residentially segregated. Of over 100 communities listed in the Israeli census, only 7 contain mixed Arab and Jewish populations. The proportion of Arabs in these 7 communities ranges from 6 percent to 30 percent. All the rest are segregated, either totally Arab (35 communities) or totally Jewish (61 communities). Segregation by area is only the beginning of the story. Arabs are located in areas that have not developed job or business opportunities. The Israeli government has opted to subsidize the communities of new immigrants rather than develop economic opportunities for Israeli Arabs. Most of the Arab communities are located in areas where job opportunities are scarce and where developments in the economy and infrastructure have been limited. The fewer economic opportunities available in Arab areas of Israel reflect the lower priorities of government investments that have resulted in disadvantaged Arab communities and have been detrimental to Arab-Israeli economic development.

The power of the government to allocate resources among areas and among groups has an optimistic side. Governments have the power to establish new priorities and redirect resource allocations to maximize a more equitable economic outcome. While it is often extremely difficult to change local cultures and attitudes, it is reasonable to direct resources in such a way as to reduce inequalities.

Arab residential segregation has an impact on educational opportunities. Schools and community institutions within Arab Israeli areas tend to be of lower quality than those in Jewish areas. But even when Arabs are able to secure educational opportunities, it is difficult to translate years of education into appropriate level jobs. Hence, the potential for the next generation of young adults to improve their standard of living is constrained. This is particularly the case when options for migration to new areas are limited and there is an expanding Arab population base. Therefore, the consequences of residential concentration for Arab men and women have been critical for education, job opportunities, and institutional developments.

The dependency of the Arab communities on the Jewish economic sector is a direct outcome of the segregation policies of the state and the subsequent increased discrimination against them in the labor market. The lack of adequate educational institutions and, most important, their lack of independence and autonomy are part of the residential concentration of Arab Israelis. These costs are important for understanding the Arab-Israeli conflict and are linked to internal ethnic tensions within the State of Israel. Government priorities in terms of economic investments and infrastructure, as well as in terms of educational institutions, have favored the European-origin population, followed by Jewish immigrants from Middle Eastern countries. Last among the priorities have been Israeli Arabs. Often investments have been made in terms of geographic or local communities and not to specific ethnic groups. Yet, ethnic segregation is so powerful that different government investments by area are identical to differential investment among specific ethnic groups.

From the point of view of the Jewish community and the Israeli government, the economic position of the Arab minority has been improving over time. That is indeed the case. The level of educational attainment and occupational mobility has been impressive among

Arab Israelis over the last two generations. At the same time, and less well appreciated, their economic dependency on the Jewish economic sector has become institutionalized. Thus, while both Arab and Israeli Jews perceive that their economic conditions have improved within the state, they perceive their access to these improvements differently. Arab Israelis are likely to perceive the economic opportunities open to them as constrained and limited not only for them but also for their children. No matter what level of education their children attain, young Arab Israelis end up working for Jews in the Jewish economy. The type of opportunities available to Arabs in the Jewish sector is likely to be viewed as open and expansive in the eyes of Jewish employers and as increasingly dependent and limited in the view of Israeli Arabs.

Arabs are less likely to succeed than the Jews that they will be competing with for the jobs in the "integrated" Israeli economic sector. Arabs are likely to pay a heavy price for occupational integration. They have to seek appropriate jobs outside of their segregated sector in competition with better-educated and well-connected Jewish persons. It is reasonable to assume that in this competition in the near term they will not be the advantaged group. Unlike in the past, when educated Arabs were in demand within the Arab sector (replacing those who left the community in the 1948 war), more of the better-educated Arabs are being pushed into the Jewish sector and into blue-collar work. Thus, there had been a nice fit through the early 1980s between higher education and high white-collar work among Arabs within the limited Arab economic sector. But a continuation of increased educational attainment without the expansion of high white-collar job opportunities in the Arab sector results in a decline in the economic opportunities appropriate for the educational level attained by the younger generation. These opportunities were expanded by the government in communities of Jewish immigrants and in the major cities where few Arab Israelis could find residences. The Arab minorities in general cannot develop new white-collar opportunities unless they are located in areas that serve the Jewish population, can fairly compete with Jewish workers, and have equal access to these opportunities. The inability to translate a high level of education into a good job is a clear form of structural discrimination. This type of discrimination may not be tied to anti-Arab intentions or culture. It is a subtle and complex form of discrimination, perceived primarily by the victims and rarely appreciated by those in power.

Educational levels of Arab men and women have increased over time in Israel with significant increases in the last two decades. These educational accomplishments have resulted in a new group of educated young persons whose opportunities are constrained both by residential segregation and by their economic dependence on the Jewish sector. Even if segregation were beneficial for some in the past, it is likely to have more negative consequences when the increase in population size outstrips the available local economic opportunities. To reduce the economic dependency of Arab Israelis on the Jewish economic sector requires an expansion of economic opportunities within Arab communities. Improving local Arab-controlled job opportunities would increase autonomy and independence of the population. But there is also an irony if such an expansion occurs. Developing investments in local Arab-Israeli communities would enhance the opportunities available to the next generation but would, at the same time, reinforce the local control of the extended family over the lives of the younger people. Thus, the reduction of dependency of Arab Israelis on the Jewish sector may result in an increase in gender dependencies. Speeding up one form of independence and equality (in the economic sector) may delay the shift to more egalitarian gender roles. Thus, there are tradeoffs between increasing the economic independence and autonomy of the Arab population, on the one hand, and the entrenchment of gender inequalities, on the other. This dilemma confronts the shapers of local and national policy in Israel.

The residential segregation of Arab-Israeli communities therefore leads to economic powerlessness of Arab Israelis, which in turn results in the development of an Arab underclass. The expanded work opportunities in Israel since 1967 did not change the status of Arab Israelis. Their increased segregation resulted in increased levels of economic deprivation, hopelessness, and deterioration, precisely at the time when objective conditions were becoming better relative to what they had been. These processes of residential segregation make the Arab minority vulnerable and conspicuous—vulnerable in the sense of being subject to economic changes, not to political harassment; conspicuous in the sense of living in places where their distinctive quality of life is retained and identifies them as a group to Israeli authorities.

Increases in the level of educational attainment among Arab Israe-

A scene of a classroom with Israeli Jewish children. This secular school has a mixture of boys and girls. Note their clothing. (1991)

lis, the availability of jobs in the Jewish-controlled market, and a traditional supportive family structure may have spared Arab Israelis some dire economic consequences. Since 1967 Israeli Arabs have been able to compare their own situation within Israel with Palestinians who have lived on the West Bank and Gaza. Israeli Arabs have seen greater depths of economic disadvantage and poverty among their Palestinian relatives. Their own economic situation looks significantly better and less disadvantaged in that comparison.

One more subtle consequence of the reinforced segregation within Israel may be the growing level of mistrust between the Arab and Jewish communities. The dependency of Arab Israelis is often translated into the psyche of the individuals within the group. An Israeli Arab describes the impact of dependency,

We have a feeling that the authorities know everything about us anyway. They're the bosses, you know, the security agents, the state, the Ministry of Education, and it's as if they've already settled everything for us in advance. They've planned out our future, and all that's left for us is to toe the line. And we really toe it.

This is a picture of an Arab Israeli classroom that is gender and ethnically segregated. Note the contrasting dress, some more traditional, other with English/American logos. (1991)

This is the way Mohammed Daroushe describes his feelings of dependency (cited in Grossman, 1993). Daroushe goes on to blame himself and his group for this situation, a not uncommon feeling among those who feel oppressed by dependency relationships.

ARAB ISRAELIS AND THE ARAB-ISRAELI CONFLICT

The examination of Arabs in Israel focuses our attention on the complex role of the state and its policies, including issues of entitlements, ideology, and discriminatory policies that shape continuity and change in Arab communities. The complexity of the Arab identity emerges from the contexts of Israeli-Arab communities, as it does from external factors. It is clear that "culture," or primordial identity, and internally imposed or externally influenced political status, do not provide adequate orientations to the changing meaning of the term Arab Israeli.

A new generation of Arab Israelis is growing up. With their higher levels of education and lower levels of occupational opportunities, they are increasing their Palestinian national identity. They are being socialized in smaller families, with higher levels of consumption and aspirations. They have nowhere to go, and little to do; they have fewer outlets for social, cultural, and political expressions. These generational changes and experiences document clearly how social changes are linked to quality-of-life issues. Arab Israelis also have a different relationship than Israeli Jews to the neighboring Arab countries and to the Palestinians on the West Bank, the Gaza Strip, and elsewhere in their diaspora.

Israel has been described by some social scientists in Israel as an "ethnic democracy," where the dominance of one ethnic group is institutionalized and has, in turn, its own tensions and contradictions. Such a system extends political and civil liberties rights to the entire population, but, at the same time, attaches a superior status to a particular segment of the population. Israel is a state of and for Jews, and it is recognized as such internationally. Hebrew is the national language, and the use of Arabic is marginal in the public domain, except of course in Israeli-Arab communities. All state symbols and national institutions are Jewish from the national anthem to national holidays, from the symbols around which national unity is organized to political symbols, flags, monuments, art, and literature.

The Arab-Israeli population was abandoned in Israel in 1948, as part of the Palestinian people and the vanquished Arab world, regarded by Israeli Jews as a fifth column, as "non-Jews" in a Jewish state. Israeli Arabs were part of a residual community; they had lost their leaders, their middle class and urban sector, and most of their institutions. Primarily they had lost autonomy and control; they became a minority. Hence, Arab Israelis were amenable to Jewish manipulation and discrimination, since assimilation into the Jewish majority culture and within its institutions was not possible. The Arab population within Israel had been granted civil rights and the status of a linguistic, religious, and cultural minority; welfare services were extended as were development funds. At the same time, they were also under military administration, largely exempted from military service; large portions of their lands were confiscated (even though they had also previously lost control of their urban sector); and they voted for Jewish political parties and protested minimally.

After 1967 their situation changed when the overall Israeli military administration was lifted and Palestinians in nearby territories came under Israeli occupation and increasingly worked within the state as day laborers. Israeli Arabs were more readily admitted to Jewish institutions and were encouraged to integrate into the working class of the Jewish economy. Educational and occupational levels increased dramatically, as did the standard of living. At the same time that they developed a bilingual and bicultural Arab and Israeli orientation, they recaptured and enhanced their Palestinian identity when their contacts with those living on the West Bank and Gaza increased. They developed a network of organizations, institutions, and leaders in their struggle for greater equality. But their leadership tended to be local—Israel has not until recently had an Arab cabinet minister or an Arab director-general of a government office. Indeed, Israeli Arabs have begun to use the democratic system of Israeli society to protest their second-class status. Ironically, their democratic protests reveal just how powerful and influential their Israeli experience has been in shaping their culture.

Palestinians and Israelis regard Israeli Arabs as part of the State of Israel. Formal separation of Israeli Arabs as a regional or territorial independent unit is not an option in the future. In contrast, they argue that partition is the only likely way to handle the Israeli-Palestinian conflict because any permanent settlement must include Palestinians outside of Palestine. The only legitimate political status for Israeli Arabs is as an integrated minority with some local autonomy but within the Jewish state. This political position must remain tenuous and conflicted given the dependencies associated with this type of minority status.

The Arab-Israeli population has experienced these pressures from a combination of population growth generated by high fertility and declining mortality, with no outlet through outmigration. The family-oriented system within the Arab community of Israel mitigated against high rates of nonmarriage or childlessness. State welfare programs in Israel prevented a reduced standard of living that would have resulted from these demographic processes. Welfare programs, combined with commuting to work outside of their communities, minimized the costs of high Arab population growth. But clearly the crunch was delayed more than alleviated, particularly with the rising younger generation of more educated Arab Israelis who could find jobs within the Jewish economic sector but not jobs that were commensurate with their educational levels. They could more readily and successfully compete with Palestinians from the administered territories working in Israel. However, they were, and continue to be, less successful in competing with Jewish Israelis in their labor market.

The combination of demographic and democratic tendencies requires a solution to the disadvantaged position of the Arab minority in Israel. Taking as a guide the value expressed by Israel's first president, Chaim Weizmann, that the quality of Israeli society will be judged by how it treats its minority communities, Israel has a distance to go to improve the quality of life of its Arab minority. It needs to set policies that diminish ethnic inequalities. At the same time, policies must recognize the powerful trade-offs to be made between residential segregation and economic development, between cultural pluralism and national identity, between the retention of the Jewishness of the state along with its Israeli-ness, with a tolerance (and supportive policies) for minority populations and pluralism. It is unlikely that the next generation of Arabs in Israel will experience full minority integration within the State of Israel. Whether Arab Israelis continue to experience economic disadvantage, whether inequalities are reduced, and whether sociocultural distinctiveness remains are open questions at the end of the twentieth century.

Chapter 4

The Palestinian and Jewish Diasporas

There has been a shift from the conflict characterized as "Arab-Israeli" to a "Palestinian-Israeli" conflict. Over the last several decades, Palestinian identity has become more legitimate (and more conspicuously selected by the Palestinians themselves). It has also become more accepted among Arab Israelis, as they have found common ground (at least in terms of their identity) with Palestinians living in the administered territories and in Gaza and Jericho. The following section describes the Palestinian population (exclusive of those living as citizens in the State of Israel). Subsequently, comparisons of Arab Israelis and Palestinians are made to identify which characteristics unite them and which divide them.

There are many ways in which to treat the Palestinian issue. In this section, the Palestinians living on the West Bank are treated as part of a diaspora, which has economic, political, and social relationships with the State of Israel. As in other new states, internal developments in Israel do not occur in an international or regional vacuum. Israel has political and economic linkages to countries and people in and out of the region. As a society with a significant Arab minority, occupying a territory that has been claimed by former residents, and having a large Arab population under its administrative control, the State of Israel has been centrally positioned in the aspirations of Palestinians for political autonomy. Moreover, as a Jewish state, Israel has important social and cultural relationships with Jewish communities around the world. Jews in these communities represent potential sources of immigration to Israel, and they are primary sources of political and economic support. Jewish communities outside of Israel have also received significant numbers of Israeli emigrants and visitors. Ethnic divisions among Jews and between Jews and Arabs in Israel are strongly influenced by events occurring outside the state. The external factors, therefore, play a complementary role to the internal changes within Israeli society in the broader contours of the Arab-Israeli conflict.

At the beginning of the twenty-first century, the external area under Israel's administrative control included the West Bank and their populations, since Gaza and Jericho came under Palestinian administration in the summer of 1994. These territories under Israel's administration encompassed over 1.5 million Arab Palestinian residents. The ongoing negotiations between Israel and Palestinians over population and territory, and over autonomy and independence, are likely to result in further administrative, political, and demographic changes over the next several years. The peace treaties and economic relations with Egypt and Jordan, and the emerging peace process with Syria, will also alter Israel's regional development and shape the Arab-Israeli conflict.

This chapter focuses on three questions. What has been the relationship of the State of Israel to the territories it administers? (This will be referred to as the "Palestinian" question.) What is the relationship between Jewish communities outside of the State of Israel to developments within Israeli society? (This will be referred to as the "Jewish diaspora" question.) What are the future prospects of the Arab citizens living within the state in the contexts of both the Palestinian and Jewish diaspora questions? (This will be referred to as the "ethnic-national" question.)

THE PALESTINIAN DIASPORA

What is the situation of those Palestinians who are residents of the areas that have been administered and occupied by the State of Israel since the 1967 war? How has this set of external conflicts with Arab Palestinians reshaped and affected changes within the country? How has it influenced the way in which Israeli society relates to its Arab minority and to the broader Arab-Israeli conflict? The territories containing Palestinians who were former residents of areas included within the state were referred to officially in Israel as "administered territories" through the end of the 1970s. These incorporated the West Bank and Gaza. When the Likud political party took over the government of Israel in 1977, these territories became known officially in Israel by their Biblical names, Judea and Samaria, rather than the West Bank and Gaza. At the same time, these territories became less identified as "administered" or "occupied" by Israel. The political symbolism of this switch is of profound importance in understanding the changing relationship of Israeli governments to these areas. Initially, after their occupation in 1967, the administration of these territories implied a temporary arrangement by Israel until administrative or political disputes could be settled. In contrast, when the territories were assigned new (old) names, particularly those grounded in traditional Jewish cultures, the political position regarding these territories became clear: Israel has reacquired areas that have belonged to Israel in the past. A new political status and legitimacy are thereby assigned to these areas. Using Biblical names for these territories was clearly an attempt by the government of Israel to reinstate politically and restore culturally the Jewish origins of these places. By implication, if not by political fiat, the renaming of these territories connoted their legitimate inclusion as part of the State of Israel. Israel would develop a different relationship to territories that once were part of the Land of Israel rather than areas that were being temporarily administered by a military force.

The population of these areas included over 160,000 Jewish settlers as of the late 1990s and over 1.5 million Arab Palestinians. The administration of these territories since 1967 has influenced population, economic development, and ethnic relationships within Israel. The allocation of resources to subsidize Jewish settlements and to control and administer the Palestinian populations living there have had a significant impact on the economy of Israel and on the identity of the Israeli Arab community, and have influenced stratification and inequalities within Israeli society. The political control of these areas by the Israeli government represents one of the core themes of the Arab-Israeli conflict.

The Israeli government has never officially incorporated the Arab-Palestinian population living in these territories into Israel, except for East Jerusalem in 1967. The political rights of citizenship accorded to Arab Israelis were not extended to those living on the West Bank and Gaza. The incorporation of the large Arab population within "Greater Israel" would have threatened the demographic dominance of the Jewish population in the State of Israel. In the 1970s and 1980s, a series of demographic projections showed clearly the higher growth rates of the Arab-Palestinian population under Israel's administrative control compared to the rate of population growth in the State of Israel. The inclusion of the Palestinian population as part of the State of Israel would have resulted in a significant decline in the percentage of Jewish persons within Israel and the risk of losing a Jewish majority in a little over a generation. Ironically, some of the most Jewishly nationalistic groups among the Israeli population argue for the incorporation of the Palestinian population within Israel. If they were successful, the demographic result would be the emergence of an Arab-Palestinian demographic majority. Hence, the more extreme among the Israeli nationalists argue for the incorporation of the administered territory within the State of Israel *without* integrating the Palestinian population.

The early demographic scenarios of incorporating Palestinians and their territories within the State of Israel were not designed to project what *would* happen but what would be the demographic consequences *if* there were no policies to deal with the future of these areas. Indeed, the alternatives to extending control over these areas to the Palestinian population have ranged from the development of a quasi-colonial relationship between Israel and the Palestinian population under its administration (which in part occurred) or the evacuation of the Arab population to be replaced by Israeli residents (which has occurred only marginally). The notion of a combined Israeli-Palestinian state shared equally between Jewish and Arab-Palestinian populations was not acceptable to the Jews or the Palestinians. Such a state would require a radical transformation of the institutions, values, and symbols that characterize Israel as a Jewish state. It would of course involve compromises on the part of the Palestinians on issues of political independence, self-administration, and control. Moreover, such a binational state would conflict with the core premises of Israeli Jewish and Palestinian identities.

The size of the Arab population of these territories is somewhat in dispute; different estimates depend on how Palestinians are defined and by which officials. One source of the different estimates is whether the de jure (legal) or the de facto (resident) population is included in the count. The former is often inflated, since Palestinians who have lived, but are no longer resident, in the areas have been included. This volume uses the official estimates of the Israel Bureau of Statistics based on the estimate of the actual resident population. There was a substantial growth in the population of the West Bank and Gaza, increasing to over 1.6 million persons from less than a million in 1970, and growing at a rate that would double the population every generation. With the return of Gaza and its population to Palestinian control in 1994, over one million Palestinians remained under Israeli administration (in addition to the Israeli-Arab population). The birthrate among Palestinians remains quite high. It is estimated at between 40 and 50 births per 1,000 population, or about 7 or 8 children per woman. The death rates have declined but have remained high. Deaths to infants in their first year of life was over 35 per 1,000 births (compared to less than 5 per 1,000 among Israeli Jews and 9 per 1,000 among Israeli Moslems). As a result, the potential for continued rapid population growth among Palestinians is high.

Indicators of health conditions and health infrastructure reveal the poor and disadvantaged economic conditions of Arab Palestinians in these administered areas, relative to Israeli society as a whole and also compared to the Arab-Israeli population. Not only are infant and maternal deaths significantly higher in these areas, but other indicators of environmental conditions, health care, and preventive medicine are significantly poorer in these areas. Sewage treatment, hospital beds, and physicians per capita reveal the poorer levels of these health indicators on the West Bank and in Gaza than in Israel. There have been improvements over time. For example, the number of births taking place in hospitals has increased dramatically from the mid-1960s to the mid-1990s (from 14 percent to 65 percent), but it still remains lower than in the State of Israel. Information on the possession of durable goods among households reveals an increase in such basic items as stoves and refrigerators but a continuing low level in the 1990s of items of communication, including telephones, bicycles, and cars.

The administration of these territories by Israel has involved political control and the presence of government agencies such as health, education, agricultural regulation, and administrative justice. This administration implied that economic decisions served the interests of the Israeli economy and that investments in local control were minimal. Local Palestinian residents have not been part of the political processes that have shaped these economic policies. Domestic needs and local economic developments have been secondary to the needs

Table 4.1
Selected Population, Health, and Economic Indicators: Arab Population in the Territories Administered by Israel, 1970–1990

		1970	1975	1980	1985	1988
Population						
Size		978	1,101	1,181	1,343	1,600
	West Bank	608	675	724	816	957
	Gaza	370	426	457	527	643
Crude Birth Rate						
	West Bank	44	45	42	41	47
	Gaza	42	51	48	45	55
Infant Mortality Rates*						
	West Bank	30	38	28	25	21
	Gaza	86	69	43	33	28
Percent Born in Medical Facilities						
	West Bank	15	30	40	56	53
	Gaza	10	21	29	47	60

		1972	1975	1980	1987
GNP per Capita					
	West Bank	410	836	1,334	2,090
	Gaza	268	605	878	1,468

		1974	1981	1985	1992
Running Water					
	West Bank	24	45	62	79
	Gaza	14	51	75	93

*The data are official estimates for the Arab population in the areas of Judea and Samaria (West Bank and Gaza).

Sources: State of Israel, Ministry of Health, *Health in Judea, Samaria and Gaza, 1988–89*, Jerusalem, April 1989; *Statistical Abstract of Israel*, various issues.

of the Israeli government, including the recruitment of labor to work within the Israeli economy and the flow of Israeli goods into the territories. Agricultural developments on the West Bank were realigned to produce crops that were not competitive with the Israeli agricultural markets, and prices were regulated. Similar control is exercised by Israel over water resources drawn from the West Bank into Israel, the takeover of some land areas for Jewish settlements and for the development of infrastructures, the introduction of Israeli firms to set up industries in the areas through financial incentives, and the establishment of export connections to Jordan and other Arab countries through the West Bank. At the same time, these administered territories have become markets for Israeli goods. According to some researchers, Israeli policies have blatantly steered the territories toward a state of economic dependency on Israel. The economies of the West Bank and the Gaza Strip lack the indigenous economic and financial institutions necessary for setting development programs and channeling savings and investment into various economic sectors.

The occupational patterns of men in these territories are revealing. Few are employed in white-collar jobs (less than 10 percent); the overwhelming majority (more than seven of ten of the employed males) work as skilled and unskilled workers in industry. The majority of these persons work within the State of Israel, commuting on a daily basis. In the 1990s, 38 percent of the employed males living on the West Bank and Gaza were working in the construction industry.

As a result of the *Intifada*, the "uprising" among Palestinians on the West Bank against Israeli occupation, increasing numbers of foreign, temporary workers have been imported to the State of Israel to replace Palestinian workers. These workers brought from Europe and Asia numbered more than 100,000 in the late 1990s. Their living conditions were often very poor and their wages (and benefits) were significantly lower than Jewish and Arab workers within Israel. They were also lower than for Palestinians on the West Bank and Gaza. The foreign workers came to Israel despite the poor wages because these are higher than they would have received had they remained in their country of origin. The resultant changing needs for the Palestinians' labor force in Israel means high levels of unemployment on the West Bank and Gaza.

With the increase in the number of Arab workers from the administered territories in the construction industry, there was a concomitant decrease over time in the number and the proportion of Jews in the construction industry. Between 1975 and 1987, the number and proportion of Israeli Arabs working in this industry remained relatively stable; however, the number and percent of Arabs from the administered territories increased significantly. By 1985 about one third of those employed in this industry within Israel were Jews (down from 52 percent), 42 percent were Arabs from the administered territories (up from 29 percent), and 22 percent were Israeli

Table 4.2
Employed Persons and Employees in the Construction Branch—
Ethnic Groups in Israel and in Territories Administered by Israel,
1975–1987

Employment Status	Numbers 1975	Numbers 1987	Percent 1975	Percent 1987
Employed Persons			100	100
Israel				
Jews	65	42	52	35
Arabs	25	26	20	22
Administered Territories				
Judea and Samaria	22	30	18	26
Gaza Area	14	19	11	16
Employees			100	100
Israel				
Jews	49	29	46	29
Arabs	21	22	20	22
Administered Territories				
Judea and Samaria	22	30	20	30
Gaza Area	14	19	13	19
Employers				
Israel				
Jews	16	13	80	76
Arabs	4	4	20	24

Source: Statistical Abstract of Israel, 1992, Table XVI.

Arabs. Looking at the employers, the evidence identifies the Jewish role in construction, in particular, and in the stratification picture, in general. While the number of Jews in this industry declined and the number of Arabs from the territories increased significantly, the proportion of employers remained overwhelmingly Jewish. Around 80 percent of the employers in 1975 were Jewish as were 76 percent in 1987. Indicators of the balance of trade and economic flows between Israel and the territories they administer reveal similar patterns with Jewish Israelis in control. The combination of poor economic development within these territories and the replacement of Palestinian workers with foreign temporary labor continues the economic squeeze in the West Bank and Gaza.

These and related pieces of evidence solidify the earlier assessment about the relative economic inequality of Arab Israelis and Palestinians. In terms of social-class hierarchy, Israeli Jews are concentrated in white-collar jobs and in service industries. Among Jews, those from European countries are more concentrated in professional occupations, followed by those with Middle Eastern ethnic origins. Arab Israelis follow with high proportions in skilled blue-collar work. Palestinians (non-Israeli citizens) are in the lowest occupational levels within the Israeli occupational hierarchy. In addition to this stratified system, both Arab Israelis and Palestinians are concentrated in particular jobs, within specific sectors of the economy, working primarily for Jewish employers. This type of occupational concentration of ethnic groups is referred to as a cultural division of labor. This translates into inequalities and the powerful overlap of ethnic origin and social class. Hence, Arabs in Israel and in the territories are likely to have very different access than Jews to the rewards and privileges associated with the middle and upper social classes.

What about educational levels? There has been a dramatic increase in the level of formal education of residents of the West Bank and Gaza between the 1970s and the 1990s. In 1970 about half of the population had no formal education; 65 percent of the women had none. By the early 1990s, the proportion with no education had declined to 20 percent overall and to about 30 percent of the women. The educational level is rapidly changing among the younger generation. In 1992, for example, over 90 percent of the Palestinian teenage boys and girls had some formal education, and about 70 percent of those age fifteen to seventeen had some high school education. Whether these educational levels will be translated into commensurate jobs within these areas remains the challenge of the next decades. In the mid-1990s, the local economic infrastructure and development have not kept pace with the new educational levels. With few appropriate level jobs available for the more educated, the value of education for social mobility deteriorates.

This had become even more serious with the entrance of hundreds of thousands of new Jewish immigrants from the former Soviet Union. These immigrants came with a disproportionate concentration in high white-collar and professional occupational backgrounds. In turn, they compete with Arab Israelis for the better jobs available. Given the priorities of the state for Jewish immigration, it is not surprising that Arab Israelis have been unable to compete successfully for the high-level positions available. It is also not surprising, on this basis alone, that the Arab Israelis would view Jewish immigration from Eastern Europe as a "threat" to their opportunity structure and a foreign element in the Middle East. Israeli Jews and the state, in contrast, view the continuous immigration of Jews as the fulfillment of the Zionist enterprise, the raison d'être of the existence of the state and of the highest priority. Arab frustration at the individual level and inequalities at the group level are reinforced in this context. The continuing conflicts between Arabs and Jews over the extent of Jewish immigration have a strong economic basis as well as a political and ideological history.

Clearly the political control exercised by Israel over these territories has resulted in the economic dependency of the Palestinians as reflected in their occupational and industrial characteristics. The identity of the Israeli-Arab population has been influenced, sharpened, and challenged in a variety of ways by the links between Israel and the Arab Palestinians in the territories. First and foremost, Arab Israelis have become linked to Arab Palestinians on the West Bank and in Gaza in their national aspirations. The links have heightened their sensitivities to the value of ethnic networks and their own national origins. Indeed, after a hiatus of about one generation from 1948 to 1967, Arabs in Israel confronted their family and former neighbors who were displaced in the exodus during Israel's War of Independence. Arab Israelis were confronted directly with the choice between continuing their self-identification as Arab Israelis or as displaced Palestinians. Studies among Israeli Arabs reveal increasing proportions of Israeli Arabs who identify themselves as Palestinians, reaching two-thirds in the late 1980s. Most Israeli Arabs favor the establishment of a Palestinian state in the West Bank and Gaza, but few of these Israeli Arabs would move to such a state. Thus, Israeli Arabs are a Palestinian national minority living permanently in the State in Israel. They are now bilingual and bicultural; Israeli Palestinian in identity but their future is firmly linked to the State of Israel.

The connections between Arab Israelis and Arab Palestinians after 1967 have sharpened the distinctiveness of the former as Israeli citizens. Arab Israelis are caught in the middle as beneficiaries of the system created to control and protect them as a minority and as citizens of the Jewish State of Israel. At the same time, they are viewed as disloyal Palestinians in the perspective of their Arab Palestinian cousins. While identifying as Palestinians in some contexts, they have been living as citizens in Israeli society for generations. They are a minority within Israel with legal rights and entitlements as citizens of the state. They have lacked opportunities to integrate residentially and regionally with Jewish Israelis and they do not serve in the military. Their identity as Israelis may be challenged and conflicted but so is their identification as Palestinians. They share many of the aspirations of the Palestinians in the territories, but they have become too Israeli to forgo the democratic rights and citizenship they have acquired in the State of Israel. They are likely to want greater political autonomy for their communities and more control over their economic and cultural lives.

Since 1967 the Israeli Arab population has risen in the social and economic hierarchy within Israel, ahead of the noncitizen Palestinians (but below Jewish Israelis). They have relinquished part of the lowest paid positions and unskilled work to Palestinian day workers or to temporary workers from abroad. They have been mobile within the Israeli social class system. While living and working, going to school, and having access to the goods and welfare of Israeli society, they are connected ethnically to Palestinians. The linkages between Israel and the territories since 1967 have reinforced and legitimated the minority status of its Israeli Arab population. These conditions have highlighted for all Israelis—Jews and Arabs—the inherent ambiguities of national identity among Arab Israelis.

JEWS IN ISRAEL'S ADMINISTERED TERRITORIES

The territories and populations living in East Jerusalem, which were under Jordanian control between 1948 and 1967, were incorporated into Israel after the Six-Day War in 1967; the area of the Golan Heights was formally annexed in 1981. Israel also took political and administrative control of large territorial expanses and populations on the West Bank, Gaza, and Sinai. The Sinai Peninsula was returned to Egypt as part of the peace treaty initiated by the leaders of Israel, Egypt, and the United States. Gaza and the city of Jericho were transferred to Palestinian administration in mid-1994.

Since 1967 there has been a Jewish settlement and population growth on the West Bank and in the Gaza area, which occurred under the auspices of, and with financial subsidies from, the Israeli government. The focus on the minority Jewish population in these areas follows from the fact that Israel subsidizes these settlements, their housing and infrastructure. Moreover, unlike the Arab Palestinian population in these areas, the Jewish population in these territories has full rights and obligations of Israeli citizenship (including military obligations and political rights), as well as the educational benefits and welfare entitlements of Israeli society. Most of the Jews in the territories work in the State of Israel, commuting to their jobs and returning to their homes in the evening. The Jewish settlers in the West Bank and Gaza areas are fully part of Israeli society, except that they are living in areas administered by the State of Israel and not formally living in the State of Israel. Their areas of settlement have developed ecologically and economically with Israeli government planning and support.

There are numerous views about the legitimacy of Jewish Israelis settling in these areas. Some Israelis, associated in large part with a political, national, and religious movement known as Gush Emunim (Bloc of the Faithful) have advocated the full annexation of these territories to Israel. They would have the territory formally part of Israel, and the Jewish settlers there would be similar to settlers of Jews in other parts of the state. A smaller Jewish minority has argued for the annexation of these areas but not the Palestinian population living there. The small number of Jews with Israeli citizenship who have settled in these areas moved their families to new housing built there, established schools for their children, and some have started small business enterprises. They obviously view these areas as legitimate areas of settlement and demand their rights as Israeli citizens. Many who live there view these areas as part of the larger territory of Palestine or the Land of Israel which they consider to be an integral part of the state. Some, perhaps a majority, view these territories as part of the religious commitment they feel as Jews to live in the Holy Land as they define it. Some view these settlements, particularly the areas on the periphery of Arab communities, as part of the security needs of Israeli society.

Some Israeli nationalists view the settlement of the West Bank and Gaza as the next phase in the Zionist territorial reconstruction of the Land of Israel. They argue that these new Jewish settlements evolved as part of the continuous policies of the Zionist movement and Israeli governments to populate land areas in order to establish Jewish political legitimacy and control. They view these settlements in the long tradition of special Jewish settlement started in the first waves of immigration with the establishment of the first collective settlements called kibbutzim. These early colonies in the first decades of the twentieth century were the first new form of the Jewish resettlement of Palestine. Subsequently, in the 1950s, the Israeli governments subsidized the settlement of Jewish immigrants in rural agricultural enclaves, known as moshavim. In moshavim, unlike the collective consumption and production in kibbutz communities, property was privately owned, but production and distribution were collective. Later in the 1950s, the government established development towns to settle new immigrants in border areas. Thus, the new settlements in the West Bank and Gaza are similar to these earlier settlement forms associated with Zionist pioneer movements and specific ideological commitments. They are important primarily because of their strong ideological origins and the financial support provided by the Israeli government, not because they are a dominant demographic concentration. In the post-1967 period, these new Jewish settlements were supported politically and economically on parts of reconstructed West Bank and Gaza areas to create political facts and security zones.

Most Israeli Arabs and probably all of the Arab Palestinians living in these territories view the Israeli Jewish presence on the West Bank as a foreign settlement on their territory. For most Palestinians, the settlements and the settlers are illegitimate and destructive of their own autonomy for which they are committed to fight politically, economically, and culturally. The presence and development of these settlements are a daily reminder of the oppressed conditions that they experience. These settlements are largely segregated ecologically, socially, and culturally from the massive Arab Palestinian population living there.

Counted formally in the 1972 census, there were 1,500 Jewish residents in the administered territories—Judea, Samaria, and Gaza—located in 15 settlements. At the next census, in 1983, 22,800 Jews were living in 76 settlements in Judea-Samaria, and 900 were living in 5 settlements in the Gaza area. By 1991 these areas and the Jewish population living there had increased to 90,300 in Judea-Samaria in 120 settlements and 3,800 in 13 settlements in the Gaza area. Of these 133 places, 10 were defined as urban locations, 9 of which had less than 10,000 Jews counted in their population. Of the 123 rural locations, 30 were moshavim, 10 were kibbutzim, and 83 were other rural settlements. There were 105,000 Jews in these territories in the beginning of 1993 and 160,000 in 1997. There are likely to be around 200,000 Jewish residents of Judea and Samaria under Israel's protection at the beginning of the twenty-first century.

More than half of the Jews in these places were living in urban localities. Many of the others have urban occupations located within the State of Israel and commute to their privately owned suburban residences in these administered territories. Economic and ecological linkages have been forged between the largest of these Jewish settlements and the metropolitan areas of Israel, since a significant proportion of the population in these settlements lives in close proximity to Tel Aviv and Jerusalem. These settlements broaden the narrow area in the center of the country that became the State of Israel in 1948 and expand the area around Jerusalem that had been divided between 1948 and 1967. The urban-suburban character of most of these settlements contrasts with the relative regional and urban isolation of development towns and the rural character of the moshavim and kibbutzim. In the larger areas around Jerusalem and Tel Aviv, there is a rather even split between Jews of European origins and Jews of Asian-African origins reflecting the ethnic composition of third-generation Israelis. In smaller places, particularly in areas of more nationalistic, ideological, and religious settlement, the proportion of Jews from Western origins is likely to be higher. The median age of the Jewish population in these areas is by far the youngest among all areas in Israel (18.9 years), ten years younger than the national Jewish average.

While the establishment of new Jewish settlements as a basis for territorial legitimacy had been a long-established feature of Zionism, the religious and messianic settlers were not ideologically "correct" in the context of Israeli socialism and secular Zionism. Their urban lifestyles and their private ownership of property contrast sharply with the older, rural Zionist ideologies of a return to agriculture which characterized the rural settlements of kibbutzim and moshavim. Their settlements were not always planned by the government and sometimes were actually in conflict with formal policies. Nevertheless, these new settlements rarely if ever occurred without government infrastructural and economic support. Their conflicts were not with an external government, as was the case between the early Jewish pioneers and the British at an earlier point in prestate Palestine, but often with the local Arab population. Their settlement activities inflamed the Arab-Israeli conflict and exacerbated the tensions between Israel and Arab neighboring countries.

The areas designated as Judea, Samaria, and Gaza under the administered control of the State of Israel had the highest Jewish growth rate (14.8 percent per annum) and the highest positive rate of internal migration per 1,000 population of any set of places in

Israel in the 1990s. The Jewish population in these areas is small relative to the majority Palestinian population and relative to the Jewish population in the State of Israel. Nevertheless, the settlers living there tend to be highly motivated persons, with strong Zionist and pioneering ideologies. Many are religiously committed to the settlement of the whole Land of Israel. They represent the political interests and commitments of the nationalist wing of the political parties to settle in these areas but have been subsidized by diverse governments in Israel.

Almost all the Israeli Jewish settlers are committed to the legitimate rights of Israeli Jews to live in these areas for nationalist, security, and religious reasons. The majority is concentrated in a select few areas that are located around Jerusalem and within easy access to Tel Aviv. These are most likely to be retained as Israeli outposts for at least another generation. There are other settlements that are more scattered and isolated and cannot sustain themselves as dormitory suburbs without support from the Israeli government. These are less likely to remain under Israeli control in the next period of time and are very unlikely to expand in Israeli Jewish population. The Jewish population in these territories administered by Israel is segregated ethnically and religiously from the Palestinian population.

The political importance of these settlers in the Arab-Israeli conflict should not be underestimated. Any resolution of the territorial and population question needs to consider the future of these settlements within the West Bank area and the Jewish settlers living there. However the settlers view themselves, however the settlers are viewed by the Israeli population that sympathizes with their settlement, or the Arab Israelis and the Palestinians, the Jewish settlers in these areas have become of considerable symbolic importance and a powerful demographic and political presence.

THE JEWISH DIASPORA AND ISRAELI SOCIETY

There are links between the State of Israel and what it defines as the *golah* or the Jewish diaspora. In major Zionist and Israeli conceptions, Jewish communities outside of the State of Israel have special connections to the State of Israel, as sources of potential immigration to Israel, as sources of political and economic support, and as part of the Jewish people. Indeed, Jewish communities outside of the State of Israel have had a powerful influence on the changing population growth and ethnic composition of the state and the political legitimacy of the state in the international arena. These Jewish communities have been Israel's financial and political backbone, supporting domestic programs and providing important aid for defense purposes. Jews outside of Israel have been partners in formulating the intellectual and ideological basis of Israeli society and have provided the political rationale for its reemergence as a state. Consequently, these Jewish communities outside of Israel indirectly influence the Arab-Israeli conflict.

A symbolic illustration of the ideological and national importance of Jewish communities outside of Israel to the State of Israel is the annual inclusion of data in the official *Statistical Abstract of Israel* on the "Jewish population in the world and in Israel." These statistical data begin with the Jewish population of the world starting in the late nineteenth century (1892) and include estimates of Jewish population size in the world and the percent of those living in Israel. No other country's statistical yearbook includes historical and comparative materials that would parallel that statistical table.

Three brief examples illustrate some of the more obvious interdependencies between Israel and the Jewish communities outside of Israel. First, the changing immigration rates and shifts in the ethnic composition of immigrant streams to Israel that we noted earlier have been strongly influenced by changes in the Jewish communities around the world. The size of particular Jewish communities and the pool of potential Jewish immigrants have varied over the last several decades in part in relation to the rate of immigration to Israel. The decline in the size of major Jewish communities living in Muslim countries, for example, accounts directly for changes in their immigration rate to the State of Israel. The end of Jewish immigration from Yemen or Iraq can be understood only against the background of the demographic demise of those Jewish communities. The commitment of American Jews to remain in the United States rather than immigrate to Israel has a major impact on the relationships between the government of Israel and the American Jewish community as well as to the government of the United States.

Similarly, shifts in the cohesion of the Soviet Union and its breakup, along with implications of these changes for the Jewish population living there, were the most immediate cause of the large-scale immigration of Russian Jews to Israel in the 1990s. The shift in the immigration policy of the U.S. government to restrict the entry of

Russian immigrants also influenced the direction of emigrants from the former Soviet Union toward the State of Israel. Thus, an examination of the impact of the timing and rate of Jewish immigration from various countries of origin to Israel must be understood in the context of these changing Jewish communities, rather than changes in the attraction of living in Israel.

A second example relates to the ways that events within Israel affect Jewish communities in the world. The 1967 Six-Day War between Israel and its Arab neighbors had a major impact on economic and political developments within the state and deeply affected the relationship of Israeli Jews to Palestinians and to the Arab populations of the region. The effect of the war extended well beyond the borders of the state. Financial aid and political support from Jewish communities around the world to Israel increased substantially in the context of the Six-Day War. In turn, the ethnic Jewish identity of diaspora Jewish communities became more firmly anchored in Israel's development. As the very survival of Israel was perceived to be threatened, the post-Holocaust generation of Jews outside of Israel responded in a variety of ways to link itself to the future of the Jewish state. These developments, in turn, led to new and more conspicuous interrelationships between Israel and Jewish communities, often involving the exchange of Jewish "ethnic" identity for financial and political support. Hence, Jewish communities outside the State of Israel increasingly became involved in, and responsive to, the broader conflicts associated with Arab-Israeli relationships. These involvements went beyond humanitarian concerns among Jews for ethnic conflict around the world but more deeply felt commitments to enhance the security of the State of Israel and reduce the sources of conflict. As Jews from Western countries—the United States, Canada, and Europe—increasingly visited Israel, sent their children on visits and periods of study, and established institutions to accommodate these interests, the conflicts between Arabs and Jews in Israel became points of personal interest not only of abstract culture, religion, politics, and economics.

A third illustration relates to the sporadic terrorist attacks directed at Jews within Israel. These have always generated political responses and concerns among Jews outside of Israel. Attacks on Jewish communities in North and South America, in Europe, and in Asia and Africa have, in turn, generated responses from the Israeli government. Israel views itself as the guardian of the Jewish people. Jewish communities outside of Israel are defined as part of the history and culture of Israeli Jews. An attack on Jews anywhere is treated as an attack on Jews everywhere, promoting a mutual, unwritten pact of accepted responsibilities and obligations. Often this takes the form of political action. At times economic exchanges or military actions are generated as well, reinforcing the bonds between Israel and Jewish communities around the world. The conflicts between Israelis and Palestinians evoke these images of concern and responsibility.

These simple illustrations can be multiplied. The major point is that important linkages exist between internal developments within Israel and Jewish communities outside of Israel which require analysis when the goal is to understand the dynamics of Israel's changing society and the changing Arab-Israeli conflict. The geographic distance of Jews outside of Israel and their major commitments to the countries in which they live result in their lack of direct involvement in the Arab-Israeli conflict.

Nevertheless, diaspora Jews have been important players in the tensions between Arabs and Jews because of their loyalties to Israel as a Jewish state. Jewish organizations and institutions have lobbied their own governments to support Israel in their negotiations with Palestinians. In several instances, Jewish leaders have been active in pursuing contacts with Palestinian leaders, when the Israeli and Arab governments were unable or unwilling to negotiate directly. Lines of communication between political units in conflict have remained open when intermediaries, not burdened by political roles, act as facilitators in the process of peace negotiations. Non-Israeli Jews have often taken direct roles in supporting and subsidizing Jewish settlements in the administered territories, enhancing the Jewish presence in these areas, often exacerbating the arenas of conflict. Most important, Israeli Jews have counted on diaspora Jews to be supportive of them in the various phases of the Arab-Israeli conflict in the past and currently in the negotiations for the larger process of peace.

A final point about the role of diaspora Jews in the Arab-Israeli conflict relates directly to how the conflict is presented in the sources of information available to Jewish communities. Within every Jewish community (and most recently on the Internet), there are news items and pieces of information about the Arab-Israeli conflict. These are transmitted in Jewish newspapers, in local lectures and presentations, and in courses held for Jewish adults in local religious and secular Jewish institutions. They are part of the core materials in Jewish educational institutions that expose the next generation of students to the nuances of Arab-Israeli relations. Thus, when Arab Israelis and Palestinians are portrayed in stereotypical form as terrorists, as evil and uncultured, the impression created and reinforced is a one-sided view of the Arab-Israeli conflict. When a dominant image of the Palestinians is a group of young children hurling stones against Israeli defense forces, the implications are clear. When the view is primarily of Israeli settlers defending their right to live in their homes and Arab terrorists who threaten the existence of the state or attack vulnerable women and children civilians, the perspective of Jewish communities outside of Israel is not to encourage a rapprochement with Palestinians.

WHO IS JEWISH IN ISRAEL AND IN THE JEWISH DIASPORA

One way to consider the relationship of the Jewish diaspora and Israel and, in turn, the Arab-Israeli conflict is to examine the ways in which Jews and their communities are one people. While these communities often consider themselves one people with common cultural and political interests, there are increasing gaps between Israeli and non-Israeli Jews. These gaps may suggest that the role played in the cultural conflicts between Israeli Jews and Palestinians may be increasingly less important to the Jewish diaspora communities than it was in the past. One source of the gap between Israel and non-Israeli Jews is at the most simple and subtle level associated with the definition of who is included as a member of the Jewish people.

The sociological response for voluntary and ethnically pluralistic societies like the United States is that ethnic group membership is by self-definition, along with the consensus of the community. A Jew in the United States is therefore someone who considers himself or herself Jewish *and* is considered Jewish by the community. Political criteria (such as citizenship) or some other formal status (such as temporary resident status) are used for other communities to define Jewishness. In some countries, the designation Jewish may be more formally noted on personal documents and more often than not has been the basis of discrimination and distinctiveness.

The definitional question of "who is a Jew" in the State of Israel symbolizes the connections, and the gap, between the two largest Jewish communities in the world: Israel and the United States. Jews in Israel are automatically entitled to citizenship and are provided with a formal document indicating Jewishness by religion and nationality. In marginal cases in Israel, mostly among those who are antireligionists, requests have been made to be declared Jewish by nationality (and not by religion). A small number of Jews claim they are Jewish by religion but not by nationality (e.g., some antinational, ultraorthodox residents). But for the overwhelming majority of Israeli Jews, the difference between religious and national definitions of Jewishness is a distinction without significance.

The definition of who is to be included within the category "Jewish" comes under the 1950 Law of Return in the State of Israel (the law that grants every Jew in the world the right to immigrate to Israel and thereby become a citizen of the state). Formally, the state grants citizenship rights to all those who are Jewish by religious-legal (Halachic) criteria of birth to a Jewish mother or conversion to Judaism by a recognized orthodox rabbi. Occasionally these formal definitions are problematic. Discussions about the criteria used to define Jewishness within Israel often occur in the context of coalition politics. These involve "religious" political parties who have often exercised power over the definition of who is Jewish at the junctures of political or life course transitions (citizenship in the context of immigration; birth, induction into military service, marriage, divorce, and death). Israeli Jews are rarely affected by these coalition bargaining tactics, and the issue is marginal to their lives, except as it reveals the political nature of Israeli Judaism. For the most recent wave of immigration from Russia, the problem of who is Jewish has become more serious again, since it is estimated that more than half of the immigrants in 1999 from Russia to Israel are not Jewish by religious or ethnic criteria, although they are Jewish by some family relationship. The inclusion within the Jewish society of Israel of large numbers of immigrants as citizens who are not Jewish by culture or religion has the potential of altering the Jewish character of the state.

In Israel, the definition of who is Jewish has been decided by Israel's parliament on "religious" grounds and implemented by the Jewish religious authorities of the state (i.e., orthodox rabbis and their institutions). Most American Jews define Israel as a very important part of their lives and central to the education of their children. Substantial proportions of American Jews have visited Israel, have relatives and friends living in Israel, and financially contribute to Israel-related projects. Israel's survival is bound up with the ethnic lives of American Jews since they consider themselves part of the Jewish people. The State of Israel has become a psychological anchor for many American Jews, the sociocultural foundation of their Jewishness, and a source of communal cohesion. "Ethnic" Jewishness and especially its Israel-centered component have emerged to replace the Judaism of ritual and belief in America.

Even though immigration to Israel is not part of the agenda of most American Jews, the State of Israel is a major source of Jewish culture, experience, identity, and history for American Jews, since it is their link to Jewish peoplehood, the quintessential form of political ethnicity. Israel is no less powerful as a symbol of ethnicity for Jewish communities, not in the "national origins" or in the geographic sense, but in its constructed, ideological form. The growing definitional inclusion within American Jewishness of persons not considered Jewish by those in power within the State of Israel represents an elementary and potentially explosive gap between diaspora Jewish communities and Israeli Jews.

CHANGING GAPS BETWEEN JEWRIES AND BETWEEN PALESTINIANS

Jews outside of Israel view their Jewishness in the context of individual choices and communal consent; Israeli Jews have a major political component attached to their assigned status. How have these relationships changed over time? Have Jews in and outside of Israel moved closer or farther apart? The "peoplehood" paradigm has a component that emphasizes "oneness" across contexts. These have been emphasized by both Israeli and non-Israeli Jewish institutions. It is symbolized by the public relations slogan "we are one" used by national and international Jewish organizations. There is some basis for this view in the long history of Jews and in Judaism, often in response to how others define Jews as part of one people and as being distinctive.

Oneness does not necessarily imply similarities in every cultural and communal sphere. Obligations and responsibilities do not mean uniformity of identity and singularity of goals and objectives or the sameness of values. Indeed, there are increasing indications that Israeli Jews and Jews in communities outside of Israel are moving apart. While the State of Israel has become the center of Jewish peoplehood, large, cohesive, and powerful Jewish communities have emerged in modern, pluralistic societies outside of Israel. These are legitimate and accepted ethnic-religious communities, with long-term roots in these societies, as well as strong linkages to Israel. While most Jews living outside of Israel are committed to the State of Israel, in their view and in their behavior they are not in "exile" or in diaspora. Their home is where they live, where they expect to continue living, and where they are raising the next generation to live. Mutual dependencies have developed between Israel and Jewish communities outside of Israel. These dependencies have changed over time as these communities have responded to each other and as technology has brought geographically spread persons into new forms of communication to exchange ideas, cultures, and people. The exchanges have flowed in both directions.

In the past, there were major commonalities of background and experience between Israeli and American Jews. Both were heavily influenced by their European origins, many were raised in families where Yiddish was spoken, and they were rooted in Yiddish culture. Many struggled with second-generation status, or being raised by parents who were not native to the country where they were living. Many shared the cultural and social disruptions of secularization and assimilation, the struggles of economic depression, the war and Holocaust in Europe, and the rebuilding of the lives of Jewish refugees. They shared in the most tangible and dramatic ways the establishment and the rebuilding of the State of Israel.

Both Israeli and non-Israeli Jewish communities had limited exposure to formal Jewish education, rejected traditional Jewish ritual observances as reflections of their discarded past, and developed ethnic-national Jewish rituals as substitutes. Israeli Jews became less traditional by becoming attached nationally to their new country; American Jews became less traditionally oriented by becoming American. In short, there was a shared sense of origins, experiences, and objectives in the past, although each was living in a different society and building a new community with an appropriate set of institutions.

New generations have emerged in Israel and in America that are more distant from Europe and from the commonalities of language. For them, the European Holocaust is history, and immigration origins are far away, as are the struggles of pioneering in Israel and upward generation mobility in the United States. The different experiences of Israel and America as societies have shaped the lives, lifestyles, institutions, and values of these communities. Not only have past commonalities declined, but new gaps have emerged. A key example is the role of women in both societies. American Jewish women have been in the forefront of social changes in their increasing independence from traditional gender roles and family relationships. Their high levels of education, career orientation, small family size, and high aspirations for themselves and their children have been truly revolutionary. Many American men have shared and adjusted to these changes in the work place and in families. In contrast, Israeli men and women tend to have much more traditional gender-segregated family and social roles; family relationships are more patriarchal; and work patterns for women are less tied to a career. Israeli Jewish women lack the autonomy of American women. This particular gap, with its implications for work and family, has increased in recent years.

A second related shift involves the growing demographic, political, and cultural importance of Jews from the Middle East in Israel. This compositional change has created new gaps at the leadership and community levels between Israelis of non-European origins and American Jews. Language barriers have increased, and limited communication occurs between these communities. Diverse social-class backgrounds and lifestyles exacerbate these differences. Jews in America have become concentrated in high educational, occupational, and income categories. College-educated white-collar professionals are exceptional among Israeli Jews and particularly among women. Social class, ethnicity, and gender differences thus reinforce the gaps between Jews in Israel and America.

Religion is the most serious manifestation of the gap between Israel and the Jewish communities external to Israel. Judaism has been highly politicized in Israel, with control over religious institutions exercised by one segment of Judaism (the orthodox). Religious leaders of Israel and of communities outside of Israel have so little in common that there is virtually no communication between them. While the Jewish populations in both societies have similar levels of secularization, the gap in religious leadership is total. The religious leaders of Jewish communities outside of Israel have much more in common, and they are more likely to interact, with the secular-political leadership of Israel than with the formal representatives of the religious establishment.

The commitment of American Jews to the separation of religion and politics contrasts sharply with the clear interrelationship of religion and politics in Israel, the long-standing power of religious political parties, and the conspicuous intervention of religious leaders in Israeli politics. Religious pluralism characterizes Jewish communities outside of Israel, and multiple expressions of Judaism are accepted and valued. Israeli society and its leadership are not committed to ethnic or religious pluralism in the way characteristic of American Jewry. The trajectories of changes in these communities are moving in the direction of straining relationships between them, not in closing the gap. As each is moving through its own development, each is moving away from the other. In the short run, at least for another generation, differences between Jews in Israel and elsewhere are likely to be accentuated, despite increasing flows of money, culture, and people between these communities.

The increasing gaps between Israeli and non-Israeli Jews have striking similarities to Palestinians in and outside the State of Israel. Members of each of these groups have common origins, but they have several features that distinguish them more now than in the past. The remnant Arab communities remaining in the State of Israel after 1948 was selective of those less able with fewer resources. A social and economic gap was evident from the beginning of the separation of these communities. Initially, Israeli Arabs experienced a period as internal refugees within Israel immediately after the establishment of the state. They were moved from their land and resettled into new areas or older Arab communities and placed under Israeli military administration. These initial experiences of Israeli Arabs were different than those of the displaced Palestinians who were relocated in refugee camps in neighboring Arab countries. Most important, these communities developed in different contexts, one as residents in Israeli society and the other as "temporary" residents in Arab countries often under the auspices of international agencies. Despite residential segregation and disenfranchisement within Israel, Israeli Arabs have become citizens of the State of Israel. They have voted in democratic elections and have been exposed to the educational system and culture of Israeli society even if that exposure has been biased toward Jewish Israelis. The Palestinians have experienced a different form of refugee status in countries not their own. They have been powerless and dependent of Arab countries and international agencies. They have had less access to economic and educational opportunities in a variety of places.

There was total segregation of Israeli Arabs from Palestinians outside of Israel in the period from 1948 to 1967. After 1967 Israel became the administrators of territories where large number of Palestinians lived whose origins were in the Palestine of the British mandate period. New relationships between Israeli Arabs and their Palestinian relations emerged. However, both groups had changed, and gaps existed between them. The social, economic, political, and cultural gaps reflected the contexts of the communities experienced by an entire generation. Many Palestinians living in communities on the West Bank and in Gaza have viewed Israeli Arabs as too "Israelified" and becoming more like their oppressors. Often they have been considered traitors to the political struggles of Palestinians for autonomy and statehood. Many Israeli Arabs viewed the Palestinians as their less-educated cousins, whose political and cultural experiences divided them from their communities. Many of the gaps between Arab Israelis and the Palestinians who were similar to them before 1948 have increased over time.

Increased communication among Palestinians and among Jews in a variety of countries has led to the recognition of diversity rather than to the neutralization of differences. The diversity has challenged the political attempt to establish "oneness" for these groups in terms of origins and current statuses. Since contexts always count in shaping the evolution of change among ethnic groups, it is not surprising that considerable diversity is characteristic of both Jews and Palestinians in and outside of the State of Israel. The increased communication among these communities may reduce the cultural conflicts that have shaped Arab-Israeli relationships.

ETHNICITY AND NATIONALISM: ARE JEWISH ETHNIC GROUPS TRANSITIONAL?

Underlying the review of the impact of Jewish and Palestinian diasporas on the changing Arab-Israeli conflict is a key question: How are ethnic divisions within Israeli society linked to social inequality? The issue of Arab and Jewish differences within Israel and between Israel and their diasporas is whether these differences are transmitted from one generation to another. There are always differences among groups. Whether these social and economic differences are continuous over time, whether they are inherited generationally, is the core issue in the perpetuation of ethnic disadvantage. Specifically, what are the contexts within Israel that reduce inequality among groups, and what are the contexts that perpetuate the unequal distribution of resources?

The major ethnic divisions within Israeli society are those that divide Jews from each other and those that separate Jews from Arabs. What can be inferred from our understanding of the sources of these differences about the relative permanence of these divisions and whether Jewish and Arab ethnic divisions in Israel are transitional? Ethnic convergences have been identified in some processes. Ethnic differences, for example, in family size and age at marriage were much wider in the past and have narrowed over time. Similarly, health differences and rates of infant mortality, which were significantly higher for immigrants from the Middle East than immigrants from Europe and higher for Muslims than for Jews, have been substantially reduced among second-generation native-born Jews and among Muslims. At the same time, other characteristics that differentiate communities have persisted through time. Residential and occupational concentration, as well as levels of higher education, continuously separates ethnic groups among Jews and Jews from Arabs. Can an assessment be made about the declining significance of ethnicity and of ethnic communities by examining the total picture? If ethnic communities are continuous features of Israel's emerging pluralism, how is national integration affected? In short, do ethnic continuities conflict with national Israeli integration? In the context of the Arab-Israeli conflict, are there signs of increasing similarities between groups that might reduce the inequalities for the next generation of Israeli Jews and Palestinians?

It is clear that the earlier entry into Israeli society of European immigrants and their socioeconomic and demographic background facilitated their relatively successful socioeconomic mobility and their access to power, resources, and opportunity. European immigrants could take advantage of their connections to the European-dominated society and economy that they found established as the state was developing. Jewish immigrants from Middle Eastern countries arrived in Israel later in time with a higher level of dependency on sociopolitical institutions. They were burdened by larger families, higher mortality, and higher morbidity, and they had fewer resources than Jews from Western societies. They came from less-developed societies and had fewer urban skills and less powerful economic networks, and they were less able to compete with European-origin groups in Israel. The timing of immigration and the cultural differences between groups reinforced these background factors which divided Israeli Jews.

The differential timing of immigration and the changing ethnic composition of immigrant streams created the contexts of residential concentration among Jews. Ethnic residential patterns, moreso than the legacy of social and cultural origins, shape what ethnicity continues to mean in the process of nation building in Israel. Residential concentration forged from political and economic considerations has become a key process marking off Israeli-born Jews from each other, as it has been the foundation of the continuing Jewish-Arab distinctiveness.

New Israeli patterns have emerged among Jews that are neither fully "Western" nor "Middle Eastern." Ethnic cultural differences remain salient, and distance from the immigrant generation continues to be an important factor in understanding social change in Israel. However, residential segregation and its consequences for access to opportunity are critical in retaining ethnic distinctiveness. Ethnic residential concentration is linked to educational opportunities and, in turn, to jobs. It is likely to relate to a reinforced sense of ethnic self-identity, pride, and culture connecting ethnic origins and families into networks of relationships. These separate patterns, almost total between Jews and Arabs, characterize significant segments of third-generation Jews when examined by the two broad Jewish ethnic categories: European (Western) and Middle Eastern.

It becomes clear that some ethnic demographic differences diminish in importance, and ethnic convergences occur over time when differences are primarily the result of the background of immigrants and largely the legacy of the past. Thus, for example, family size and family structure differences among Jewish ethnic groups have diminished with each passing generation, as mortality differences have disappeared among the foreign-born first generation. In contrast, when the sources of ethnic differences are embedded in Israeli society, ethnic communities remain salient and unequal. These are the result of the patterns of emerging residential segregation—concentration in particular jobs and in local schools. Ethnic cultural expressions and values legitimate these Israeli features, as do the prejudices of those in power and the discrimination against selected minorities who are powerless.

Ethnic residential concentration among Jews and between Jews and

Arabs reinforces the overlap of ethnicity and socioeconomic factors through the impact of location factors on access to educational and economic opportunities. Together, residential and socioeconomic concentrations shape the continuing salience of ethnic distinctiveness in Israel. When groups have been integrated residentially, ethnic differences have become marginal in their social, economic, and political importance. When residential segregation within Israel has persisted, it has become the primary engine of ethnic persistence and inequality. While ethnic segregation is associated with poverty and lower socioeconomic status, it also implies supportive and family networks that shape the lives of many Israelis. Ethnic-family networks, economic networks that are ethnically based, and some local institutions—religious institutions, community centers, health clinics, and leisure-time and cultural activities (sports and music, for example)—are concentrated among particular ethnic groups. Jewish ethnic loyalties and identities persist despite government policies and ideological orientations to deny the salience of ethnicity.

These same processes of economic concentration, residential segregation, and institutional separateness drive the Arab-Jewish distinction. It also reflects the political legacy of the broader Arab-Israeli conflict, the role of Palestinians in their quest for national identity, and the importance of Jewishness in the political shape of Israeli society and its symbols. The ethnic identity of Arab Israelis can never be fully Israeli as long as being Israeli involves a clear and unmistakable Jewish cultural component, Jewish historical constructions, and dominant Jewish symbols.

Arab Israelis cannot seriously relate to the Israeli national symbols because of their Jewishness. Consider the Israeli "national" anthem that refers to the longing for Jewish statehood for the Jewish people—"We have not lost our hope for 2,000 years, to be a free nation in our land, the land of Zion, Jerusalem." Can Arab Israelis citizens of the state join in the singing of this national anthem? National events and their symbols are infused with Judaic religious distinctiveness (e.g., national religious holidays such as Passover and Israeli Independence Day celebrations) and Jewish historical meaning (e.g., the Holocaust). They are annual reminders of the distinctive status of Arab Israelis and the Jewishness of the state. Jews can celebrate these national Jewish occasions in their distinct and diverse ways, but they identify their celebrations as Jewish. Arabs cannot.

The economic integration of Israeli Arabs into Israeli society makes their distinctiveness sharper and their powerlessness obvious, and it does not increase their social integration. Conferring political rights and welfare entitlements cannot erase the effects of their Palestinian identity and their minority status within Israel. The Arab population of Israel is likely to struggle with the conflicts of their identity and their unequal access to opportunities as citizens of the state for at least another generation.

These arguments suggest that convergences among ethnic groups in some aspects of social life do not necessarily provide clues about total ethnic assimilation. Increasing similarities in family structure or educational level among Jews from different ethnic origins are a poor basis for concluding that assimilation is proceeding to eliminate ethnic communities. Ethnic communities have been redefined away from specific countries of origin toward an amalgamation of broader ethnic groups that represent new forms of ethnic differentiation. The diminished significance of Polish, Romanian, Algerian, and Tunisian ethnicity among Jewish immigrants to Israel does not preclude their recombination into new ethnic categories that are specific to Israeli society and have importance as "European" and "Asian-African" Israeli communities. These new ethnic divisions, which mark Jews off from each other, have significance only in the context of Israeli society. The conspicuous differences among Jews in the second and third generations negate the melting-pot response to the integration of ethnic populations. The resultant Jewish ethnic divisions do not imply that individuals do not move between ethnic groups or into a third ethnically neutral Israeli group. The fluidity of boundaries does not imply their absence. Ethnicity may continue to be a characteristic of groups and communities, although it may not be an ascribed feature of each person's identity.

By the standards of ethnic assimilation, in Israel and in other pluralistic societies, the Arab-Israeli distinctiveness is embedded in the structure of Israeli society, its values and political culture. In contrast to ethnic differences among Jews, Arab-Israeli distinctiveness has been perpetuated generationally. Jewish-Arab residential segregation within Israel and the resultant disadvantage of Israeli Arabs are unlikely to be resolved without major internal changes within the society, its institutions, values, and political system. Barring such fundamental changes within the Jewish State of Israel, the residential segregation of Arab Israelis will continue, and the consequences for socioeconomic inequalities will persist. Only local control over institutions and the development of local opportunities for socioeconomic mobility within Arab-Israeli communities can reduce their disadvantaged status. How Israeli Arabs will be linked to autonomous Palestinian areas and Arab states remains unclear.

There are only beginning answers to the consequences of changes for ethnic communities and cultural conflict in the context of nation building in Israel. In thinking through the broader question of the conditions under which communities retain their salience and the contexts that facilitate integration, our orientation is to emphasize the role of ethnic networks and ethnic institutions in the context of residential concentration. Clearly, and for different reasons, neither the Jewish diaspora nor the Palestinian diaspora is about to join the State of Israel, but new relationships will emerge that will link these peoples to the state and the society. As the twentieth century closes, it is clear that these relationships, whatever their particular nuance, will be different from those of the past.

WHEN PEACE ARRIVES: HOW WILL THE ARAB-ISRAEL CONFLICT BE RESOLVED?

Some Israelis and some Palestinians view giving up land as a violation of a fundamental ideological principle. Others are more willing to consider trading territory for a process that would lead to security and peace. Palestinian control over land occupied by Israel for a quarter of a century is countered by arguments over who has the "right" to the land, constructed as "divine" or as "political" or as "historical" rights. There is the Israeli concern that terrorism and uncontrollable conflict, not peaceful neighborly relations, will result from Palestinian autonomy and statehood. Fear and distrust have been replaced often by hatred and the suppression of Palestinian self-determination by Israeli power. This may be slowly changing, but it is a long process that requires time to unfold. The *intifada* (or uprising of West Bank Palestinians against the Israeli occupation) had its most violent expression among Palestinians.

The international situation in the world in the 1990s has altered, particularly with the collapse of the Soviet regime and its diminished influence in the Middle East, the changing role of the Gulf States, and the increasing ethnic-national identity of the Palestinians. Israel and the Palestinians are talking to one another, but terrorism continues. Syria and Israel appear to be more open to negotiating control over the Golan Heights. Russia is overwhelmed with its own national and regional economic problems and is less involved in power politics with the United States over the Middle East. It is clear that Israel will give up territory (how much and when is not clear) and the Palestinians will have increasing control over their own autonomous political unit in the West Bank, parallel to the developing institutions and infrastructure within Gaza. There will be an end to the Israeli military presence on the West Bank and a diminished control over local Palestinian institutions (health, education, welfare, and economic). The indicators all point to a set of processes that will result in new relationships between Israelis and Palestinians. Whether and when this will involve a Palestinian state with control over internal and external affairs will become clearer over the next generation.

In the late 1930s and 1940s, when faced with a similar dilemma, the Jewish government in Palestine, under the leadership of Ben Gurion, opted for people over land and accepted the idea of the partition of the British mandated Palestine. It was a decision that was not reached without considerable pain and internal conflict. Faced with a similar choice, the current political leadership in Israel has reached similar conclusions. This appears to reflect the current consensus in Israel as evidenced by the election results in 1999. Ehud Barak became prime minister in direct elections as a representative of the Labor political party defeating the incumbent Benjamin Netanyahu of the right-wing nationalist Likud party.

The costs of continuing with occupation and violence are high. The importance of economic growth and peace is real for internal development within Israeli society. The toll in the quality of life in Israel and in the territories Israel administers is very high to justify the continuation of the status quo. The dependency of both populations on other nations and outside support is too great for either side to follow only its ideological imperatives. So a peaceful resolution is likely of the Arab-Israeli conflict in its end-of-the twentieth-century configuration. Few legitimate voices on the Israeli side take the extreme position of incorporating the whole territory of the West Bank and its populations within the State of Israel. Even fewer argue for the incorporation of the territory without the Palestinian population. Few Palestinians argue for control or their rights to the whole of Palestine, including the State of Israel and its Jewish population and institutions. So the questions are twofold: Which territories will become part of a Palestinian controlled territory? And what kind of independence or autonomy will emerge?

Viewed historically, there is only the option of partition of the areas previously designated as Palestine under the British mandate. Each side has in the past taken the position that all the land was theirs, and each side is faced with the reality that there are others who make similar (and legitimate) claims. There are two stories that are invoked when issues of territorial divisions are discussed. One is the biblical story involving King Solomon who was confronted with deciding which of two mothers was the mother of a surviving child. Each mother claimed that the one surviving baby belonged to her. The king suggested to the mothers that the surviving baby be divided in half. The first mother agreed. The second mother suggested that the baby be given to the first mother, since splitting the baby in half would kill the baby. Solomon concluded that the second mother must be the actual mother of the surviving baby. According to some observers in the Middle East, recommending an equal division of territory would result in an unnatural separation of the territory and must therefore be a sign of deceit and illegitimacy. Yet, the challenge remains to divide the land claimed by both parties without removing the core claims of each of the parties.

There is another story discussed in the Mishnah (a fourth-century compendium of Jewish laws). It involves a dispute over the ownership of a piece of cloth, with each side claiming ownership of the whole. The cloth, the Mishnah argues, has to be split into "equal" shares and distributed to the claimants, even when that may destroy the value and integrity of the whole fabric. Land is not a fabric, and what each side defines as "equal shares" in the Arab-Israeli dispute has been shaped by history.

Analogies are never exact, but they are helpful in allowing us to see the possibilities of resolving conflicts and assessing the costs of continuing with the status quo. Long-standing conflicts often are viewed as having no resolutions, just consequences. There is every reason to proceed with a cautious optimism that the long-standing Arab-Israeli conflict will also have resolutions that the claimants can work together to implement equitably. This is not the direct lesson of history, but it may be the critical turning point where we can learn from history without repeating it.

PART II

DOCUMENTS

The documents extracted in Part II give voice to the players in the Arab-Israeli conflict. Some reflect on the lifestyle of Israeli Jews and Arab Palestinians in and outside of the State of Israel. Others reflect directly on the consequences of the Arab-Israeli conflict on their lives. The overriding themes reflect the experiences of generations from the early Jewish settlers in Palestine to the more recent Jewish settlers on the West Bank, from Arabs who remained in Israel after the establishment of the State of Israel to the refugee Palestinian population living on the West Bank. The powerful sources of the Arab transition from majority to minority status under Israeli occupation are highlighted, as are the transitions from immigrant to ethnic group statuses among Jews. Whereas immigration and the ensuing relationships between the generations and among ethnic groups have shaped the Jewish Israeli experiences, the displacement and powerlessness of Palestinians become clear from these selections.

Part II is divided into four chapters which reflect the changing historical and substantive issues in the Arab-Israeli conflict. The selections in Chapter 5 focus primarily on the ethnic clashes among Jewish immigrants and the impact of exposure to Israeli society on the generational gap. The ethnic Jewish clashes described are between Jewish immigrants from European countries, who controlled more of the resources, and the later immigrants from Middle Eastern countries. These ethnic clashes occurred as part of the adjustment of immigrants to a radically different society than that in their communities of origin. The descriptions relate to the patterns of assimilation of immigrants and the divided society emergent in Israel based on national origin. Two important conclusions emerge from the descriptions in the first two sections. First, Jewish Israeli society is not homogenous. These divisions by ethnic origin need to be understood in addition to other divisions that characterize all societies—for example, social class and gender. The interrelationships of the ethnic and the social-class variations have major implications for the inequalities shaped by the diverse immigrant groups in Israel.

The second conclusion concerns the distinctive Jewish experiences in the State of Israel relative to the experiences of the Arab population in Israel and the Palestinians who were displaced. These different experiences of all Jewish immigrant groups remain a major source of continued distinctiveness in the second and later generations. In turn, the distinctive experience of Jews in their national homeland prevents the simple integration of the Arab minority as Israelis.

The selections in Chapter 6 deal directly with the Arab-Israeli conflict. There are new Israeli pioneers in the last two decades of the twentieth century—Jews who settled in the Israeli-administered territories of the West Bank. Their views of their own rights to the Land of Israel and their commitments to the ideals of living in Israel are impressive. Their presence among Palestinians who outnumber them and who resent their being there is a major source of tension and confrontation. Their voices must be heard since, from the point of view of Israeli governments, they are full citizens of the State of Israel and not only have rights to the land but also rights (and obligations) of citizenship. They have received major financial subsidies from the Israeli government and have in the main received political as well as economic supports.

These new settlers have also earned the enmity and criticism of Israelis who view their presence, as do the Palestinians, as a source of continued conflict in the relationship of Israelis to Palestinians. Chapter 6 begins with two selections of Israeli Jewish voices who have been critical of the Israeli role in the Palestinian conflict, in general, and of the Jewish settlers, in particular.

The voices in Chapter 5 and 6 are those of Israeli Jews who are reflecting on the meaning of their distinctive experiences and are expressing their views on the Arab-Israeli conflict. The selections in Chapters 7 and 8 capture some of the feelings of the Israeli Arab community in Israel and some of the depths of anguish and pain experienced by the Palestinians who are living in the West Bank and elsewhere in exile. The selections in Chapter 7 begin with three reflections on the meaning of the establishment of the State of Israel in 1948. There was euphoria in the Jewish community, as well as around the world, when the new State of Israel was established, particularly among the stateless of the European Holocaust survivors. Many thought that finally the dream of the Jews in exile for 2,000 years had been fulfilled with a Jewish state of their own. The dream of the Jews, however, was the nightmare of the Palestinians. Uprooted and displaced and used as pawns in international politics, they often felt as if they were the new "Jewish" wanderers in the desert. On the celebration of the fiftieth anniversary of the establishment of the State of Israel in 1998, the *Journal of Palestine Studies* asked several prominent Palestinians to reflect personally on *al-Nakba*, the tragedy of Israeli statehood. Their views are a reminder that wars and displacement have both losers and winners, and the deeply felt perceptions of the events are radically different on both sides.

The poignancy of the Palestinians returning to "visit" their former homes in the State of Israel is clearly conveyed in the selections included in Chapter 8. The description of the feeling of coming "home" and still being treated as a foreigner by those who are "foreigners" to them is moving and tragic. The parallels between the feelings of Palestinians coming to their home in what was Palestine and now is the State of Israel with that of Jewish immigrants coming home to Palestine/Israel to live in their national homeland can be clearly observed. Minority status was not a positive experience for the European or the Middle Eastern Jewish immigrants in their countries of origin. Minority status is not a positive experience for the Israeli Arab. The absence of a homeland for generations of Palestinians living under some other government control finds striking parallels with the dreams of the early Jewish immigrants to establish their own homeland.

Chapter 5

Ethnic Clashes among Jewish Immigrants

The selection from the novel *Requiem for Na'aman* by Benjamin Tammuz reveals the issues of generational conflict and describes the variety of social class and diverse ethnic backgrounds of Israeli Jews of the *Yishuv*. Here the conflict between Middle-Eastern-origin Jews (Sephardim) and European-origin Jews (Ashkenazim) are described as well as their relationship to Arabs in Israel. Some of the language used is informative. Note the use of the word "pogrom" for the Arab attacks on Jews in 1921, a word familiar to the European experience of Jews. The point about language and translation appears regularly in Israeli literature.

REQUIEM FOR NA'AMAN

Memorandum

For the attention of the Superintendent of the Jerusalem Police.
Copies to the Minister of Justice and the Prime Minister.

I, ABRAHAM CORDOVIERO, now known as Abie Cordo, eighth generation in this country on my father's side and second generation on my mother's side, with the intention of putting an end to the rumors and slanders that have been piled upon me by various liars and villains, hereby declare that everything written herein is complete truth.

On my father's side we belong to the family of King David, and we had the proofs of this in written documents and they were with me in my flat, when I was married, and all these documents were burnt in a fire when the burning was in the above-mentioned flat, which was lit by Bibi Turgeman . . .

• • •

. . . I am a Sephardi Jew, of the purest Sephardi stock, and I saw in my childhood the Ashkenazi Jews coming from all over the world and grabbing positions and rudely elbowing their way in and pushing us aside to the corner. And all these newcomers have jargonesque names like Rabinowitz and Schmendrikowitz. And what do they do with their names? They change them. Rabinowitz becomes Rabin and Schmendrikowitz becomes Alouf. I said to myself: If they rule over us, I'm in the Diaspora. And if I'm in the Diaspora, I will change my name from a Hebrew one to an outlandish one exactly the opposite of what Rabinowitz does.

That is the reason for the change of my name, and that is one of the reasons for my departure to the Diaspora.

When will I return to the land of my forefathers? This is a solemn oath, a saying of honor and truth: When the Ashkenazis fold in their rude elbows and become a minority. The day Jerusalem has a police superintendent from our people, and in the House of Parliament there will be a Prime Minister of ours and in the army a Chief of Staff of ours—then I shall know that no danger is imminent for me, and I will return to my father's house and to the motherland; as long as she is occupied by you, I am waiting outside. And from time to time I come to see, with my own eyes, if there have been any changes.

Respectfully yours,
A. Cordo
An Israeli citizen, with foreign citizenship, according to the law.

• • •

20.

ONE DAY IN 1921 Ephraim was making his way from his settlement to Tel Aviv, and when he passed close to the eastern quarters of Jaffa, among the orchards, he met Arabs on his way, and their faces were not as in times past. He knew in his heart that the events which were taking place there were not good, and he turned from his way and arrived in Tel Aviv by a circuitous route, through the fields of Mikveh-Israel.

When he reached the house of Sarah and Aminadav, carrying with him the two baskets of fruit and vegetables, he found the household busy trying to revive Oved. The boy had gone to the Herzliah Gymnasium in the morning and there he had seen people gathering and whispering. Then a corpse was brought in, wrapped in blankets, and it was laid down in the yard. Oved nudged his way between the legs of the gathered people and saw Brenner the teacher lying there stabbed, with closed eyes, on the blanket, his beard stained with blood. He had come home and had been vomiting all day, wailing and not answering when spoken to.

"So, it's a pogrom," said Ephraim. "The Arabs are trying to do to us what the Ukrainians and Russians did."

That year the Jews in the Land of Israel started to stock up weapons and organize themselves for self-defense. The older pupils at the Gymnasium were made to swear an oath at night on the Bible and a revolver. And in the settlements the farmers went out on guard by themselves and the Arab guards were dismissed from their positions.

In 1929, when the second pogrom erupted, the sixteen-year-old Oved was already a unit commander of the Haganah,* and spent his nights away from home, in flats at the end of Ha-Yarkon Street, opposite Hassan-Bek Mosque, on the border of Jaffa. During those riots it happened that an Arab lemon-sorbet hawker fell upon a Jewish cart-driver and started to stab him with a dagger; Oved, standing at a window, aimed his revolver, shot the Arab, and killed him. When he came home in the morning, to sleep and regain some strength, he could not fall asleep. But he did not vomit and he did not wail, and when at noon his mother offered him lunch, he sat down at the table and ate, as in days gone by. His younger brother, fifteen-year-old Elyakum, was cleaning Oved's revolver and noticed that the barrel was fouled.

"Did you shoot last night?" he asked his brother in admiration.

"Do your own work and don't ask questions," Oved scolded him from his place at the table.

Obligation to secrecy was a basic principle in the Haganah.

• • •

In 1934 the wedding of Oved and Rachel took place in Jerusalem, and the Ben-Zion family and the Abramson family went up to Jerusalem and stayed at the Warshawsky Hotel for three days, to celebrate the matrimonial alliance and to make the acquaintance of the Cordoviero family.

Rivka sewed herself a special dress for her grandson's wedding and Ephraim wore the suit he had taken to Europe twenty-two years earlier. An expert tailor from the settlement of Rehovot let it out in the necessary places, and after ironing the old seams were almost invisible.

Nevertheless the two of them looked somewhat like beggars, or com-

---

*The left-of-center underground military organization of the Jewish population in Palestine.

moners, dressed up for the day, when compared to the splendid presence of the Cordoviero family.

The distinguished Sephardic Jews of Jerusalem in no way resembled the few Sephardic Jews who were in the settlements and in Tel Aviv. Not only were their houses furnished in European taste of the nineteenth century, and there were Persian carpets, Damascus copperware, and cabinets inlaid with mother-of-pearl and silver and gold threads, but also they had an ancient, dignified appearance. It was perhaps the dignified appearance of famous and resolute rabbis, perhaps the dignified appearance of great merchants from the towns of Russia and the Caucasus in times past. But these Sephardis were not Russians, they were an exotic kind of human being, whom Ephraim suspected of being too close to the Arabs, or the Turks, or other creatures of the Orient.

The Cordovieros received the Ben-Zions and the Abramsons with lofty cordiality, but Ephraim felt that they were exaggerating their hospitality to conceal a heartfelt contempt, or a kind of pity, or perhaps even fear and suspicion; and he was in a foul mood during all three days of their stay in Jerusalem.

According to the standing of the household and according to what people said, Ephraim had no ground for regretting the match. Especially as he had no worries, God forbid, about Oved's fate. The lad was like that cat which, if he fell, would land on all fours and not get hurt. And yet Ephraim felt that his grandson was going beyond the grasp of the family and that, one might even say, he was going beyond the grasp of the tribe, the tribe of the Abramsons from Russia, farming pioneers of the Land of Israel.

"Never mind," he said to Rivka, after the couple had come out from under the canopy, properly married, true, but nevertheless married by a Sephardic rabbi, in a black robe and with a black turban on his head, who had chanted nuptial chants such as Ephraim's forefathers had never known. "Never mind, let it be a good omen and good fortune. Oved will find his way even beyond the remote, Dark Mountains, all the more so among those Jews, who in the end are no less Jews than we are.

• • •

Whilst the guests were still congratulating the couple and turning toward the tables laid out with all manner of good things, Elyakum was enjoying the company of some youths from among the dignitaries of Jerusalem, Sephardis and Ashkenazis, who had been invited to the wedding, some on the strength of family relationships and some on the strength of the legal profession or the land trade. And there were also some Arab guests there, from the most venerable families in Jerusalem. And in that company, when the wine had been poured and the glasses had been clinked against each other, and the guests had already become heady, Elyakum was carried away in his speech and talked effusively and said: "I have a question to ask, and I want to understand . . . simply because there's one thing I don't understand: where are you headed, all of you here? Look here, my brother has already become a lawyer, and all of you too . . . what are you? Merchants, speculators, money-rakers, or what? Where does all this lead to? In other words: what for? And aren't we dealing here with the Land of Israel . . . that means a dream. Or how shall we say it? An ideal. . . . Want to put right something that has been flawed, to change, to remedy a kind of defect, or, let's say, to remedy a disease. . . . Yes, a Jewish disease, but also a world disease. . . . I will say it clearly, without any circumlocutions. . . . Shall we say it like this: we've returned here after two thousand years, so why the hell did we go to all this bother in the first place to come here? That is the question. Why are people killed and dying here? What did we have all this for? And I say: To realize a dream . . . a dream. So what did we dream, then? We dreamed a beautiful world, beautiful human beings, a kind of purity, a different kind of joy, new, not to be found in exile. . . . And here, what? Lawyers, banks, cheap labor, exploiting the Arabs, licking the asses of the English and receiving all kinds of jobs. . . . What is it? It's filth. For this it's not worth it, gentlemen. . . . Think for yourselves and answer me: was it worth it to come to swamps and malaria and murders, in order to be lawyers and to work in a bank? . . . Look to the window, gentlemen, and you will see what a splendid light glows upon Jerusalem, how the stones burn, gentlemen. . . . Here there's a wonderful fire, go out into it and get burned in it, purified in that fire, gentlemen; this is an opportunity that comes to our people once in a thousand years, once in two thousand, in fact. . . . So what then? Lawyers, clerks of the court, clerks, petty speculators, ha? That's it? I ask, why all of a sudden?"

His voice soared higher and higher and all the guests heard the ends of his statements and some of them were astounded, whilst others chuckled and wondered and asked each other: Who's the joker? And when the wedding guests learned that he was the bridegroom's brother they were dumbfounded, because Oved had indeed made a good impression.

And the Arab guests were told that the bridegroom's brother had made a speech blessing the marriage.

• • •

Benjamin Tammuz, *Requiem for Na'aman*, trans. Mildred Budny and Yehuda Saffran (New York: New American Library, 1978), 55–63, 143–46.

This selection is by Ilana Sugbaker Messika, a native-born Israeli who grew up in a rural moshav, an agricultural settlement of immigrants from Morocco, Egypt, and India. She reflects on her Indian upbringing and the role of ethnic origins in her life and in her community. The way in which ethnic groups coalesce and remain distinctive in their own eyes and in the eyes of others is revealed with great insight and sensitivity. The tensions between becoming Israeli and retaining the culture of one's family and community underlie this essay.

MEMORIES OF AN INDIAN UPBRINGING

So it turns out I'm an Israeli from India, that is, I was born in Israel but my parents came from India. In the eyes of many, I'm a "Yemenite," because of the color. Once, years ago, when women soldiers used to hitchhike, this conversation repeated itself again and again:
"Yemenite?"
"No."
"Persian, right? Moroccan??"
"Indian."
"Indian? It doesn't show."

Or: "How come I didn't think of that?" My mother does invitations for an "Indian" evening in Jerusalem. Years after I had left, yearning for an Israeliness that could be taken for granted. Like every year, thousands of the *Bene Yisrael* from India gather in Jerusalem, to see and be seen, to experience the shards of a culture still existing in them, the civilization of India. It's very *in* to talk about immigration, Ethiopians, tradition, Russians, Israeliness, Bukharians and whether or not the news about a community of six million Jews in Kashmir is true or not. Would it be good if a couple of million Indians come to the country? Under the condition that they're Jews, of course, why not? It's interesting to see what the leaders will put together for the community's annual evening, an evening of color, Indian clothing, great food, art, music, and Indian dance. Other people, all eyes upon them, with *"good manners,"* are not jostled in, to the women's clear, ringing laughter.

• • •

Crossing walls on the Tel Aviv—Moshav Masliah road. Preparing "Punjabidaras." Tel Aviv summer, get your mount ready for winter. At the last minute, I prefer pants and a white shirt, something casual. At parties with friends, I'll arrive Indian, Oriental, or Arabic with a *gallabiya* or something else. That's fine. But for there, for an Indian evening, I hesitate. The deference, the scrupulous observation of Indian aesthetics, the agreement down the length of the skirt, the pitch of the hips holding the wrap in place . . . but with me, the train of the sari falls right down, helplessly plodding along my shoulder. I'm awkward, I don't have the right moves to grapple with clothes like that. But I love them so much, they're so beautiful to me. But not *on* me. It's better not to even get tangled up in all that.

We're on our way, my mother Abigail, my father Menahem, my sister Sarale in a festive top embroidered in gold, my brother-in-law Asher and me. Just before we get on the bus coming from Ramallah, my mother warns: "We'll probably have to wait two hours because they won't start on time."

I know, but nobody cares, everything's cool. In the back of the bus, a group of kids, boys and girls, start singing Indian songs from the movies. I'm compelled to look: kids with shaved heads and a lock of wild hair dipped in gel, curling down to the neck. Young girls with waves in the style of Shuki Zikri or some other famous Indian star (is that her name? I don't even follow Indian movies anymore). The finest fashions for the young, those whose parents were probably already born in Israel and work for the Aircraft Industry or at El Al. Amongst them, second-generation immigrants sing songs in Hindustani.

The mid-fifties, my parents after the Gate of Ascent and before Moshav Masliah, at kibbutz Yagur. I'm a chocolate baby. Often, on walks through the paths of the kibbutz, in the area designated for immigrants from India, a comrade from the kibbutz would stop to express astonishment at the dark baby. I was a *sabra*, the pride of the family. These days, an unplanted *sabra* doesn't sound like much. The third of five children, but with the sole and special right to be a *sabra*, a real Israeli.

Binyanei Ha-Uma, in Jerusalem. In the parking lot, two women in white and violet saris rush towards the entrance. I'm struck by the colors. My mother says: "No taste." How come? Because you don't wear a sari that distance from the ankles, you cover them. And the wrap is too short for the shoulder. And the folds of the fan are vulgar. Got it? A different aesthetic, unfamiliar. She's right, my mother Abigail—and the sari takes on a different meaning.

August 91, *Binyanei Ha-Uma* in Jerusalem. Huge signs greet us: *"WELCOME TO THE ANNUAL GATHERING OF DESCENDANTS FROM INDIA IN ISRAEL."*

"The *Benei Yisrael* aren't even mentioned."

"What?"

"Didn't you notice that they don't even mention the *Benei Yisrael*?"

"I wonder why."

"They want us to forget."

One assumption takes the place of another and it is no longer *Benei Yisrael* but "Jews of Indian descent." And why should that really be important? We're all Israeli. Whether by chance or not, today marks India's day of Independence.

• • •

Indians came to Israel from a number of regions for, after all, India is half a continent, gigantic; to get from one city to another you can spend three days on a train, easily. Not like here. The Cochinis came from the south, darker than us, pattering another Indian, clanging along like silverware, quickly, quickly, quickly. Funny. Avi the Cochini from the preparatory course in Jerusalem, now a successful lawyer, says the Cochinis integrated into the country well. The *Benei Yisrael*, those who came from around Bombay (like me), were not absorbed as they should have been, and many went downhill. I'm surprised, I always thought differently; after all, there, in India, the Cochinis were mostly peasants while we had the businesses, the education, the respected professions, the posts in the government and the railroad. How did that happen? Different services during immigration? The nature of the ethnic group itself? Maybe he's not even right? There are also Baghdadi Indians, Jews from Iraq who lived in Bombay for several generations. We, the *Benei Yisrael*, helped them out at times to fulfill the commandments of the ransom of the firstborn or the *bar mitsva*. There are no "kohens" in our community. We are Marathi speaking *Benei Yisrael* from the region of Bombay. The *Benei Yisrael* of the Bible are not the kind of *Benei Yisrael* that we are. We don't exist in any of the history books on the state of Israel. And there are even Indian Jews in Persia.

I almost forgot the degradation of the sixties. Then we were denounced as illegitimate, bastards, perhaps not even Jews. There was something suspicious there but nobody knew exactly what, before '67, before the Panthers, way before. Right around the time of Kennedy's assasination. Maybe after. Suddenly they told us we weren't Jews! Not Jews? Just like that, a discovery! And we're already here ten years, settling down the place and settling in our heads, on some "succesful" combine, Moshav Masliah, with our Egyptian neighbors (who think they're better educated than we are!), and Moroccans who also think a lot of themselves. Can you imagine? Why should we be less Jewish than anyone else? And why don't we have an alternative?

In those repressive years of the sixties, the competition between the three ethnic groups on the Moshav concerning the debate over who is "more modern," finally changed into who is "more Israeli." No one wanted to be primitive. It was agreed-upon that the Indians are reserved, the Egyptians diligent and the Moroccans . . . well, you know about the Moroccans. With the Egyptians, there were strong family ties; on the Sabbath, echoes of their joy even reached us, and we witnessed the sight of their two ringing kisses, one on each cheek, for "Sitti," or "Umti," and the trilling ululations at every festivity. When the children finished high school and the army, they went to work, permanently. Welders, careers in the military, mechanics, factory workers. R. Darwish was the first Egyptian girl from the Moshav to go into the army. A notch above me. At the end, she married out of the community. At first, the kids used to bring their salaries back home to their fathers, but that stopped later and they began to save for their own dowries; they bought a refrigerator, a stove, pots and pans. The sons even built houses for themselves. And with no warning, they made us Indians not Jewish. So degrading, so insulting.

We were seized by a kind of modesty that went right along with our reticence and patience from the absorption years in the homeland. How did the story end? We got what we wanted. We demonstrated. Quietly, in exemplary order, precisely following the commands of the police. Time after time we waved huge slogans opposite the Parliament: *"We Are All Benei Yisrael!"* Both men and women. At the rabbinate or amongst the politicians, they all said: "Things will be fine." But they continued checking our family trees. Comparing notes in black and white. Since then, the immigrants from Russia have undergone these tribulations. With them, though, problems are solved behind closed doors. And the Ethiopians. Only it doesn't look like things are going that easy for them. If at all.

It's better not to even go into it. A delicate matter, even these days, when an Indian wants to marry someone from another community.

The first *sabra* in the family. I was given a Hebrew name to cleave unto the land. I had the privilege of being their first Israeli. What would I have been there, in India, had my parents stayed in Bombay, like my two uncles? A teacher, perhaps, or maybe a diligent clerk. Maybe even there I would have had to struggle to get to the university, fighting my way forward, tooth and nail. Father would have been able to arrange a good, stable job for me. Mother would have worried if I was twenty-two and not married, the age she married my father. A tough age. No one ever came to ask for my hand. Were they afraid of me? Had I, in their eyes, become a heretic? Maybe even in India I would still be the same person. Yet, the hope to be part of a dream was implanted in me. I grew up with a great love of the Land, the earth was enclosed within me, the olive and the lemon trees, the Valley of Ayalon.

My sister Sarale, the oldest, was born there, in India. In the kibbutz, the "le" was appended to her name. She and her friends aroused jealousy when they wore fluttering skirts and bright scarves. In protest, I stuck to boy's shirts and jeans. A protective wall between me and the world. To be "modern" meant to look like someone from the kibbutz. I didn't want to look trashy, like a cheap slut giving her body away to everyone with a thin blouse, a miniskirt and high-heels. But Nissim Sarussi was a heartbreaker:

> I can't bear to see them go
> hand in hand anymore

while she left me here alone,
Oh, why did she leave me so?

And Aris San and Aliza Azriki and the Oud Ensemble. . . . Wrapped up in a man's shirt. Cheap imitation of a *kibbutznik*, it seemed like I had turned into an "Israeli" everyone could recognize, even my parents, maybe even out on the street.

The annual gathering. Tables spread out with all kinds of artwork made by the community's sons and daughters. Drawings, tiny dolls dressed in the choicest Indian apparel. Different kinds of saris, styles from different regions of India, and the colors! Deep, warm, impeccable combinations of violet and red, dark green and bright pink. They weren't satisfied with the six basic colors there! All the colors were respected, even those unfamiliar to the West. In the middle of the display area there was a small table with a reduced model of a map of India on it, done up in the colors, so familiar to me, of the Indian flag. To the side of the flag, two dolls dressed in saris woven of the same colored cloth grip flagpoles with tiny flags. Between the two dolls, *"Blessings Upon the Indian Nation on Their Day of Independence,"* is written. I bump into Hilda, my cousin from Dimona. She's wearing a violet sari with red embroidery, pure silk. Spectacular. Hilda had been an excellent dancer, she'd even danced in the movies. How jealous all the girls in the Moshav were of me. Hilda, my cousin. She got to the country at the beginning of the sixties, ten years after us. Silently laughing, she and her sister Edna, may her memory be blessed, adorned with incredibly styled, golden ornaments, exuded magical scents, beauty and brightness. Her weight had gone up since then. She stopped dancing on her wedding day, and she was already a grandmother.

A girl in a sparkling pink sari was on stage, happy to be dancing about the love of nature. Members of Parliament are there too. Women wrapped in saris or Punjabi-daras embroidered in gold, men in Punjabi shirts, custom made, brought in directly from the finest shops in Bombay and London. There are also more than a few long braids, "ambra" and, here and there, smooth black hair as well, proudly flowing down to the hips. And some are dressed in the elegant, sporty style of Zahava or Ophra Haza. Not Margalit Sa'anani, though, or hardly at all.

And there are members of Parliament. My mother says again and again that, for an evening like this, the little girls are really superfluous. The kids should get their time on Hanukkah or Sukkoth. But not at a gathering of grown-ups. Asher, my brother-in-law, gets fed up looking at five year olds. The little ones arouse the amazement of the minister for religious affairs who had come to make a blessing. Avner Shaki, a member of Parliament, says that it's fine to continue being Indian as long as you remember that you are a Jew. Ah, I say, Judaism, again it comes down to whatever suits them. Let me be, it's not my problem, I'm Israeli through my Indian culture. The five-year-olds haven't been forewarned: all over the country they've got classes in Indian dance: in Or Yehuda, Ashdod, Dimona, Lod, and even Petah Tiqva.

Parliament member Eli Ben Menahem unfurls a speech, shooting from the hip. He calls upon the Indian audience to stop "withdrawing," to become Israeli. Hold it, hold it, hold it, hold it just a second. If Eli Ben Menahem is saying something like this, what is he doing here? He didn't even want to accept the flowers of honor, according to the Indian custom (because his shirt would have gotten damp and left spots on it); so let him take it out of the "bonus" they "organized" for themselves. Members of Parliament, corrupt as usual. Or better yet, he shouldn't have even come or done us any favors. The audience is silent, not reacting, waiting. Member of parliament Eli Ben Menahem finds it necessary to point out the community's mute docility: "They never came complaining and they built synagogues for themselves from money contributed by members of the community and not through aid from the government." Then, as if by chance, he finds it necessary to mention that of course he was born in India but his parents came up to Israel when he was a year old. The hall is silent: automatically those sitting in couples begin looking at those not sitting in couples.

"He's not *Benei Yisrael* at all."

"His parents came to India from Baghdad."

"From Bukhara."

"He's just cashing in on it."

"Just like Abie Nathan, the Persian born in India."

"The one who spoke well is the guy from Yavne, he was here last year, Meir Chetrit; he said he loves to pray in an Indian congregation."

"I heard that."

"You did? When?"

"At the gathering last year."

"You mean he always says that?"

"Sure, whenever he appears before Indians."

"What a crock."

The audience suffers the torment patiently until the flowery speeches are over. The young people in back clap from a lack of interest, they want to sing and dance, groupies of the Indian band from Lod. Why don't they show that group on TV? They already showed Kiryat Malakhi, so why not Indian dances by ten-year-old Israelis?

The evening is conducted around a competition of singing and dancing, held now for five years in a row at *Binyanei Ha-Uma* in Jerusalem, always with an audience of thousands. The young men and women reach the competition after qualifying in a first round; five representatives, four men and a woman. Out of the five, four chose sad songs. One of the songs is at least forty years old. And the songs are untarnished—boistrous and full of longing, interlaced with the beauty of childhood. As for hidden regions, it's doubtful there were any. Shlomo Bar says that Indian music is composed for different times of the day. There is music meant for the morning that depicts awakening from sleep to the aroma of flowers in the gentle, sunny air; for early afternoon, when nature is mercilessly laid bare with brazen clarity for all to see, there is different music. And so on for evening and for night. Interesting.

The orchestra comes on stage. Four kinds of drums. A set of tablas, a set of pop drums, two sets of African congas. String instruments: a sitar or bulbul tarang, a bass guitar, an accordion, and an organ. The crowd reacts with a cheer. Way in the back, like up in the balcony to the left of the stage, young men enthusiastically sing Indian songs. This year the liveliest crew came from Dimona. The ones from Ashdod were quieter. All boys except for a few girls here and there, but they aren't rabble-rousers. They just chuckle with excitement. The emcee is charming, polished Hebrew, no sign of an Indian accent: "r," "r," a French "r," pampered. The host is colossal. He participated in the singing competition last year and took second place. Hebrew is foreign to him so he conducts the evening in Marathi, the language of Bombay.

Almost the third singer, the host says: "The next song is from a movie that is familiar to all of us, *Bajai Baura!*" Cries of surprise and contentment are heard from all sides. The movie, as everyone knows, is sad, really sad. A philosophical movie. The hall is silent. A young singer, maybe twenty-five or thirty, gets up and bursts into a scintillating *mawwal*, with incredible embellishment—this is no fake. He is good. A first-rate *mawwal*, definitely in the league of Muhammad Rafi, the famous Indian singer. Bajai Baura is a small, poor town that suffers from constant pillaging by thieves. A pair of lovers whose song is like the song of the gods. Questions of existence, power over fate, the value of honor. Tough world, a war for change. Classically Indian. The song is musically complex and the words are in the form of a supplication to mortal beings:

> There were mortals, guests in our world,
> there were decent people. And those
> who think they have the world in their
> hand, grasping the movement of a cloud,
> the passage of water. Oh, bitter fate:
> when lightning strikes, there is no saviour.
>
> Time forever enduring, my time, our time
> is but a drop upon a cocoa shell borne
> in the heart of the spacious ocean.

The opening is riveting. An awesome silence reigns throughout the audience, the accompanying group blends in just when they should, leaving room for the quiet sitar. No one moves, the song replenishes hollow hearts.

Now, it should be pointed out that the Indians (or the so-called Indian immigrants), are not really still Indian. They're Israeli. More Israeli than Indian? They prefer the automated electronic beat of a drum machine going along to "Boogie, oh boogie, boogie," or "Love to love you, kudi, shugi, bugi." So Shlomo Bar's words light up my somber thoughts.

Applause from all sides. Indian songs, just like Indian dances, have a very complex structure but they remain alarmingly flexible. Through improvisation, the depth of the inner structure is maintained, intuitively. There is space to breathe and you can get lost. Exhilarating. The little guy on stage is improvising, really stretching out, breaking through the barriers put up between long years of disconnection. A society that knows what it wants imparts a rich existence back over to the other side. A society with narrow horizons, in eclipse. Now that we've gotten acclimated and learned how to get along, to be maniacs like everyone else, we can spare some time for music, to improvise, to ease the pressure.

The crowd keeps a record of what's good and what isn't. Wild applause. No matter what you think, it's a tough song that not everyone is up to singing. To sing like Zohar Argov, or Arik Einstein. So here comes this little guy, he takes the risks, and sings. Flawless execution. The audience is transfixed. It touches that nerve, of once upon, of times obscured, stinging the neck. Now, the long, sad days come back to us. . . . Now they are the long, sad days. In the end, he only picks up third place. Everything's fixed.

People mill around at the intermission: a friend from Yavne, another from Kiryat Gat, a chance to greet a relative who came this month from India—father went to school with her there.

On her second cassette, Zahava sings an Indian song. An Indian song in Hebrew. Zahava singing an Indian song. So what? But I still feel a little weird about it. Zahava takes something that is "mine" and interprets it the way she wants. After all, Zahava is Moroccan with a heavy Turkish influence, right? So Zahava sings an Indian song, what's the big deal? Nevertheless, deep within me that same chord strikes, to sing, to dance. Just like in the movies, like in the songs, to be beautiful and have long hair, to be a great dancer. But, really, what do I have to do with Indian songs? Zahava sings an Indian song. Actually, that's nice. I would even say, really nice. Great, Zahava. Ten and a half.

The dancers have pure skin, their clothes are bright. With tiny bells on their ankles, they perform classical and modern pieces, to the pleasure of everyone. Long, fake braids. Sequins. Flowers. Movies. The winner is declared. A dancer in violet: a charismatic dance, but lacking spirit. They're well trained, these dancers from Kiryat Shmone, Beersheba, Dimona, Ramla, Lod, Ashdod, Kiryat Ata and Or Yehuda. Twenty year olds, at most. Salt of the earth. Israelis, like me. Like you.

• • •

At the grocery, everyone wishes each other a good New Year. The days flow on again, streaming off in hidden torrents. A magical spring, stories about life, stories from life. Once tales gathered the spirit in. Now a heat wave does it.

Allenby, the summer is full of sounds from the banks of the Volga, accordion tunes from Broadway, and I struggle not to dole out a cent. At the Carmel Market, Russian immigrants grunt as they inspect the loads of meat displayed at the butchers. Pork is at a premium. I see their eyes pop out at the huge, tender pieces. Craving for a taste. They're hungry, starved to the soul. For them, the Carmel Market isn't the crowds and the awful stench, the misery and oppression, not even the vulgarity. On the contrary, they don't even look at the people. Their gaze is transfixed. They can't get enough of the abundance of food displayed. Lusting vision. I take a look: Damn straight, there is a hell of a lot of food in the market. That the prices are high, that's another story.

What fascinated my parents when they came to the country? What surprised them in their first years? I don't know. My, my, am I sinking into all the miserable baggage that goes along with those days again? The dark fifties? My mother claims that if the water here is tainted the way it was there, that is, in India, then what was the point of coming at all. We were infected. Father, still an innocent boy, loves the country—he discovers innovative methods to raise chickens in the Moshav. The conveyer belt produces like a wood-chip factory in Taiwan. Taken hostage by technology. Something or other simply blinded them, one of the enchanted country's miracles. Maybe the army, maybe proximity to the revered West, maybe the myths of peoplehood.

Each generation and its immigrants, new immigrants and their distress.

It came to blows between Russians and Ethiopians at some hotel. It happens. So what? How touching. Maybe they were flabbergasted because they were black and had a different culture. They see strangers and strangeness in them and they're pushed aside according to some hidden, racist criteria under which society operates. So they'll become a social problem, so they'll live as if they're spiritually impaired (to say black is beautiful is another story altogether). The Ethiopians aren't interested in my sympathy. But I still feel for them, despite that. I'm no fanatic, not at all. They too will spend years passing through the obstacle course of the alien homeland. Some will fit in, some will never find their place and draw the line. And the blacks will continue to be likened to the ape, particularly by the Moroccans and the Poles and the Persians and the Iraqis and the Russians and the Kurds. And even the Indians. Of course. So?

The boardwalk. The end of August, one of "those" Tel Aviv nights. I love this city. Me, the farmer from Moshav Masliah, finally loves the city, fifteen years after I got here. At least for now. Or maybe altogether. By the circular plaza, a crowd takes up positions to watch some dancers. On stage, there is a disc-jockey and a dance troupe. Kids happily leaping. The beat of a samba freely flows into the lambada. Lam-ba-da. Two boys and two girls wave their hands and shake their legs, their heads rocking. The crowd is happy. So are we. A three-year-old jumps to the beat, a captive fan of the ten-year-old in the super-short fluttering skirt. And they are most becoming, and so cute, their eyes filled with joy.

I look over to the side, as usual, but my eyes continue to the left, a few people down from me, to a tall man with clear glasses and a stylish shirt. Good-looking. I quickly shift my eyes back, so as not to transgress the limits of politeness in staring at a stranger. A second later, I look again. Quiet, a concentrated look, soft eyes, no tension in his body. The same calm, the same look. Next to him is a very pretty woman. Her fingers are long and thin, adorned by rings of gold set with delicate, exquisite rubies. Her beauty is enhanced with strong colors. Her hair is black and short. She, too, has a calm look. Positive identification: Indians. He looks at me, she looks, our eyes converge: "Indian? *Benei Yisrael?*" And I think to myself: "New immigrants, from Kashmir." As one, our eyes shift back to the stage, back to the audience of elderly folk sitting comfortably on the municipality benches, watching the South American deejay, watching the children of Tel Aviv from the Yemenite Quarter, Ramat Israel, and Yad Eliyahu jump to the beat of the lambada. Children from Persia, Iraq, Morocco, Greece, Libya and Romania. The salt of the earth.

Bear well, my brothers and my sisters, bear yourselves well for another sad year that is about to come upon us. At the Moshav, they are wishing for rain. Rain also fell there in the summer, in India, steaming tropical rain. Maybe this year it will come on time, maybe this year it won't tarry in alluding to the signs.

From Ilana Sugbaker Messika, in *Keys to the Garden: New Israeli Writing*, ed. and trans. Ammiel Alcalay (San Francisco: City Lights Books, 1996), 221–31.

Chapter 6

Voices of Israeli Jews

This chapter contains three short reflections made by Israeli Jews on Arab and Palestinian issues. The first is by Gideon Spiro, an Israeli of German origin, who was a soldier in 1969 and is a journalist living in Jerusalem. His strong position against the Israeli occupation of Palestinian areas is readily revealed, as is his orientation to Israel as a colonial state. Hannah Safran echoes his strong critique of Israeli policy in the second selection. She is a Jewish Israeli born in Haifa of Eastern European parents. She also has arrived at a political position that recommends national statehood for Palestinians, rejecting the position of Golda Meir, former prime minister of Israel, who denied that "Palestinians" existed as a people. The third is a letter that was written by a Jewish Israeli living in a West Bank community. Her genuine, deeply felt reflections on the peace process in the late 1990s convey a position that characterizes not only settlers living in the administered territories but also a significant portion of the Israeli Jewish community who have strong religious and nationalistic commitments.

ISRAELI JEW OF GERMAN ORIGIN

There was a time when I was not so concerned about whether Israelis and Palestinians reached a peace settlement . . . Of course, during my army days between 1954–1957 it was still early in Israel's history and we were all still in a very patriotic phase. I was for the survival and the flourishing of the state of Israel. I was a paratrooper, part of the elite troops. I wanted to be a pioneer in our army, in the forefront of the fighting. In the 1956 war, the Sinai campaign, I received a medal for participating in the Mitla Pass jump.

• • •

. . . In the 1967 war, I participated in the occupation of East Jerusalem, and found myself for the first time confronting a civilian population as a soldier, which caused me much discomfort. I had hoped that this would only be for a short period, a transitional period. No one thought in 1967 that the newly occupied territories would become a permanent part of our society. . . . For over half of our country's history, we have been an occupying power. As the occupation increasingly became a permanent part of our society, my liberal side became more and more dominant. I found myself becoming more active in various activities against the occupation, activities for Palestinian human rights, and against the oppressive measures of the Israeli army. More and more we came to adopt a colonial mentality; racism developed and grew.

• • •

. . . I was the only Israeli who was ever taken to court for public criticism of government policy while being a state employee. While working in the Ministry of Education during the war in Lebanon, I wrote many newspaper articles and letters calling upon everyone who has a human conscience and who is committed to human rights to refuse to serve in the war. The state prosecutor decided to sue me for being in violation of an obscure law which forbids government employees to criticize the government of Israel. In Israel, we don't have human rights principles that are guaranteed in the law. . . . In the end, I lost the case. The punishment was severe—I was dismissed from my position. I was also disqualified from holding any government position for five years, and my pension rights were cut as well. This means that my children, too, will suffer. It was clear that this was a vendetta because of my political views, not because of the severity of the crime. Of course, if I compare my situation with that of the Palestinians, I am still very lucky—no one is demolishing my home or sealing it; I'm not under administrative arrest. But it can happen in the future; it's all part of the Israeli law system. Everything we are doing in the occupied territories can eventually be transferred into Israel itself.

• • •

... The Palestinians were mistaken forty years ago when they refused to accept the partitioning of Palestine, but they have since accepted reality—they don't need to love it. Now Israel is the refuser. It's a combination of biblical beliefs with contemporary security considerations, a very dangerous mixture. It's fuel for fascism, the mixing of religion with nationalism.

Gordon Spiro, "Israeli Jews of German Origin," in *The Struggle for Peace: Israelis and Palestinians,* ed. Elizabeth Fernea and Mary Hocking (Austin: University of Texas Press, 1992), 206-7.

ISRAELI JEWS OF EAST EUROPEAN ORIGINS

... For a long time I was brought up to believe that Palestinians did not exist—the Arabs, yes, somewhere, but there were no Palestinians. You know Golda Meir used to say, "There is no such thing as a Palestinian." Even today there are people who would say the same. This is the way we were brought up, the way we are taught in school. We are told that there were no others here when we came. Even though in Haifa until 1948, half of the population was Arab and half of the population was Jewish, they don't really mention it [the Arab population], it's not spoken about. I used to live in a neighborhood where ten minutes from us there was an Arab school and an Arab community but we never knew about them. And this is not unusual, it's a common thing in Israel. . . .

Later, in 1967, when I was seventeen, it was obvious to me that we had conquered places that didn't belong to us, and that for peace we would have to give these lands back. Since Israel did not annex the territories right away, and even Jerusalem was not annexed until very recently, it shows that even some of the leaders of the time saw that this would be an asset to negotiate peace. . . . But there is another reason why Israel did not annex the territories immediately—if we have a democratic state where each individual gets a vote, then we won't have a Jewish state anymore. Now . . . the occupation of these areas . . . we have the Palestinians there who have never been allowed to vote for any form of government. They are denied the basic rights of any democracy and this is only the beginning. Now they are in conditions of having nowhere to work and little to eat.

• • •

... [A]t this particular place and time in history, the Palestinians need a national identity. This is a small country and it's unfortunate that there are two peoples here, but we cannot deny it, and the solution is to divide it. Many times I quote the Bible, the story of Solomon, where there are two women arguing over a child. Each woman says, "The child is mine." Solomon tells them that they have to divide the child. You know, in Palestinian reasoning about the history of the conflict, they ask, "Why did the Jews choose in 1947 to partition Palestine?" They say the Jews are like the mother who agreed to the partition of the baby in Solomon's story—she agreed because she was not the real mother. They did not agree because they were the real mother. Maybe they are right . . . but not completely.

• • •

Hannah Safran, "Israeli Jews of East European Origins," in *The Struggle for Peace: Israelis and Palestinians*, ed. Elizabeth Fernea and Mary Hocking (Austin: University of Texas Press, 1992), 199–200.

ISRAELI JEW LIVING IN EFRAT, ADMINISTERED TERRITORY

Dear Mark,

I am sorry that I have been so busy lately. Between all the holidays, my soldier son and the other kids, work and all my volunteering, I feel like I am just over my head. Sitting in front of the computer for a shmooze is a tremendous luxury.

The peace process is indeed moving ahead, and it is just amazing that it is going so quickly and as you say, there is little heard about the way Israelis feel. Perhaps they feel numb.

I have been thinking about the changes in our country lately. And I have begun to feel that the powers that be perhaps do not want us to feel too strongly tied to any place in this little State, because everything, including Jerusalem (excluding Tel Aviv and Haifa) is on the chopping block.

To me it is depressing. I am sorry that I cannot be enthusiastic for a peace process that puts an entire nation in jeopardy.

I think things really came to a head for me during Sukkot. It started out with a simple family moment together and then I began thinking about everything happening around me in our tiny country. Thinking has been dangerous for me lately.

You know that I am a very community-involved person, and usually it is all too rare when I have the opportunity to take a walk with my children—to enjoy the beautiful evening air and share a few words. But, thanks to the *Yomim Tovim*, I was able to take pleasure from a few family walks.

On our first outing, I heard the sounds of firecrackers breaking the stillness of the night. "Those are not firecrackers," said one of my older sons. "Those are gun shots." "Who could be shooting?" I asked. "The Arabs," he said. "They're probably having a wedding. They always shoot at weddings."

Well, when I next went out after the completion of Simchat Torah hakafot, the streets were so still, you could hear a butterfly sneeze. Suddenly, firecrackers once again. "Arabs shooting," I said. Then I remembered a report by Mordechai Sones (didn't I send it to you) on the Arab preparations for a first strike to overrun the settlements, G–d forbid.

Let them, whoever they are, tell us the shooting is a result of an Arab wedding. (Their caterers must be making a fortune on all those nightly weddings.) I will hope the firings are from weddings, but I am ready to accept the fact that they may indeed be training exercises to attack the yishuvim.

Well, unfortunately nothing would surprise me anymore. I mean, whose country is it anyway? Or whose country would they like us to think it is? The government, the media and even teachers have gotten together to make us cast doubt about our right to be in the land and the about the righteousness of our Zionism and love of the land.

Our new history books tell us that we got the State of Israel because of our might and our power, and not because of the miracles that G–d wrought for us. They say the Jewish people are conquerors, occupying land that is not ours. They forget what every Torah-educated first grader knows—that the One who created the world gave the Land of Israel to His people.

And so, our own government gives away more and more of Yesha (soon to be 42%). Then as a freebee, it takes even more Jewish land literally from beneath our feet. Without telling anyone, it has taken 2,998 dunams of Jewish land in Gush Etzion and given it to the PA [Palestinian Authorities]. It was a sneak deal, a freebee to add on to the percentage that is publicized to the PA. How ironic that Gush Etzion, the area everyone considered part of the consensus and the area that all thought was the strongest area in Yesha is the first that the PA tried to grab a foothold in. (Meanwhile the government is looking into it . . .) But the Arabs are smart. They're trying for ALL of Israel in anyway they can—42%, through the peace deal so far, 1% through Gush Etzion under the table deal, and then another percent or two in other parts of Yesha. But they don't only wish for pieces of the hills of our little yishuvim in Gush Etzion, but are demanding Latrun, Maaleh Adumim, Yaffo, kibbutzim on the Kineret, and Jerusalem itself.

Whose country is it anyway? The United States Congress acknowledges that Jerusalem is Israel's capital, and as such, its embassy must be relocated there. And our own officials do not insist that this must be done. Moreover, they are "satisfied" with a Walt Disney World Epcot exhibit that mentions Jerusalem as the center of three religions, but will not dare say that Jerusalem is the capital of the Jewish State.

They stand by as the US Secretary of State, a Jew (despite all her actions to prove otherwise) calls our communities "destructive settlements." And although the US State Dept. actually defines destructive settlements as anywhere that Israel has settled beyond the 1967 Green Line, including "the west bank, Gaza, the Golan AND all the new neighborhoods in Jerusalem since 1967," not a protest is raised.

Whose country is it anyway? We see the red danger line in the Sea of Galilee. The drought is fully upon us with no water in sight, and yet we're prepared, G–d forbid, to give away all our precious water resources—the Golan Heights, and the land upon which our settlements stand and where under ground well water is gathered. It reminds me of Marie Antoinette's tragic wit when her people were starving for bread, "Let them eat cake." When our taps run dry, will our leaders intone, "Let them drink Coke."

We have turned precious land over to the Palestinian Authority without worrying about our resources that are now trapped within Area A. Take as an example, Efrat's electricity. Almost every night for a month, the 1200-family strong community of Efrat has suffered blackouts—once, twice, nine times a night. And despite the complaints and the shouts, there is nothing the electric company can really do. Efrat's main electric wires run through Chalchul, and the repair crews cannot reach the problem without a joint-Army escort, because they are stoned and attacked when they try to clean the wires. (And that is during peace! What will happen Heaven forbid if it is NOT so peaceful.)

And while we are cutting off our Jewish communities from one another, we are planning roads and bridges to connect Gaza with Ramallah and Chevron and Beit Lechem.

Whose country is it anyway? Not only can we NOT enter newly-turned over Palestinian Authority communities, but we are soon to allow "safe passage" of Arabs from the PA to drive upon our roads and enjoy political immunity within their own cars. We are opening our own drivers to the constant threat of accidents by non-licensed or martyr-crazed Arab drivers, and our communities to possibility of robberies or terrorist attacks, G–d forbid.

We have released hundreds of Arab terrorists and murderers, and we have allowed them to be enlisted in the Palestinian "Police" force, soon to be the Palestinian Army—which will have familiarized itself with our country because it has traveled on our safe passage roads and will know how to strike, chas v'shalom, thanks to their nightly "weddings."

Israeli Arabs, trained in the Palestinian Authority, were involved in two bombings in Haifa and Tiveria. Firmly believing in G–d's promise to gather in the exiles from throughout the world, it is Arafat who says there will be no peace until 3.6 million more Arabs (these raised in the hatred of Arab refugee camps) are allowed to return to their pre-1948 homes in Israel. They don't want peace, Mark, they want Jaffa and Beersheva and Har Nof.

A group calling itself the Rabbis for Human Rights is crying out against a fictitious government intention to demolish a fictitious 6,000 illegal Arab homes. But who is crying out when the government says it will review the building tenders for 2,600 homes in Yesha. And instead of screaming and shouting for the sake of their people, former Yesha leaders, like Gush Etzion's former Mayor Shilo Gal (whom you met at Kfar Etzion) and Yesha Council's Aharon Domb, are lining up to announce to the media that Jewish communities might have to be uprooted, or that they personally will accept the dismantling of settlements.

Burger King boycott, Disney boycott, Sprint boycott, Benneton boycott. Do I have to go on? The Arabs are deciding whose country this is, and we are all watching silently, as if it has nothing to do with our lives or the lives of our children.

Some of us are beginning to feel that it is not rightly our country. Some of us are beginning to feel that we are powerless to act in the face of the constant actions against us. Some of us are beginning to believe that we must give up our land, our water, our air, because G–d cannot guarantee our future—only Clinton, Arafat, Hussein, or Assad can.

Yet despite all the actions that would remove G–d's Divine Hand from the Land of Israel, that work to dishearten our faithful people, and that would try to sever the loving relationship we have with our Creator, they will not succeed. Despite our enemies from without and from within, the words of the prophets will be fulfilled boldly and grandly. "Thus says Hashem, a voice is heard in Ramah—lamentation, bitter weeping: it is Rachel weeping for her children. She refuses to be comforted, for they are away. Thus says the L–rd, 'Refrain your voice from weeping, your eyes from tears. Your work shall be rewarded,' says Hashem. 'They shall return from the land of their enemy. There is hope for your future,' says the L–rd. The children shall return to their borders." (Jeremiah 31)

G–d knows the borders of His country. He doesn't need a withdrawal map, or an Oslo map, or a Wye map, or a Sharm map. He created all the maps of the world, and the countries depicted upon them. And Hashem will gather the Jewish people, who have been scattered among the nations of the world. And despite temporary land-give-aways, safe passages, Arab refugees and boycotts, the Jewish nation will return to the Israel of His map in gladness and song. And the walks that we take with our children will be filled with laughter and whispers and happy memories.

All the best and Shabbat Shalom.

Sharon Katz, letter to Mark Schwartz, October 1999.

Chapter 7

Voices of the Palestinians

Chapter 7 presents the voices of Palestinians, three of whom reflect on the year the State of Israel was established, 1948. On the celebration of the fiftieth anniversary of the establishment of the State of Israel, the *Journal of Palestine Studies* asked several prominent Palestinians to reflect personally on what is described among Palestinians as *al-Nakba*, the tragedy of Israeli statehood. These reflections review some of the same history of the Arab-Israeli conflict but from a very different perspective than their Israeli Jewish counterparts. The essays are rich in their expressions of feelings and challenging in their interpretation of Israeli political and social actions.

REFLECTIONS ON AL-NAKBA

To most Palestinians, 1948, the year of al-Nakba, is the formative year of their lives. This is true irrespective of age, background, or occupation, or whether the person is a refugee or not, or lives in Palestine or the diaspora. On this fiftieth anniversary of al-Nakba, JPS asked a number of Palestinians of different generations and walks of life to write short pieces on what this event has meant to them.

In JPS's letters of invitation, the "guidelines" suggested were to avoid political and historical analysis in favor of personal reflections. The following are the results.

Mamdouh Nofal

Mamdouh Nofal was born in Qalqilya, Palestine, in 1944. He has held a succession of high military posts in the Palestinian movement. In Tunis as of 1988, he was a member of the Higher Coordinating Committee for the intifada. He participated in the Madrid Conference in 1991, served on the Higher Steering Committee for Palestinian Negotiations, and is a member of the PLO Central Committee. Permitted by Israel to return to Palestine in March 1996, he lives in Ramallah. He is the author of two books (in Arabic) on the peace process.

The closest I can come to explaining what 1948 means to me, and how it affected the path I took in life and the choices I made, is to tell about growing up in Qalqilya, on the frontline with Israel.

When the dust of 1948 settled, Qalqilya itself had not been occupied, falling in what came to be called the West Bank. But it had lost more than 90 percent of its agricultural lands, its main source of livelihood, which were now farmed by the Jewish colonies across the railroad tracks that had once linked Turkey, Syria, Palestine, and Egypt and which now formed the border with the newly created State of Israel. The war had also transformed Qalqilya into a main station for refugees fleeing the massacres and the fighting in Kfar Saba, Abu Kishk, Miska, Byar Adas, Shaykh Muwwanis, and al-Tireh, who increased the town's population by half.

It is difficult, after the passage of fifty years, to sort out my own memories from those of my family, neighbors, friends, and schoolmates, from the collective memory of my hometown. But it seems to me that of the battles for the defense of the town, I have vague memories of the young men organizing night and day guard shifts and of the Iraqi army camp and the Palestinian military formations near town. I also remember the throngs of refugees in the mosque next door to our house. The girls' school and the boys' school were also turned into refugee centers, and there was chaos everywhere as the town didn't have the means to absorb such a huge influx. Some of the refugees settled in our town and live there to this day, while others moved inward to other towns or onward to exile, due to the difficulty of making a living and the scarcity of water resources.

So our town, which had been self-sufficient and relatively comfortable, became destitute virtually overnight, cut off from its livelihood of orchards and farmlands on the coastal plain and cattle breeding and trade with al-Tireh, al-Taybeh, Jaffa, Tel Aviv, Lydda, and Ramla. The conditions of the original townspeople abruptly deteriorated to abject poverty, such that there wasn't much difference between them and the refugees. Hunger spread, and if it hadn't been for the huge quantities of dates provided by the Iraqi government, many would have died. I remember that we children used to gather the date pits and sell them to bakeries—a full basket for one piaster. We were also set to gathering firewood and dry vegetable stems for cooking fuel and grasses and wild herbs for the rabbits and sheep.

The dire situation of Qalqilya's inhabitants was taken into consideration after the United Nations Relief and Works Agency (UNRWA) was set up in 1950 and welfare cards were distributed along with emergency and fixed rations to everyone, except that the rations for Qalqilya's original citizens were only half as much as those given to the refugees. I will always remember the number of my family's welfare card: 58610405. That same year, the United Nations established a hospital on premises that the Iraqi army had used as an emergency center and opened schools for refugee children. Thus international aid became Qalqilya's main source of livelihood. I still remember the long queues for milk in the mornings and the little skirmishes that sometimes broke out when provisions were distributed.

A National Guard was set up in Qalqilya, and many of the young men joined, their main job being to keep watch on the Israeli border from the trenches dug on the outskirts of town. We children used to amuse ourselves running back and forth between their positions, and some of the guards would send us on errands to buy cigarettes or matches they had run out of. We also used to compete in seeing who was boldest in sneaking into the old orchards and placing rocks or pouring motor oil on the railway tracks, hoping the Jewish train would skid. But the train kept moving back and forth relentlessly, blowing its shrill whistle each time it neared our town.

After the establishment of the State of Israel and the departure of the Arab armies, Qalqilya's inhabitants began to realize that this would be a long story. The educated youth set their minds on going abroad. Some entered the Gulf countries illegally, and some even died of suffocation hidden inside oil tanks. Men sold the jewelry of their women and tried to reclaim the poor mountainous lands that remained on our side of the border, digging out rocks and filling the holes with soil to plant vegetables. They also dug many artesian wells using primitive methods, and we kids used to hang around while the work was going on. They bought generators and pumps to irrigate the orchards that were left and set up what could be described as small agricultural cooperatives, some of which are still functioning.

Throughout the years, the people of Qalqilya and the refugees dreamed of returning to their fields and villages. During the earlier years, their sleep was disturbed by nightmares involving Jews hounding them and chasing them out, and they brooded about how the Arab countries had conspired against them and the whole world shared in the injustice meted out to them.

As time went on, al-Nakba was transformed into a memory that the people of Qalqilya went on commemorating with school holidays and demonstrations in the streets and near the Israeli border. As children we would roam the streets, happy with our holiday from school, brandishing flags and banners denouncing the Partition and demanding the return of refugees to their homes, and chanting in imitation of the grown-ups: "Down with Britain! Down with Israel!!" and "Hajj Amin, the Sword of Islam!"

Some of the town's imams saw Qalqilya's tribulations as a sign of God's anger at Palestinians for having gone astray. Many people resorted increasingly to religion, some even joining the Islamic Tahrir Party. A handful reacted by turning their backs on religion, saying God had abandoned them and had not stood up for the holy places in the blessed Land of Palestine (though they refused to join the Communist Party because the Soviet Union had recognized the State of Israel). My father, who was practically illiterate, joined the ranks of the independent nonbelievers. My illiterate mother, on the other hand, became more devout and urged me and my older brother to pray, to fast, and to learn the Qur'an by heart. Following her instructions, I prayed five times a day and often repeated the *ayat al-kursi*, which she said would protect whoever memorized it from the devil and the attacks of the Israelis. For many years, I would race to be the first to reach the mosque after the dawn call to prayer, sometimes arriving before the imam, and I would stand right behind him in the front row of worshippers. This earned me the reward of sweets from a devout relative. Later on, this same relative used to give me schoolbooks and pencils, particularly during the numerous stretches that my father spent in Jordanian prisons for "infiltration" into Israel.

After the Free Officers Revolution in Egypt in 1952, a strong Nasirist current spread among the youth; when I was older, I myself joined their ranks. Those days, whoever did not own a firearm tried to get one, though weapons had to be carefully concealed as the Jordanian police frequently conducted searches and confiscated whatever they found. Many young men carried out a variety of dangerous actions inside Israel, and some established relations with the Egyptian Secret Service. Many were imprisoned by Jordan, where infiltration was an act punishable by prison (the sentence could last several years if a firearm had actually been used). Many of Qalqilya's sons were killed, including fathers and relatives of friends of mine, when they sneaked across to "steal" a cow or horse or some clothes or water pipes or whatever they could lay their hands on in the Jewish colonies or harvest whatever crops they could in what had been their orchards and fields. No one in our town could be convinced that the fruits of their lands, still within sight just across the tracks, did not belong to them anymore.

There were countless such "infiltrations." Our town was often awakened by the sound of gunfire between its young men and Israeli troops or guards from the Jewish colonies. On such nights, people would wait tensely, ready to move to neighborhood mosques better able to withstand shelling: people still believed that "the houses of God had a Lord to protect them" and that God could deflect artillery if He so desired. And people would pray, "May God spare us! O Merciful Lord, drive the Israelis blind and be merciful to our men!" Many times, my father was one of those in need of such prayers.

When one of the men was martyred, everyone would know because the wails and screams of women and children would tear through the stillness of the night, and all the inhabitants would be at their doors. The children would wake up, all anxious and perturbed, clinging to the skirts of our mothers, and if the town was under shelling we boys would rush out into the alleys once it stopped to be among the men. As kids, I remember how our anxiety would be calmed as we listened to the men's talk, eavesdropping on the latest news which we would carry back to our mothers, scared and worried. The town would live through a state of genuine sorrow after the loss of a martyr. To show solidarity, everyone would walk in the funeral procession after prayers over the dead man's body and then sit with the family throughout the three days of condolence offering. And during these times we children would hear the stories of infiltration into the colonies and skirmishes with the Jews, of courage and cowardice, of life and death, of paradise and hell, of the special status of the martyrs before God, and of the behavior of the Jordanian Secret Service. They were exciting and terrifying stories, almost like mystery tales, imprinted in our memories.

The *mujahidun* and the infiltrators from our town harassed the neighboring colonies for over five years. Israel stepped up the pressure on Jordan, which it held responsible for the security of the borders, and did not hesitate to use artillery and machine-gun fire against the town or to position snipers to shoot whoever came near the border. A number of men, women, and children (including relatives and schoolmates) were killed that way. In the early 1950s, the Israeli troops began to follow a more aggressive policy, carrying out numerous punitive raids against houses of alleged infiltrators and the town's wells. In 1953, Moshe Dayan threatened to raze Qalqilya to the ground. As Israeli pressures on Jordan increased, so did Jordan's pressures on Qalqilya. The Jordanian Secret Service, police, and army clamped down on the infiltrators, and Jordanian courts meted out harsher sentences on those who got caught. The better known among the infiltrators were imprisoned for long terms even if they had not been caught red-handed. My father was one of these. The families of the imprisoned men were left without any source of income. My own family lived off the meager sums that other infiltrators paid in order to use my father's old machine gun.

Despite all the measures taken by the Israelis and the Jordanians, frequent skirmishes between the people of our town and Israeli troops and the colonists continued until 10 October 1956. At 9 P.M. on that date, Israeli forces launched a large-scale offensive against Qalqilya. Ground forces, including tanks, attacked from three directions, and warplanes bombed the town. They targeted the police station, which they destroyed completely, killing everyone inside. They also destroyed the wells the people had dug. The men of the National Guard and the regular Jordanian army unit stationed in town fought bravely, and over twenty were martyred. In return our men killed many of the attacking forces, including the commander. After Qalqilya was occupied in 1967, some Israeli officers built a memorial on Soufin Hill where he had been killed, the remains of which are still there.

I still have clear images of the martyrs pulled out of the debris of the police station, and I will never forget the funeral procession, when all the men, women, and children of the town walked from the mosque to the local cemetery. For days on, my siblings and I accompanied our mother in visiting the homes of the grieving families, and I vividly recall the wailing of the bereaved and the incantation of Qur'anic verses by blind shaykhs. For weeks afterward, my schoolmates and I would rush out the minute classes ended to inspect the ruins of the police station and other blown-up buildings.

When Israel conquered the West Bank in 1967, Moshe Dayan remembered his threat to raze Qalqilya. His troops drove out all the inhabitants and brought in bulldozers to plough the town under and erase it from the map, just as they had done with the villages of Bayt Nuba, Yalu, and Imwas. Qalqilya's inhabitants were left without shelter, and it was only thanks to direct American intervention that they were allowed to return a month later, after about a third of the town's houses had been destroyed.

By that time, I was gone. I had joined the Arab Nationalist Movement in 1961, and a few years after that, when I was twenty, I joined its military wing, The Heroes of the Return. From that time on, I devoted myself to military work within the Palestinian Revolution in Jordan, Syria, Lebanon, and Tunis.

Fawaz Turki

> Fawaz Turki was born in Haifa, Palestine, in 1941. He is the author of a number of books, including *The Disinherited: Journal of a Palestinian Exile* and *Exile's Return: The Making of a Palestinian-American*. He has lectured around the country and has been published extensively in the American media. He has been a writer-in-residence at both SUNY Buffalo and the Virginia Center for the Creative Arts. He currently lives in Washington, D.C.

By the middle of 1968, I had been around for twenty-seven years. And if you want proof that youth is indeed wasted on the young, what I had done with my life up till then is proof enough. For here I was, a Palestinian boy from the refugee camps, buzzing around the Australian bush, shearing sheep, working with road gangs, and toiling in the iron ore mines in the northwest. Palestine was several time zones away, and its memory was already beginning to fade in my mind, like ash cooling in the grate.

Truth be told, there was more to it than that. When I'd arrived in Australia at age nineteen, I was some sort of a runaway, seeking an alternative order of at-homeness. I wanted to escape my roots. I didn't need my damn roots nagging away at me the whole time or have them daily shoved in my face, as they had been when I was growing up in Beirut. I didn't need others to remind me of my otherness whichever way I turned. In short, I was too young to be Palestinian.

I belonged to a people who had been brought to ruin by a fiercely parochial settler movement feeding on the drug of racialist hatred and aggression that it had brought with it from Europe, a movement that in a relatively short time had put us in desperate flight across our borders, reduced us to being squatters in other peoples' lands, and tried to hound us out of history.

I could not have chosen a better place to flee to. The forbidding landscape of the Australian outback has a way about it—about its searing heat, its unfamiliar rhythms, its influence on the human imagination, its rock and ash and echoes, and the expanse of stars in its night sky—that makes a man jump outside the skin of his past.

But that, I discovered after a while, I could not escape. For it would always come back, that past, as if it were an ache, an ache from a sickness a man didn't know he had. Like the smell of ripened figs at a Perth supermarket that would place me, for one blissful moment, under that big fig tree in the backyard of our house in Haifa. Like the taste of sea salt in my mouth as I swam in the Indian Ocean that would take me back to the Mediterranean, our own ancient sea. Like the apocalyptic images that my mind would dredge up, out of nowhere, of our refugee exodus twenty years before, as we trekked north on the coastal road to Lebanon, where pregnant women gave birth on the wayside, screaming to heaven with labor pain, and where children walked alone, with no hands to hold. Like the memories of my first year at Burj al-Barajneh—a makeshift refugee camp on the outskirts of Beirut—when I was always hungry. And cold. And angry. Angry that the tricycle that my dad had bought me a short time before our flight was left behind in Haifa and that some Jewish kid was now riding it around.

These evocations loomed large in my consciousness, where they had taken irrevocable tenure. I could no more escape them than I could my skin. The sheer force of my Palestinian past had seeped into the quick of my very being and had a mastering grip on my identity. There was no escaping that—Australian bush or no Australian bush. As a Palestinian exile, I carried some mighty heavy cargo on my back, and when I was, as it were, driven to unpack it (what is it in, and about, that moment of immediacy in our lives that drives us to do that?), I would feel that anger again, that same anger from twenty years before, welling up in me like vomit.

And here I was in Australia, a Palestinian kid with a name too difficult to pronounce and a patrimony too difficult to locate, talking to myself and waiting for Godot.

No matter. For unlike Beckett's two vagrants, I was destined, as were other Palestinians of my generation, to meet that mythical character. Our massive silence, it turned out, our I-me dialogue, our self-address over the previous two decades, was itself a kind of rhetoric.

In an inexplicable, almost mystical synchronicity, the youth of the world was to mount one hell of an uprising that year, and mount it with the uninhibited, brutal directness of feeling that only youth possesses.

Nineteen Sixty-Eight. There was something magical about it all: Here were these young people, oceans apart, seemingly disconnected by geography, culture, and historical experience, coming together and jelling as one, as if they were all tuned in to the same sounds from the same bell. You know it when the bell tolls for thee.

It happened all over the planet, all at once, all the same year: From the general rebellion in France, known as *"les événements,"* that brought down the de Gaulle government, to the antiwar movement in the United States that brought down the Johnson administration; from the Tet offensive in Vietnam to the Cultural Revolution in China; from the Tupamaros in Uruguay to the civil rights movement in Northern Ireland (when Catholics and Protestants marched together for the first time); from the student takeover of Columbia University to the hippie dropout in Haight Ashbury; from the student protests against communist rule in Poland to those similar protests against the Russian invasion in Czechoslovakia; from the Beatles releasing their "Helter Skelter" album to feminists disrupting the Miss America Pageant; from the bloody confrontations in Chicago outside the Democratic Convention headquarters to the "three M formulations" (Marcuse, Marx, and Mao) of the New Left.

That was the year you were afraid to scratch your head in case you missed something. It is no wonder that Jimmy Morrison was singing then, "We want the world, and we want it now."

And we were there too. Part of it all. We the Palestinians were there doing our own thing—in Karameh, in March of that year.

Except for one thing. Everybody else was saying: There is no looking back.

Are you kidding? Our movement was all about looking back. We could not move forward in 1968 without looking back to 1948—looking back anew at what had happened to us during the two decades on either side of that year.

And the looking back began with the question: So the bastards think they have gotten away with it? Hell, no. These people have walked off with our home and homeland, with our movable and immovable property, with our land, our farms, our shops, our public buildings, our paved roads, our cars, our theaters, our clubs, our parks, our furniture, our tricycles. They hounded us out of our ancestral patrimony and shoved us in refugee camps. They so thoroughly destroyed our villages that nothing was left of them but the wind that now blew through them. And they even robbed us of our name.

Yes, even our name got lost in the shuffle in 1948. Those of us in exile became known as "the Arab refugees." Those in the West Bank became "Jordanians." Those few who stayed behind became "Israeli Arabs." And those in Gaza, well, heck, no one even knew what to call them.

They really thought, with that cozy vulgarity with which they had viewed us, that was going to be that. A bunch of Arabs merging into the Arab world. Soon to vanish into thin air.

We were the people that history was supposed to have forgotten and that God was supposed to have given His back to.

Excuuuuuse me! I guess both needed a bit of a nudge. And we gave them that in 1968.

This was only a short time after the "Israelis," as they came to call themselves, were able to conquer and occupy that 23-percent remnant of our country, the West Bank/Gaza, that they had left us twenty years before. Now they were astride the whole of historic Palestine and then some, jubilant at their new role as latter day colonial overlords. It was also the time we grabbed them by the throat, as it were, insisting on contract, dialogue, and reason. Sorry, fellows, the accounts between us do not balance. I am a Palestinian from Haifa. You owe me. And you owe me big. You robbed me of my city and my property. You owe me reparations (which I know that you, or your children, will one day have to pay, and under duress if need be) for all the pain and unspeakable suffering you have put me, my family, and my fellow exiles through.

If the Israelis feared us at the time, what they feared was not our military might—we had none—but the resurrection of our name. For once we wrested control of our name and etched it on the conscience of the world, we raised a question that became a deadly threat to Israel's very legitimacy: If these people are Palestinians, the world wondered, then they came from Palestine, and if they came from Palestine, then why are they not allowed to return there? Logical question, yes? (I remember reading about the innocent editor of some paper in the Midwest cabling his reporter in Beirut, in August 1982, when everybody was wondering where the Palestinians were going to go after their evacuation from the Lebanese capital, and asking him: "Why don't these people just go back to where they came from?" Why indeed!)

Proclaiming our existence, as Palestinians, as one people, nagged at the

Israelis and drove them to suffer gusts of murderous exasperation. That is why Golda Meir at the time was prepared to raise very serious doubts about the professional skills of her optometrist by stating that "there is no such thing as Palestinians." For so long as we were around, saying our name over and over again, we made them responsible to history. We mocked their claims of turning desert into orchard.

They had not, of course, turned desert into orchard (except for the Negev, there was no goddamn desert in Palestine to turn into orchard in the first place); what they had done rather was to turn our lives into a nightmare of destitution, statelessness, and alienation.

They are the biggest liars in history. And theirs is the biggest crime that any people has committed against another.

They robbed us (I keep using this word because no other will do) of our homeland, superimposed their own state on it, and then proceeded to define what they had created in isolation of its impact on our lives and national destiny. Now they have the chutzpah (a word they coined) to celebrate their crime this year, with much fanfare, exactly half a century after the fact.

Look, I'm angry. Still angry after all these years.

Here's one reason.

A while back, on the eve of the Gulf War, I returned to the old country for a visit—yes, these people would allow a Palestinian Arab (with a Western passport) "to visit," but welcome a Russian Jew "to live," in Palestine. I went to the house where I was born. The house with the big backyard and the big fig tree. The house where I had left my tricycle behind in 1948. The house where I had made my original leap to consciousness. The house where God had willed me to be born, like all His creatures, to an inviolate freedom. The house I was to grow up and acquire a past in.

I knocked on the door and some low-life immigrant, with an Eastern European accent, opened it, and when he realized who I was, refused me the right even to look around.

Will I ever forgive this man? Just ask yourself if you would had you been a Palestinian.

I will never forgive these people. These people who have (again that word) robbed us, ever so brazenly, of our patrimony and relegated us to a place in the world, unchosen and unwilled, that we have had to inhabit all these last fifty years.

But wait! Our remembrance of where we came from has not torn at the edges. We have not, even after these fifty years, been hounded into oblivion. Palestinian exiles, wherever they are, share that same historical preoccupation, that same turn of phrase, that same communicative internality, that same love for the hammer beat in *al-awda* song that we all grew up singing ("Who am I? / Who are ye? / I am the returnee / I am the returnee") and that we today hum to our children as we tuck them in every night.

We'll still be around fifty years from now, and if Israel is still around—a doubtful proposition, if you ask me—we'll be knocking on its door, asking to be let in. And if there is no response, we'll break the door down.

We'll break the door down, baby.

If God is my witness, we'll break it down.

My children are not growing up in refugee camps as I have done. They are not living in a host state whose authorities snarl at their heels, or place them close to the door for easy eviction as their father had lived in Arab host states. But they do realize that, though they are loyal Americans, only in their ancestral homeland would their larger identity be housed, and only through the struggle to liberate it do they become enduringly defined.

And here we are, after the suffering that followed 1948 and the sacrifices that followed 1968, in 1998. The Palestinian leadership (and I will spare Palestinians the indignity of identifying it as "our leadership") is bickering with Netanyahu, and all the other yahoos in his government, over the fate of a yard here and a yard there in the West Bank.

West Bank, West Shmank. That ain't got nothing to do with us. Life is too short to be worrying about pretentious trivia like that. We have a new struggle to organize, an old homeland to liberate.

Musa Budeiri

> Musa Budeiri was born in West Jerusalem, Palestine, in 1946. He is the director of the Center for Area Studies at al-Quds University, where he teaches political science, and is the author of *The Development of the Arab Labor Movement in Palestine* [in Arabic] and *The Palestine Communist Party 1919–1948: Arab and Jew in the Struggle for Internationalism.*

I am doubtful that there can be such a thing as a collective Palestinian memory of the events of 1948. I use the term "events" consciously and deliberately; the term "nakba" has a cataclysmic ring that sounds hollow. Perhaps this is a generational thing, but I feel it is more than that. The plain fact is that Palestinian society was not only socially and economically differentiated, and consequently affected in different ways by 1948 and its aftermath, but it was also geographically differentiated. Physical uprooting, expulsion, destitution—this was the experience of a sizable segment of the Palestinians, perhaps the majority, but by no means all. For those who stayed put and whose towns and villages were not conquered by the Israeli army, I am not sure that 1948 constitutes a watershed. British rule in Palestine lasted a mere thirty-two years, a brief interlude after the centuries of Ottoman rule, and there was no hopeful expectation that this would be a lasting state of affairs.

For those who remained in what became known as Jordan's West Bank—and I am coldheartedly discounting the thousands of refugees who populated the camps—the "nakba" came much later. Perhaps in June 1967, but more probably as a process over a number of years starting with the occupation and culminating in the Oslo Accord and the beginning of the implementation of the autonomy agreement. If on the individual level this did not result in physical expulsion or material destitution, on the collective level the abandonment of hope and resignation to defeat constitute a "nakba" of much larger proportions. Although I hesitate even to allow myself to think this (at least most of the time), I sometimes imagine that after 1948 there was not a single Palestinian people, but numerous ones, all appearing outwardly to cling to the same identity (though even this is debatable), yet without much in common. But perhaps an analysis grounded in material reality is not part and parcel of "imagined identities." And in time, thanks largely to Israel and to the postcolonial Arab state system, the Palestinians have indeed come to regard themselves as a single people with shared interests and a common identity. This is so notwithstanding the widespread recognition that there are Kuwaiti Palestinians, Jordanian Palestinians, Lebanese Palestinians, Syrian Palestinians, Israeli Palestinians, and of course *Sulta* Palestinians, to name only the larger concentrations. Thus the question of whether or not the Palestinians have become one people has not lost its relevance.

Growing up in "Jordanian" Jerusalem in the 1950s, what strikes me most today is the total absence of Palestine and things Palestinian in my then-worldview, both as a child and as an adolescent. True, on my daily trip to school I walked in the shadow of the wall built by the Jordanian army presumably to protect people from Israeli sniper fire, but the task it actually fulfilled was much more ominous—it rendered not only the enemy, but Palestine itself, invisible. East Jerusalem and the West Bank, as the name implied, were no longer Palestine but Jordan; "Palestine" was *over there*, beyond the flimsy wall that started at Damascus Gate and stretched all the way to Shaykh Jarrah.

Things were not much different at home. I can barely remember references to Palestine or to the events of 1948, not to mention prior to 1948. At various stages I had garnered some rudimentary facts, such as that my family had lived in the Qatamon quarter of West Jerusalem, and that some time not long after the Haganah blew up the Semiramis Hotel not far from our house, my mother fled with me and my elder sister in tow to Gaza to stay with relatives, after which she continued on to Alexandria where she was joined by my father. Some months later, prevented from returning to their own home in West Jerusalem, now occupied by Israel, my family managed to return, and not without difficulty, to the Jordanian-occupied part of the city. This was the sum total of my knowledge up to 1967. I had once asked my father, who had an obsessive love for books, why he did not have a library, and he replied that he used to have one, but that it was lost in 1948 along with *everything else*. He did not elaborate. The conversation ended there and then. Why? I am not sure I have an answer to this day.

The outbreak of the June 1967 war coincided with the end of my first year at university. Having been shipped off to school in England on the occasion of my sixteenth birthday, I had little awareness of the events taking place in the Arab world beyond the little that I could glean from the tightly controlled media during my annual visits to Jerusalem for the summer holidays. Even before that, having grown up in the culturally arid atmosphere of Jordanian-ruled Jerusalem and attending St. George's, a British-run Anglican missionary school where the language of instruction was English, my knowledge of the Arab world and the social and political currents within it had been minimal. There was, however, a striking war atmosphere in the British media following the closure of the Straits of Tiran, and it seemed certain that the region was heading toward war. Curiously enough, this did not cause me much concern. Having derived my information from the British media, which emphasized the overwhelming superiority of the Arab side in terms of numbers, armaments, and so on, I was confident that the Arabs would beat Israel. I had no personal recollections of the Suez War, but I accepted the prevailing Arab opinion that grew in its aftermath, first that it was a victory, and secondly that Israel would have been defeated had Britain and France not stepped in. This time, Israel was going to be defeated. I did not speculate much beyond that, and I did not see the approaching conflagration through a Palestinian prism. This was a war between Israel and the Arab states, but the object was not the liberation of Palestine. Not that I lacked enthusiasm, but my worldview was not very colored by my Palestinian identity. If I remember rightly I used to identify myself at the time as a Jordanian of Palestinian origin. Being Arab was more meaningful to me. The Arab defeat when it came was too swift for me to be able to deal with rationally.

Shortly after the war, I made the trip to the Israeli Embassy in London and demanded to be allowed to return to Jerusalem. I refused the explanations of the stonewalling official regarding my Jordanian passport, and I remember clearly affirming that I *went with Jerusalem*. Since the Israelis were now in control of Jerusalem, they had to find a way of getting me back to it. In retrospect, perhaps this is the strongest attachment I have felt, despite the fact that unlike many others, I have never been able to discern Jerusalem's physical charms, nor do I have fond memories of childhood or adolescence. Even my recollections of the city's physical contours in the 1950s are vague, and when I talk to contemporaries, I am amazed by their recollections of the changing physical aspects of the city to which I am oblivious.

Filastin to my mind is inextricably linked with Israel. I cannot separate the two. When I make the short drive from Jerusalem down to the coast and stroll around Shenken Street in Tel Aviv or browse through Shouk Ha Karmel, I feel I am in Palestine. I know it is not Jaffa *'Arus al-Bahr*, that this was not some Arab quarter that had been taken over and "ethnically cleansed," but I also know that *Filastin* in 1948 *was* ethnically cleansed. Nevertheless, I cannot help but feel whenever I make the fifty-minute drive to Yaffa/Tel Aviv that I have arrived in Palestine. I don't have this feeling in Nablus, nor in Amman, by far the largest Palestinian city in the world. The fact that Tel Aviv is teeming with Jews is itself an intrinsic part of this feeling. I cannot visualize *my Palestine* without Jews. I try to keep myself under control by recalling numbers and hard facts: the Jews were a minority in 1948, their ownership of land was minuscule, and so on. I know that this is not what Palestine would have looked, smelled, and felt like before 1948. But I have no recollection of *Filastin*, not even a second-hand one. The Palestine I know is the one I discovered on that first visit to Jerusalem and points westward after the June war, though I only really came to know the place in the aftermath of September 1970. And this Palestine was already Israel.

June 1967 was the historical divider between "before" and "after," but in retrospect the events of September 1970 drove home in personal terms the meaning of identity and the dimensions of defeat. I had traveled in the summer of 1970 from London to Amman, lured like thousands of young Arabs (and numerous non-Arabs) by the promise of "the armed struggle" and its empowering potential. The rude awakening came with the swift defeat at the hands of the Jordanian army and what I perceived to be the disintegration of the Palestinian leadership. Some prominent leaders who fell into the hands of the Jordanian army made radio appeals calling for an end to the fighting, while those who remained at liberty saw their salvation in the intervention of "friendly" Arab states—the same ones they had denounced for their dismal performance in June 1967. I believe it was then that I decided that I wanted to go back and live in Jerusalem. This was the closest I could get to *Filastin*: an occupied and a divided city to be sure, but I saw that as an advantage. Living in Jerusalem would enable me to overcome at will what was both an imaginary and a physical border.

Until the outbreak of the intifada in December 1987, the occupation had in fact reunited Palestine, or at least effected a re-Palestinization of the West Bank. There were negative sides, to be sure. One was the separation from the Arab world, which resulted in a lack of social and cultural development. The West Bank, as many Palestinian returnees discovered to their dismay in the early 1990s, was frozen in time. I began teaching at Birzeit in 1974 and despite all the hype soon discovered that the university, modest in its resources and not particularly blessed in its faculty and administration, functioned essentially as an export factory for the manpower-hungry economies of the Gulf. Although I did not realize it at the time, it was foolish to expect the place to be an island of enlightenment. Socially and culturally it was part of its natural environment, a closed and conservative society nurtured by the sterile years of Jordanian rule on which was superimposed the arbitrary rule of the military occupation (though Israeli interference in the daily workings of the university was, to my surprise, less than I had expected).

All these shortcomings notwithstanding, I felt myself particularly lucky. I wanted to live in Palestine, and for the time being Birzeit was the vehicle that allowed me to do so. I could cross the imaginary border at will, traveling to Nazareth, Beersheba, Shafa'amer, Rameh, Ramat Aviv, or wherever. Unlike many of my acquaintances, I never saw myself as an outsider in Israel. Although I am sure that for most Israelis I was an unwelcome intruder, I saw my presence in the smallest and most remote corner as one of *right*. One instance I particularly remember was looking for somewhere to stay in the occupied Syrian Heights and, unable to do so, finally ending up in a kibbutz guest house on the Israeli side of the border. Kibbutz Hagoshrim, I soon found out, made its living by manufacturing night sights for Israeli tanks. With my one-year-old son in tow, I took up the advertised offer to see their products exhibit. Although I have no particular interest in tank sights, I felt I had to make my presence known. Irrespective of the Jewish inhabitants, the kibbutz, the tank sights, this was *my Palestine*.

There has always been an unresolved tension when the issue is reduced to flesh-and-bone Israelis. I mean Jews, of course. There is also a tension where Arabs who reside in Israel are concerned, but this is usually quickly overcome. Both sides go out of their way to accommodate each other. This is of course a temporary arrangement and recognized as such by both. With Jews this is not the case. As far as they are concerned, I feel I remain invisible. They do not see me, they definitely do not recognize my presence in their midst, although they are an integral part of *my Filastin*. Irrespective of the length of my stay in Jerusalem, the only Jews I meet are the ones I have to meet—that is, officials of all sorts, whether civilian or military (though mostly, of course, of the latter type). While living in London, I had a large circle of Israeli friends and acquaintances, yet living in Jerusalem with no physical barrier between the Arab and Jewish parts of the city, there seems to be an insurmountable chasm that militates against any kind of social interaction. Hundreds of Jews travel daily on the road in front of my house on their way from West Jerusalem to the Hebrew University campus on Mount Scopus. Not infrequently, some stop to ask for directions and fall speechless when I respond to their questions in Arabic. The presence of Arabs in the city always comes as a surprise to them. The use of Arabic in itself seems to pose a dangerous threat. This was driven home to me on the occasion of a protest meeting at a Tel Aviv University forum in the aftermath of the Israeli invasion of Lebanon, when I happened to meet General Aharon Yariv, a lukewarm dove even by Israeli standards. He addressed me in Hebrew, and I replied in English that I did not speak Hebrew. His rejoinder was a revelation: "It is not that you do not speak Hebrew, it's that you *refuse* to speak it," he said. Although it took me some time, I eventually came to see the wisdom of his words. Now, everywhere I travel in Israel/Palestine I insist upon speaking Arabic. In *my Palestine*, Arabic is the lingua franca. I have made my *historic compromise*. Now it is the turn of the Jews.

"Reflections on al-Nakba," *Journal of Palestine Studies* 28, no. 1 (Autumn 1998): 5–13, 31–35.

Chapter 8

Issues of Identity

Several short selections written by Israeli Arabs and Palestinians reveal issues of identity and nostalgia for their homeland. The confrontations between returning Palestinians who are visitors to their family home in Zichron Yaakov, or in Lod, in Haifa, or Akko, convey more than a sense of personal loss. There are issues of relationships to the land and confiscations, injustices, and competition with Jews in school, of reactions to moving and the *intifada*. Fawaz Turki, a Palestinian, born in Haifa and exiled in 1948, writes as a Palestinian American. He returns to visit his home in Haifa and notes the changing names of streets and that someone of Eastern European origins occupies his former home. The switch in identities in this selection is of particular importance.

The views expressed in this section about Arab worker and Arab labor are in sharp contrast with the Israeli Jewish view. The ways in which Israeli Arabs who remained in the state differ from the Palestinians who were displaced and live on the West Bank should be noted. This section begins with a short but revealing piece about the problems of communication written by the former Mayor of Beer Sheva. The intended meanings and messages are very different than the actual translation. The problem of communication, connecting what people say and mean to what people hear is a particularly vexing issue in cross-cultural descriptions within and between places.

THE BEST OF ARIEL

On the eve of Independence Day, 1954, a reception was held at the military governor's office in Beersheba for the Beduin sheiks and elders of the Negev. When the guests were all assembled, the military governor stood up and addressed them in these words: "Honoured sheikhs, the government of Israel extends greetings to you on Independence Day and invites you to the spectacle which the Israel Defence Forces are putting on tonight at the stadium in Ramat Gan. The government of Israel expects that this year, as every year, cooperation will increase between yourselves and the ruling institutions, and assures you that as long as you continue to be cooperative, the government will continue to be helpful towards you."

But this is how Aminadav Altschuler, known to all as *Hawaja* Amin, proceeded to translate the governor's speech into Arabic: "Esteemed sheikhs, the government of Israel invites you all tonight to a great feast at the village of Ramadan, such a banquet as you have never witnessed in all your born days, even at your mothers' weddings, and it is incumbent upon you to conduct yourselves appropriately. And the military governor demands that you obey the government in all things and carry out all the commands of the police officers and soldiers and clerks and if you do so, the government will release all the abandoned lands to you, and will give you work and buy you tractors, and give you loans for the sowing season and bring water to the entrances of your tents, and build clinics and schools for you. The government will buy shoes for everyone and look after you and you will be pampered and nurtured and treated as tenderly as can be imagined. But, on the other hand, should you fail to obey the government and refuse to do what the police officers, soldiers and clerks tell you—then, by Allah, you will eat bird-droppings, and you will be cursed in the names of your fathers' fathers' great-grandfathers, and it would be better not to delve into what else will befall you . . ."

David el-Natour, "Three Tales," in *The Best of Ariel*, ed. Asher Weill, trans. Judith Cooper, *Ariel Magazine* (Jerusalem), 1993, vol. 183, 132.

THE STRUGGLE FOR PEACE

We were sure it was impossible to get a license for a new cooperative project [in Beit Sahur] such as a dairy farm under the martial law of the occupation. Others have applied many times for similar local projects, but in vain. Yet, we took the risk and went to an Israeli *kibbutz*, bought eighteen cows, and brought them to a special place very near town. Well, we started taking care of these cows, but a month later the authorities discovered them and it seemed that they thought a dairy farm was a very dangerous thing. The military governor, the Shin Bet people [the Israeli secret police], the civil administration officers, and a lot of soldiers went to the farm, surrounded it, and they took photos of each cow, with identification numbers. Then they gave us a military order to close the farm within twenty-four hours or else the military governor would order the place to be bulldozed. They said that the cows were a security threat. I asked the military governor myself, "Just please explain to me, I can't understand it, why this is so dangerous for you? How can eighteen cows be so dangerous for the state of Israel?" He said that I didn't need to understand; that they understood well enough what's dangerous for Israel and what's not. So, there was no explanation. We had no other alternative but to go late at night and move the cows secretly. So when the military governor went the next morning to the farm and didn't find any cows, he got very angry—it seemed like he had lost eighteen terrorists. So he did something very strange—at least for our area, it was the first time such a wide search campaign was organized. People say hundreds of soldiers participated, even with helicopters, looking for the cows, those terrorists. The soldiers carried photos of the cows, showed them to people, and asked them "Have you seen these cows?" It was amazing. Sometimes we wonder why they didn't put up "Wanted Dead or Alive" posters for them. After ten days of searching, they located the cows. They found them with a butcher, and a butcher has a license to buy cows in order to slaughter them afterwards. He told them, "I have bought these cows, here are the papers. I'm going to slaughter them later for the meat." The military governor was very pleased; the problem was solved. So they waited a week before coming back to check whether the butcher had indeed killed the cows. They found them still there, though, and indeed, there were then twenty-three cows instead of eighteen because all of them had been pregnant when we bought them and five had delivered. They didn't know what to do. Then they started harassing the butcher's family, so we soon decided that it was time to move the cows again. Once again, we moved them at night, this time away from Beit Sahur. It was a transfer. And I'm afraid that this is what is going to happen to the people of Beit Sahur, also, because what has been going on here since the beginning of the occupation is a slow transfer of people. But I can tell you something, the cows are still hidden somewhere and they are still providing the children of Beit Sahur with the milk of the *intifada*.

Jalal Qumsiyah, "Profiles of Israelis and Palestinians," in *The Struggle for Peace*, ed. E. Fernea and M. Hocking (Austin: University of Texas, 1992), 210–11.

EXILES RETURN

I am home.

Yet as I say that to myself, I know how facile and illusory that outcry is. It is tawdry, I tell myself, for me to be saying that. I cannot return here, after forty years in exile, with my alternative order of meaning, my comfortable notions about homelessness being my only homeland, and say that I am home. The house is no longer as habitable as when I left it. The toys are no longer in the attic. An awry force in history has changed the place, and my own sense of otherness has changed me. This place could not be lived in by anyone other than its new inhabitants, and they have already stripped it clean of everything but themselves. From time to time I come across something here and there, inherited from nature—the view of the Mediterranean below, the cloudless sky above, the richly green trees around—that had always independently declared their own form of being, but apart from that, Haifa no longer speaks to me.

A few feet away, a man with a skullcap is holding a child on his shoulders. The child, a girl of five or six, is crying. As she cries, she leans so far out from his hold that I think she is going to fall. Her father sits her on his lap, claps her hands together, and begins to speak to her. In English. With a Brooklyn accent. Elsewhere, I would not have found this scene charged with any meaning beyond the touching sight of a father out for a walk with his child. Here it is a scene with the unlogic of dreams and reality turned on its hinges.

This land is so pervaded by symbols, so defined by them, that even the people who live here have themselves become symbolic. I could not even see a father and his daughter in a park but as a symbol of disruption in my life. He is from America, and this place is now his. I am from this place, and America is now mine. In between his trip and mine, as we changed places, something happened to me. People who live in exile guard their names the way they shield their eyes from the sun. In exile everything is excitable, like storms in wintertime, the only season you know there. Without your name, without those lips from childhood's mirror, you will be forgotten inside the American dream. I'm a first-generation American, still covered with the blood of ancient wounds.

I leave the park, wander down to the port (port areas remain the same, like the sea), and walk a few blocks north in search of the house where I was born. Something in me, in the central knot of my being, is still saying: You're back home. *Home*—a mystical, healing incantation that affirms that the link between the world in me and the world around me has not been irreparably ruptured.

There is the house, as nondescript as ever, standing at the corner of Miknass and Talal streets. The names, like everything else in this city, have been changed. Three steps lead up to the front door. I climb them and knock. The glow from the sun is so powerful that when I close my eyes they are instantly flooded by red. For a moment I swim in it. I feel the floor rock like the deck of a ship. A man in his late sixties opens the door and says something in Hebrew.

What can I say to this man? What am I doing here? Why am I driven to return to this country, this city, this street, this house, after forty years in exile?

Perhaps there lurks in each of us who have been severed from our homeground a craving to return. Whatever it is, I know I came here to remember. "I will remember," wrote Thomas Wolfe. "When I come to the place, I shall know." Here and there, I will meet Palestinians who, unlike me, had remained anchored to what they remember. They will help me to know.

"Do you speak English, sir?" I ask the old man.

He tells me, in a heavy East European accent, that he does. And I ask him if I could just look around the house a bit. He has wrinkled eyebrows and a pouting underlip that expresses his puzzlement at my odd request.

"I was born here," I offer, in the way of explanation.

He lets me into the hallway without saying another word.

"You want that I show you the house?" he asks.

"That'll be very kind of you."

"You do not speak Hebrew?"

"I'm afraid not."

"And you were born here?"

He obviously thinks I'm Jewish, but I don't want to deceive him, so I say: "I am not a Jew. I am an Arab."

He looks at me uncomprehendingly. I can see the man has arthritis and his hands are shaking.

"I mean I'm Palestinian. I'm not an Israeli," I add redundantly, but this only excites the language of his wrinkled eyebrows and pouting underlip, and he looks at me as if I had smacked him. His hands begin to shake more visibly.

"I mean, like, you know, I'm actually American," I blurt out defensively. But the man wants me out of his house. His house. My house. Our house.

I leave without either of us saying another word.

I should have told him I wasn't there to reclaim the place, just the passions it once housed. I think he would have understood. He too was once in exile, after all. I should have shared my memories from this place and the memories I acquired outside it.

Fawaz Turki, *Exile's Return: The Making of a Palestinian American* (New York: Free Press, 1994), 4–6.

RESISTANCE BEHIND THE GREEN LINE

I was born in Ein Mahil village on the ninth of July, 1962. We are a big family. With all my brothers and sisters, we are eighteen. It is a family which grew for more than 400 years in our village. No one left the country after the massacre and the war in 1948.

My grandfather was a big leader in the village. All the people still remember Mohammed Ibrahim, my father's father. He has the reputation of a man who supported the people, who cared for all the village, not for himself. I still remember the stories that my mother and father and my big brother told me: that he always gave land to other people in the village who needed land to build houses and establish themselves; and that when someone wanted to take a loan from a wealthy man in Nazareth, they would take my grandfather to guarantee that the loan would be repaid. My grandfather didn't establish a big house for himself. Although he had much land, he didn't care for us more than he cared for all the people in the village. It's an integral part of our tradition that you can't be in a situation with a lot of land while your neighbor is living in a small area.

My mother said, "Your grandfather gave a gift of land to all these people and now you haven't any piece to establish a house for yourself." I said, "OK. I agree with him." Because I still hear the good reputation of my grandfather. I don't need land if the people hate me. I need the love of these people. I was arrested during the Gulf War in 1991 and when I came back home, all the village people came to shake hands and to say, "We support you and we hope that you will be like your grandfather."

Ein Mahil has had a bad relationship with Jewish settlements. Bet Qeshet was a Jewish settlement that tried to control Ein Mahil. Partition was established before 1948; there was a pact between Ein Mahil and Bet Qeshet. But in 1948 there was a battle in a small village less than two kilometers from Ein Mahil, and Ein Mahil lost eight men in this battle.

People from Ein Mahil, Kufr Kana, Reina, El Mashad, Dabouri and Aksal didn't leave, and many people from Nazareth didn't leave the country in 1948. I asked my parents why they didn't leave in 1948, and why in all this area people didn't leave. They said, "We understood that if we left, we would not find a place where we could live in freedom. All of us heard about many people who had lost their lives on the road between Palestine and Lebanon in 1948. There was no chance that we would be able to maintain our future in Lebanon or Jordan or Syria. Our decision was to stay here, in our homeland. If there was going to be a confrontation between us and the Jewish settlement, we had to be here. All of us agreed. We were going to continue to struggle here until the last man." This is what my parents said. I think that the battle between Ein Mahil and Bet Qeshet was what made them decide to stay here.

I still remember the lifestyle of my family. At five in the morning we would go to the fields together. We would take tomatoes and grapes and water. The fields were far away, about three kilometers from our house. We spent the time there working on our land because we were villagers and the land was our main resource. When we came back to our home at 6:00 or 6:30, we cooked some food. I still remember how we ate together, eighteen people in the same room. I still remember the traditional food. I still remember that in our home, my grandfather's house, we had two bedrooms and a big salon. The big salon was for the many visitors who came to my grandfather to talk about the issues in the village, about our problems and about our future. This style of life gave me a sense of belonging, that I am an integral part of this family.

I learned from my grandfather and after that from my father and mother, that we have to be together, we have to struggle, we have to love the people. We lived in my grandfather's home until he died and when they separated the land between the brothers, they gave this house to my father. When the land was separated between me and my brother, my brother gave me the house of my grandfather and of my father. I live, I sleep, I sit in the same house as my grandfather and my father. These things keep me believing that I have to continue in the same style of life, to struggle with my people. When I talk about land confiscations and about my village, it is not as a private case. I protest for all Ein Mahil villagers.

Land Confiscation

We have to look at the confiscations of land as a continuous process from 1948 to the present.

In 1948, land which had belonged to the British Mandate now belonged to Israel. The land of people who were "absent," who escaped or were forced to leave, was taken by the Israeli authority and given to the Jewish population. Other land was confiscated for a "public purpose."

They came to Ein Mahil and they said, "We want this land for a public purpose." They took many thousands of dunums from Ein Mahil and the surrounding villages, and they said they took it for a public purpose. While our population was increasing, they were taking the land.

Ein Mahil in 1948 had a population of 862 people with 14,000 dunums. The population increased up to 7,100 in 1992, and after all of the confiscation, we have only 4,100 dunums.

Take another example, Kufr Kana. In 1948, Kufr Kana had a population of 1,000 and 19,500 dunums. In 1992, there were 13,000 people and only 5,635 dunums.

Let's talk about Reina. The population in 1948 was 750; 15,777 dunums. The population has increased to 8,000 and in 1992 Reina has only 6,764 dunums.

El Mashad had a population of 823 people in 1948; in 1992, 7,000 or more. Land, in 1948, was 10,805 dunums; 5,420 in 1992.

The main issue is that there is an Arab majority in Nazareth and the surrounding villages, and the Israeli authority is trying to establish and maintain a Jewish majority and an Arab minority in the future. They can't maintain a Jewish majority if they don't have land for them.

From 1948 until 1964, the Israeli authority used military rule. If you wanted to move from Ein Mahil to Kufr Kana you had to have permission. If you wanted to buy anything in Nazareth, you had to have permission. The military situation made people more and more afraid and frustrated. People heard about the Deir Yassin massacre. People heard about the Sufsaf massacre. They heard what the Israeli authorities were doing to the Palestinian people and they were afraid that if they made any kind of protest, any kind of resistance, especially related to the land, the Israeli authority would take them outside the border. And who would care? The United Nations? No one would care. The people decided to be silent. You have to understand the frustration, the hopelessness.

After the 1967 war, after the abolition of military rule in Galilee and after connections were made with the West Bank and Gaza Strip, we had more and more students who finished secondary school, more students from the university, more understanding of what was going on, and more capacity to protest. We had parties. We had leadership. We had money. And we had resistance. We had the knowledge that we had to do something.

The First Land Day

In 1976, I remember the Land Day when the whole Palestinian population moved to the streets in Ein Mahil, in Kufr Kana, in Reina and Arabeh and all the villages, and I was one of them. We were protesting against the land confiscations and the Israeli policy of surrounding us. The West Bank and Gaza Strip supported us by protests on the same day.

Confiscation orders had been issued on March 9, 1976. It took us three weeks to organize everything with maps, with slogans, everything. It is my impression that the first Land Day was organized by two political movements, Sons of the Land, and the Democratic Front for Peace and Equal Rights, with the support of all the Palestinian population.

Issues of Identity

On March 30, 1976, all the people moved from Ein Mahil to Kufr Kana and in Kufr Kana there was a big protest. Then all the people moved from Kufr Kana to Arabeh, and to Sakhnin, and to other villages, to show that we were unified. It was not a case for Ein Mahil or for Reina or for Arabeh. It was a case of "to be or not to be." We had to fight against these confiscations of land.

In Sakhnin, I remember, we were in the protest and people began to say, "We'll sacrifice our blood in the name of Galilee." This meant, we'll not give you this land. We will not sit down and see you take this land.

Then the police began to shoot, to use force. I was not far away: I was here and the woman who was killed was there [about 30 yards]. The people were screaming, "Bring the ambulance! There is a woman killed." They took the woman to the hospital.

We didn't move. We stayed there. After an hour they said that she had died. Anyone could have been in the same situation. She was just part of the demonstration. Her name was Khledija. She was 23 years old.

The people were angry and they moved toward the police. The police began to use tear gas. And they arrested many people after that.

Until this day, the Israeli authorities say that they made a mistake to use force against this demonstration. It was a provocation to put themselves among the people when the people were angry and didn't want to see any symbol of Israeli authority.

After Land Day in 1976, the Israeli authority decided they would not go inside the village on Land Day. They would try to maintain security from outside the village. They understood the risk. On the thirtieth of March, 1992, they said, "You want Land Day? OK. You want to protest? You want to dance? OK. You are inside. We are outside. We will maintain the roads. We are not going to go inside the village." Because they understand that if they go inside the village, the same problem as in 1976 will happen again and again.

I think Land Day had an effect on the historical process. From 1948 until 1967, the Israeli authority tried to take the Palestinian people away from their political connection, from their social atmosphere, by confiscation of land, by taking them to work in the industrial area, by trying to move villagers to cities and to the Hebrew language and Hebrew culture. Go to Tel Aviv and you can see the lights, the cinema and everything.

They were successful with some people. Some say, "I am a Palestinian in Israel." Some say, "I am an Arab Israeli living in Israel." And some say, "I am not Palestinian. I am an Arab Israeli." Some of them work and support the Shin Bet activities.

After 1967, the border opened with the West Bank and Gaza Strip. There were many refugees who moved from here to the West Bank. We found our brothers there, we found ourselves there, and we began another historical process, which meant to come back to our roots. After Land Day in 1976, we came back to our roots more and more.

The Israeli authority had pushed this people to work in the cities without maintaining their social situation—no food, no house to sleep in, not enough money, no security. By land confiscation, they were surrounding us, and in 1976, the confiscation came to the borders of our homes.

Through Land Day and cultural activities and the connection with the West Bank and Gaza Strip, I think people now understand, without any hesitation, that they are Palestinian in their identity at the same time they are residents of Israel. Now, more and more people declare that we are Palestinian.

• • •

The Israeli authority has begun to control the confiscated land. They cut our olive trees and they have begun to establish 10,000 houses at the edge of my village for the new immigrants. They established another three factories beside the houses.

If the farmer does not remove the trees from the confiscated land, he has to pay for the trees to be cut. It's about 2,000 shekels, depending upon how many cuts and what machine they use. Some of the farmers cut the trees because they have no money to pay. Some of the farmers refuse to cut the trees; it is difficult to order the farmer to cut his tree. If you will not pay, they are going to take you to jail. That's Israeli legitimacy. They confiscated the land and cut the trees and they try to force you to pay the money to the court. Justice!

Ghanem Habib-Allah, in *Homeland: Oral Histories of Palestine and Palestinians*, ed. S. Lynd, S. Bahour, and A. Lynd (Northampton, Mass.: Olive Branch Press, 1994), 288–91, 295–96.

HOMELAND

"Wherever we are, as Palestinians, whether inside or outside Israel, we are a whole people."

Mohammed Burgal: My father and my grandfather and generations before them were here in Lod. Historically, we didn't come from some other place. This was our home. It seems that Lod is a very old city. No one knows when it was built. It was before the Assyrians and the Babylonians.

I remember, when I was a boy living in the slums of Lod in a section called "Mahatah." (In English, "the Station.") There was a certain holiday in Israel called Lag B'omer. They made fires everywhere and they would circle around the fires and dance. We saw them put a puppet of Gamel Abdul Nasser on the fire and, as children, we asked why they did that. We loved Gamel Abdul Nasser. His picture was in all of our homes because of what Nasser symbolized. As a response to that, I remember, we burned a puppet of Ben Gurion.

The Arab schools had classes on Saturdays. Every Saturday, when we would go to school, we would pass through the Israeli neighborhood where the Zionists were. (I say "Zionists," because not all Jews are Zionists.) They knew that we were Arab and they would attack us. Every Saturday we had a struggle with them. They threw stones at us and we responded. Our mother would try very hard to dress us well but when we arrived at school we no longer looked well dressed. That was life from the first to the eighth grade in school. Everywhere we went, we understood that we were Arab. There was tension and there could be a struggle or cursing. It would lead to conflicts.

We think about the reason why. At the beginning, I admit, we had just a general understanding: These are our enemies. They took our land, and they hate us. They don't try to let us live as human beings. They do not let us make progress as Arabs. They want us as just a lower class. They want to get more from us without giving us anything.

Also, we asked our mother and father. My father didn't want to speak about his experience. He fought in 1948 and was wounded in his thigh. He sold his horse to buy a weapon. He did not speak about that because he was afraid that if he said anything, it would make us more angry and we as young guys would try to do foolish things.

But we heard from my mother. For example, my brother came home from school and asked my mother, "Why do we think that Jews are not good, the Israelis are not good? Our teacher told us, they gave work to our father and now we have money and they protect us from burglars and enemies outside."

So my mother answered him. She felt she had to tell him the truth. I remember, she took him and sat with him and told him: "Look. If someone came now and took your house, this house over us, and then told us just to stay in the store; and he let your father work on the land that was his; and he killed your sister, which made your brother so afraid that he fled from the house; and then he told you, 'I am good enough to you to let you live here and you must accept the fact that you have to pay rent and you have to work and I will give you a little food.' Is that good enough for you?" my mother said. "Of course, it's not good. It's not fair." So, by that, she explained to him in a very simple way the whole Palestinian issue.

Before 1948, my family had a house and land. After 1948, they had no house and no land. The authorities confiscated the land and the house on it; it is now the property of a committee that is responsible for abandoned land. Even though we remained inside Israel, we are considered to be like those who left. It is ridiculous—we exist but we are considered as nonexistent—that is the law. Now my family pays rent to live in a house that belongs to them.

Little by little we came to understand that what we heard on the Israeli radio was false, that the state did not want anything for our benefit and that they were trying to cheat us. When we heard the Arabic stations, we heard very good songs about the necessity to liberate Palestine.

Where I lived, there were separate schools for Arab children through elementary school. In high school, I went to the Jewish school. Otherwise, I would have had to travel to Haifa and my parents would not accept that.

I had to enter into competition with pupils who had already studied in a Jewish elementary school. It was very hard for me to continue in high school with these students and subjects and with the program made for Jews. But it was the only opportunity I had to continue.

The official goal of Israeli education, according to the law of education, is to establish the culture of the people of Israel. The program of study includes the Holocaust, Israeli achievements in science, loyalty to the State of Israel and to the people of Israel, and there is no mention of another people who lives in this same land. You can see it in practice. What we are learning in the schools is without any mention of our history, without any mention of us as a nationality. It is systematically planned to diminish any feeling of our nationality or of our Arab minority inside Israel.

I had to study the Bible and Hebrew literature as if I were a Zionist student, not an Arab. In the schools for Arabs, they taught the Arabic language, grammar and literature, but they did not stress the history of our people.

The separation into Arab and Jewish schools was also discriminatory because the classroom hours that were given to the Arabs were two-thirds of those that were given to the Jews. So, the Israelis, the Zionists, had enough hours to be ready to succeed at the university examinations. They gave the Arabs the same examination questions but they did not give us the same opportunity to prepare.

I had Arab teachers in the Arab school. But Arab teachers—and only Arab teachers—had to pass a Shin Bet security examination. The Shin Bet is the Israeli security service. A person could really want to teach and he could be qualified enough, but he could not teach if the Shin Bet would not accept him as a teacher. And every headmaster had to be approved by the Shin Bet.

The whole system makes it nearly impossible for the Arab students to achieve progress. You can see it also in the percentage of Palestinians in

Israeli universities. The percentage of Palestinians does not reflect their actual percentage in the whole society. It is much lower. In my pre-law year at the university, there were 360 students. Twenty were Arab students and I was one of two who succeeded and went to law school. Even though the requirements for Jews and Arabs to enter certain subjects are the same, it is much more difficult for Arabs to excel in the Israeli curriculum.

There is hard competition among Arabs. The academic fields for Arabs are mainly law and medicine, because nearly everything else is connected with security. If an Arab wanted to study electricity or electronics or engineering, as an Arab he would be regarded as too dangerous to be in such a sensitive position.

The only way that is open for an Arab is to go outside Israel. When a young adult sees how the world feels living in freedom, you can imagine that he is persuaded to live abroad. He thinks twice whether to come back or not. If he succeeds in his field abroad and has good conditions to work outside Israel, and if he finds a woman to share his life, then all of his life will be outside. But it is very hard for him to leave us and live abroad, because it will be difficult for him to continue living as an Arab.

Wherever we go, we have to understand our situation. It is part of our life. We are under the authority of a government and a law that is not serving us, an authority that is just capturing us in every facet of life.

Mohammed Burgal and Lawahez Burgal, in *Homeland: Oral Histories of Palestine and Palestinians,* ed. S. Lynd, S. Bahour, and A. Lynd (Northampton, Mass.: Olive Branch Press, 1994), 296–98.

THE SECRET LIFE OF SAEED, THE ILL-FATED PESSOPTIMIST

Twenty-four: Saeed Anticipates Real Arab Nationalism by a Frenzy of Work in a Frenetic Age

One spring I met a girl from Tanturah,—Tanturiyya let's call her. This is not her real name, of course, but a reference to her village lying beside the sea. There she was born thirteen years before that village fell. The eviction of the villagers came suddenly, while she was visiting relatives in the hamlet of Jisr al-Zarqa, which also lies on the coast. She remained there, perhaps fated to share my troubles with me if only for a season.

The story of this hamlet, Jisr al-Zarqa, is a strange one. How was this tiny place along with its sister village, Fraydis—"Paradise," that is—able to withstand the catastrophes of war and dispossession, when such gales tore up all the other Arab villages on the shore between Haifa and Tel Aviv? The list is long—al-Tirah, 'Ain Hawd, al-Mazar, Jaba', Ijzim, Sarafand, Kufr Lam, 'Ain Ghazal, al-Tanturah, al-Buraikah, Khirbat al-Burj, Qaisariyyah, Umm Khalid, Khirbat al-Zababidah, al-Haram, Jalil al-Shamaliyyah, and Jalil al-Qibliyyah. Weren't these in fact stronger and more deeply rooted than Fraydis? Yet it survived to fulfil a purpose that Jacob had in mind.

Now this Jacob was not my master Jacob of the Union of Palestine Workers but a certain James (Jacob) de Rothschild who had established nearby the colony of Zikhron Yaqub "in memory of Jacob," at the close of the nineteenth century. Its settlers, who had all come from Europe, began producing fine wines. Nowadays the summer resorts of the Arab world place these wines, which have acquired so many different names, on the tables of Arabian princes from the Empty Quarter. The wines reach them via the "open bridges" across the Jordan, and the princes enjoy them mightily. Their songsters celebrate it thus, in the very poetry of the ancients:

> Oh Bishr, no swords, no wars for me;
> My star for fun and frolic stands,
> Song, wine, lovely dancers to see,
> And sleep with a sweet girl demands;
> Now there's an Arab Knight to be!

Then these drunken princes roar in fury, accusing of treason those who demand implementation of the resolutions of the United Nations Security Council!

Yes, it's a fact that the people of Fraydis were saved from the storms of war by the grape juice in Yaqub's jars. It's true to say that they make huge profits at Zikhron Yaqub, won from the toil and sweat of the people of Fraydis.

These settlers, then, laughed good-naturedly when the following story about them spread (it was related to me by my master Jacob). The elders of Zikhron Yaqub disagreed about the following problem: Is it lawful for a man to sleep with his wife on the sabbath, or is the act a kind of work and therefore not lawful on that day? They went to the rabbi for a decision as to whether it was work or pleasure. The rabbi thought long and hard, and then he ruled that it was pleasure. They asked him for his reasoning. He replied: "If I had ruled it to be work, you would have given it to the Arabs of Fraydis to perform!"

My, how we laughed at this story—Jacob because he hates the Ashkenazi or "Western" Jews, and I because he laughed.

And who would be so unfair as to blame the people of Fraydis for owing their preservation to vintage wine? Who, after all, erected the tall buildings of this country, cut and paved its broad streets, dug the trenches, and fortified the shelters? Who planted, plucked, and ginned the cotton, then wove it into clothes for the lords of Raghdan and Basman, palaces in Amman, to wear so proudly? It was said that the National Union would have them make one standardized uniform from this cloth, so that all its members would be equal to one another, similar as the teeth on a comb. And then no Arab would feel himself better than any non-Arab, except for their kings and for the way they wear their *kuffiyya*, their headdress, the very symbol of their national identity. When their Arab blood boils they muffle their faces in the *kuffiyyas* and silently invoke the name of God. When it bursts within them they squat down, fuming and foaming about a "better life" and hold forth against all "foreign imports." Except, that is, for kingship, cloth for *kuffiyyas*, air planes, bars, photographs (both to take and to pose for), the kissing of hands, the crown prince, and "how the rich enjoy the hunger of the poor," to quote Ali the son of Abu Talib. And that's not to mention exploitation and injustice to workers, with livelihoods being cut off, and debauchery in this age of skirts raised high. Yes, who erected the buildings, paved the roads, dug and planted the earth of Israel, other than the Arabs who remained there? Yet those Arabs who stayed, stoically, in land occupied by our state received never so much as a mention in all the files of Ahmad Shukairy's ringing speeches.

How often in Ajami Square in Jaffa I have seen those fresh-faced young men from Gaza, Jabaliyya and so on, swaying in the back of contractors' trucks, like the tombstones of those martyred brothers that have been seen moving in a Gaza graveyard. I have come to believe that the living too can indeed remain in their own land.

When I see such men in Lower Haifa, there in Paris Square, (previously known as Hanatir ("carriage") Square and before that as Khamrah Square), awaiting the trucks of the contractors, who will feel their arms and scrutinize their trim bodies and then pick out those with the strongest arms and the firmest legs, I recall how we were twenty years ago and have faith that this nation of ours will never die. At sunset I often see them again being crammed into old trucks just as they have all day crammed boxes of potatoes and piles of beetroots into trucks newer than the ones that will transport them back to their towns and villages at night. Except, that is, for those whom Mr. Contractor pretended not to see and allowed to spend the night in some unfinished building. These workers must cover themselves with bricks to protect themselves from their two likely attackers, the early morning cold and the nighttime police. When dawn arrives, they will roll up their sleeves and start working again.

Seeing them reminds me how we were twenty years ago, and how my master Jacob would ask me to choose between losing Tanturiyya, as I had lost Yuaad before, or rising at dawn to visit the workers who had fallen into the clutches of contractors, to save them from the claws of the Communists, "just as the old Christian women saved the priest's beard from being plucked as he stood in prayer before the altar."*

I came to believe that all this was our predetermined fate, and that "what will be will be," as in the Italian song, the sense of which may be translated poetically thus:

> The path we're fated for, that we walk;
> All fated with a path, that we stalk.

But the people of the village of Jisr al-Zarqa, close relatives of my Tanturiyya, did not walk a single step. They never left their undiscovered village: that is the secret of their survival. They remained, fishing at the river's mouth, safe and secure.

All except her, that is, my Tanturiyya.

Twenty-eight: Saeed Becomes a "Man with a Mission"

"Get some sleep now," I told her. "Everything will clear itself up in the morning."

But I did not sleep. For I realized that our path to that treasure was fraught with danger. If I did not arrange it all most carefully, we would be ruined, neither attaining our treasure nor preserving our secret. If that house my brother had built on the shore had become property of the state of the big man, of small stature, how would it be with an iron chest in the sea only a few yards from shore and therefore most definitely within Israel's territorial waters?

Baqiyya realized as I did how dangerous it all was, critically dangerous. For she even believed, really and truly, that the Arabs who had remained in Israel were themselves also government property. She told me that it was the village chief who had told her that, and that the government had told it to him.

One night I asked her: "Didn't your uncles own land in Jisr al-Zarqa?" She replied that they did once, but that the government had confiscated it along with the rest of the land in their village.

"But didn't your uncles have recourse to the law?" I asked.

She was clearly amazed at my question and replied, "The village chief informed us how they had told him: 'You fought and were defeated; therefore both you and all your property have legally become ours. By what law do the defeated claim their rights from the conqueror?'"

"Great! Great! So that's it!" I exclaimed. "That's why the big man was

---

*This is in reference to the ostracism of the communists by the Vatican at the beginning of the fifties. A rumor circulated in Haifa to the effect that the communists had planned to pluck the beard of the priest, and that that was the reason for their ostracism by the Church.

so keen on preventing the Communists from entering your village and others like it isolated by nature. And if nature did not isolate them, then the government did it with barbed wire."

Immediately I wished I had not said this, for Baqiyya opened her eyes wide and rained questions down on me. "Who are the Communists?"

"Ungrateful people who deny the blessings."

"What blessings?"

"The blessings of life which victors bestow upon the conquered."

"But such blessings come from God."

"Well, they deny God. They're heretics."

"How are they heretics?"

"They claim, God preserve us from them, that they can change predetermined fate."

This explanation made her even more eager and persistent.

"However could they be that powerful?" she demanded.

"Perhaps they found, as we did, chests their fathers had left for them, hidden along the beaches of their own Tanturahs."

This answer inflamed her imagination all the more. Her eyes gleamed and she knit her brows in determination and insisted, "Then we must seek help from the Communists."

I realized now that I had plunged into a bottomless well and that no matter how much I wanted to drag her out of this Communist business, the deeper I would fall into it. It disturbed me to realize that if Jacob had heard this dialogue he would have accused me of spreading Communist propaganda. I whispered to her how necessary it was to be cautious.

And since my father, God rest his soul, had left me no worldly goods at all, just my sense of caution, I set about offering this inheritance to her every morning and evening. "My father," I told her, "warned me that people eat people, so never trust those around you. You should suspect everyone, even your own brothers and sisters, from your own parents. For even if they do not in fact eat you, they could if they wished."

I lectured her endlessly on the need for circumspection and caution until she fell asleep in my arms. But I remained awake all night myself, pondering the problem of the chest and how to recover it.

Emile Habiby, *The Secret Life of Saeed, the Ill-Fated Pessoptimist*, trans. Salma Khadra Jayyusi and Trevor Le Gassick (Columbia, La.: Readers International, 1989), 79–82, 90–92.

STILL SMALL VOICES

The following excerpt is from interviews with Miriam Levinger, a Jewish Fundamentalist living in Hebron. Her religious and political passions reveal the potential for additional conflict between some small group of Jews and Arabs who take religious positions on political questions and where compromises with political issues confront directly deeply held religious convictions.

Miriam Levinger is a figure of controversy, a hero to some, a canister of hatred to others, well known throughout Hebron and much of Israel for her daring, defiant demonstrations of Jewish determination to establish a presence in the Arab city. She is Miriam, a daughter of Abraham, sister of Aaron and Moses, a woman whose calling it is to fulfill the words of the Bible. When she and her husband came to Hebron twenty years ago, they came because they received a signal, a sign that they believe said, Go and settle this land of the ancients. After the Arab-Israeli war in 1967, when the Jordanians lost the West Bank to the Israelis, Miriam and Rabbi Levinger knew it was their job to lead a handful of Jews and return to Hebron. "The Six-Day War was of the Arabs' doing, so for me it's a sign from God," she says. "All this land where my forefathers trod came suddenly into our possession again. My husband said, 'God did His; so we have to do ours!' "

On this torrid June day, dressed simply in a short-sleeve blue-and-white plaid blouse and brown pleated skirt, with thick support stockings on her legs and practical black rubber-soled shoes on her feet, she walks alone, contemptuous of the crowds, daring the Arabs to disturb her from her daily chores. She moves slowly past shops that sell plastic dolls and cheap toys, ignores the stalls where gold necklaces and earrings are sold by their weight, glances at the big bins of powdered spices—curry, cumin, oregano, and pepper—and looks purposefully at the open baskets of fresh vegetables—plentiful supplies of potatoes, ripe red tomatoes, yellow onions, white onions, several varieties of lettuce, radishes, zucchini, and aubergines. She stops for a moment and nods her kerchiefed head toward a basket of onions. "How much?" she asks the vendor in Hebrew. "Two shekels," he replies in her language. She carefully chooses two dozen onions, weighs them, and pays the old man his price. Now, head held high, she walks briskly a few hundred feet and stops before a small dark shop where the air inside is dank with the heavy smell of sesame and olive oils. Again she asks how much, and the seller answers her in Arabic. "Ten shekels." "Are you kidding?" she says brazenly in pidgin Arabic. "Last week it was eight shekels." The man turns to his boss, who shrugs his shoulders and nods in concession. In the style of generations past, he presses out a liter of thick golden oil. Satisfied, Miriam pays him the money. "It isn't the two shekels I care about," she says later. "But if I let him get away with it, then next week it will be twelve shekels and the week after, fourteen. After all, this is the Middle East."

Miriam Levinger came to the Middle East an idealistic eighteen-year-old, who had left New York against the wishes of her parents and set off on Passover to make *aliyah*, uncertain where God would lead her. Now, nearly thirty years later, her supporters call her a seer. "She is the spirit of Israel," says Israel Harel, one of the leaders of the settlers' movement. "She has set the way for many people."

In the spring of 1968, ten months after the Six-Day War, she and her Israeli-born husband, Moshe, a rabbi, came to Hebron. Their professed reason was to celebrate the eight days of Passover, the holiday that recalls the Jewish exodus from slavery in Egypt. In reality, they were determined to claim the ancient lands of Judea and Samaria. Tricking the Israeli government, whose policy at the time was not to let Jews move into Arab cities and to allow the Arabs to lead their normal lives, the Levingers told the military governor that they wanted to spend Passover in Hebron, and took rooms at a hotel near the dusty entrance to the town. But after the holiday was over, the Levingers refused to leave. They yearned to be near the burial site of Abraham and his wife, Sarah; of Isaac and Rebecca; Jacob and Leah. Their goal was to settle in Hebron, this holy place where Jews had lived from the days of Abraham until the destruction of the Temple. Even afterward, small groups of Jews had lived there until the Arabs massacred sixty-seven of them in 1929 and the rest were forced to leave.

Seventy thousand Israelis have followed in the Levingers' footsteps, settling the sweeping hilltops of Judea and Samaria, boldly building their starkly modern compounds that look down so brazenly upon the old and crudely built Arab towns. For each of them Miriam Levinger is a model of the Jewish matriarch, a proud, persistent, pious woman, who rears her children in the spirit of Sarah and Rebecca and risks her life so that the Jews may live in the biblical Eretz Yisrael.

But the Arabs who have been living here were not so easily convinced nor so ready to give up their farms and their homes. Miriam Levinger's Jewish detractors—and they are many—believe that she has carried the word of God too far, defying the government of Israel and jeopardizing the lives of her countrymen. Since the days when the Levingers first arrived in Hebron, the town has become a microcosm of the conflict between the Palestinians and the Israelis: hundreds of Arabs and dozens of Jews have been killed; the Levingers' son-in-law has been imprisoned for life; Israeli politics have been torn asunder; and the very soul of Israel has come under question.

Around the corner from the teeming market is a small square where the mood is quieter and the air is still. Here a stone plaque marks the place where Aaron Gross, a nineteen-year-old talmudic student, was murdered and chopped up by four Arab boys several years ago. A few feet away, an enclave of white stone houses rises out of the earth, buildings so at one with the land that they look both ancient and modern, cavelike and contemporary. Israeli soldiers, wearing olive-green uniforms and carrying walkie-talkies and machine guns, stand on guard, some on the rooftops, some on the ground, placed there ostensibly to protect the few dozen Israeli families who live here from the Arabs. But some would argue that the defense force is present just as much to protect the Arabs from the Jews.

Above the soldiers is the old Jewish quarter of Hebron, where a dozen old houses cluster around the sixteenth-century Avraham Avinu synagogue. A flight of winding stone stairs leads up to the figure of a woman highlighted in the brilliant sunshine. Miriam Levinger stands proudly in front of her door, her hand resting near the mezuzah that proclaims this a Jewish home. In the tradition of orthodox women, her head is covered, a brown cloth pinned to her graying brown hair. She uses no cosmetics. A thin gold necklace and a plain gold wedding band are her only adornments.

She welcomes her visitors and brings them inside the thick stone house with its curved walls and arched ceilings that date from four hundred years ago; now she and her family rent their sparsely furnished home from the Israeli government. Up a few stone steps and to the right is the square kitchen, where a barely adequate refrigerator and small stove take care of the family's needs; although it is still early in the day, the smells of Shabbat dinner float through the air. A few more steps lead to the bedrooms where Miriam and her husband and the youngest five of their eleven children sleep. In the days when the Jordanians occupied this town, they razed the community's Avraham Avinu synagogue and used this house as a goat pen. Miriam laughs now as she refers to her children's dormitory as the "kids' room." She guides her guests to the living room with its cool tile floors and walls lined with leather-bound books, nods toward the sofa, covered casually with a gray jacquard cloth, and settles herself in a hard wooden chair.

"Do you mind if I smoke?" she asks in an accent that still smacks of New York, and lights a Montana, an Israeli cigarette. She draws in on the tobacco, admonishes herself because smoking is considered inappropriate for religious women, and compares her precarious existence now with what it was. "Life is easier here than in the east Bronx," she laughs. Her clear brown eyes smile from a face that has few lines, kept smooth perhaps by the purity of her vision. When she speaks seriously, her eyes have a distant, almost mystical gaze as though she were looking back into the past as well as into the future. At fifty years old, she is secure in her knowledge of who she is and why she is here.

"I am part of the Jewish people and I must do individually what the Jewish people as a whole has to do," she says. "Because of that I am sitting here in Hebron."

Hebron, the land of the patriarchs where Abraham paid four hundred shekels for a burial place for his wife, Sarah; Hebron, the land that David ruled for seven years before he went to Jerusalem; Hebron, sister city to Jerusalem and the second-holiest city for Jews. Miriam Levinger feels it is only natural that the Jews should be here now. To her, Hebron represents the beginnings, the place where the Jews grew as a biblical nation, and the place where they must grow again. She is a child of the Bible and believes that its message states clearly that Israel is the land of the Jews, the land where the Jews belong, and the land that they must serve.

"There are certain main themes in Jewish history," she says emphatically, "written down in black on white." She is a daughter of the Diaspora, a woman driven by the words *Next year in Jerusalem* and by the principle of Eretz Yisrael. Over and over she repeats the words of the Bible, "Israel I gave to you, I gave to Abraham, to Isaac and Jacob, Israel I gave to you." She takes her lessons from the rabbis of the Talmud, the prophets who begged the Jews to return from their exile in Babylon. She speaks of the wise men who blamed the Jews themselves for the destruction of the Second Temple in A.D. 70 because the Jewish people, content with life in Babylon, refused to return to Israel to rebuild their land. Miriam quotes Santayana ("If you don't learn from history, then you will be forced to relive it") and Barbara Tuchman ("She says there aren't really any reasons for anti-Semitism; there are always excuses"). She talks of the Holocaust, and of the blindness of the Jews in all of Europe—particularly in Germany, from which her husband's family fled, and in Hungary, from which her own grandparents could not. She tells about her cousin who now lives in Tel Aviv, but who more than forty years ago was an inmate in Auschwitz. There in the concentration camp, she watched as her mother, her sister, and her grandmother were led to the ovens and burned. Now Levinger says she takes it very seriously when Arab leaders say they want to destroy the Jews.

Miriam Levinger sees the future strength of Israel in the lessons of its past. "For the Jewish people to come into their own, after two thousand years of Diaspora, they have to start all over again," she says. "That begins from the tie to Israel." All Jews, she insists, "whether they are orthodox, reform, or secular, must recognize absolutely that there is only one place in the world to which they truly belong—and that is Israel."

At three A.M. on a cold April night during Passover, 1979, Miriam Levinger roused her seven small children from their sleep. Pulling them from their beds against their will, she squeezed their bare feet into their socks and shoes and buttoned up their coats over their pajamas. Over and over the children cried and complained and tried to climb back into their beds, but Miriam would not be stopped. Listening to her children's protests, she fought off fears that maybe she was crazy and told herself to remember the words of Rabbi Nachman of Breslau: "When a person wants to do a good deed, all the objections in the world suddenly rise up before his eyes." Several times she reminded herself of these words and fought off her own impulse to quit. Then, as the last child was buttoned up and ready to go, all of the children seemed to come alive and fall into the spirit of the plan. And at that moment, Miriam knew that the rabbi's spirit was with her and what she was doing was right.

When they had arrived in Hebron in 1968, the Levingers and their followers had gained a concession from the government and for the first two years were permitted to live as squatters inside the compound of the military governor. They continued their struggle, and in 1970 a compromise was reached: the Levingers were granted the right to live not inside but outside the city. They were given homes and land to settle in an area called Kiryat Arba. But after several years Miriam Levinger was still frustrated in her dream to penetrate the town. From the beginning she had told her husband, the spiritual leader of the settlement, that she wanted to establish a foothold smack in the center of the city. Now was the time to do it.

The Levingers conspired with several other couples, all of whom lived at Kiryat Arba, their compound in the hills above Hebron. Together the men had come up with a plan to take over a building once used by the army but now abandoned, save for a few Arab shops in the rear. The building, known as Beit Hadassah, had been established as a Jewish clinic, one of the first Hadassah projects completed at the beginning of the twentieth century. It was the site where the family of a Jewish pharmacist named Gershon was brutally murdered, the first victims of the Arab massacre in 1929. Now, by this very act of reclaiming the building, the settlers would begin to avenge the death of the Jews and, says Levinger, to "wipe out the shame of 1929."

Knowing that the government was against the idea of Israelis provoking the Arabs by living in their town, the settlers plotted to make their move under cover of darkness. They sent the women and children first so that the Israeli soldiers would neither attack them nor try to eject them from the house. With their thirty little ones bundled up, the twenty women, some of them pregnant, climbed onto the settlement's truck and lay down on the floor, hiding from the Israeli soldier on duty at the gate. They drove the few miles down the road to Hebron and steered the truck to the large stone building that once served as both a clinic and a school. From the truck they took a long ladder and leaned it against the building's walls. Slowly the women and children climbed up the ladder and, through a broken window, entered the house. To keep their offspring warm during the night, the women fed them oranges and matzos, and by daybreak the children started to sing. When the soldiers finally found them and asked how they had arrived, the youngsters told them they had been led there by Abraham, Isaac, and Jacob.

For more than a year some of the families lived in the house. At first the Israeli soldiers would not permit them to leave and reenter, and for six months they lived without water, electricity, or men. But after a while life became more normal, until January 1980, when Yoshua Saloma, a yeshiva student walking in the marketplace, was stabbed to death by an Arab. Saloma's murder became a rallying cry for the settlers. "Your death will be a service to our cause," Rabbi Meir Kahane, leader of the fanatical Kach movement, announced to Saloma's mourners, and the cycle of violence had begun.

After much debate in the Knesset, the government finally decided to give the settlers three locations inside Hebron: Beit Hadassah could be used as a yeshiva and home for several families; the decaying handful of houses and the synagogue in the Jewish quarter would be turned over to them; and the tombs of the patriarchs would be open to them for private worship at designated times.

The Arabs, finding the decision offensive, reacted in a panic and the mood turned black. The mayor of Hebron, Fahd Kawassme, organized mass gatherings and militant demonstrations in the streets. On the evening of May 1, a group of *cheder* yeshiva students on their way from synagogue to Beit Hadassah were attacked and shot by Arab terrorists. Six of the students, who were combining their studies with military duty, were instantly killed and several others badly wounded. Later that night the mayor of Hebron, the grand mufti of Hebron, and the mayor of neighboring Halhul were all deported.

Those who know the story from the Arab side tell it somewhat differently. Darwish Nasser, the Palestinian lawyer for the attackers, claims that the house called Beit Hadassah was not abandoned at all, but had been occupied by Arabs since 1929. "Arabs lived in the house," he says. "The women came and occupied the house and after that they threw the Arabs out." Adds Nasser, "Many, many ministers and officials condemned this step by the settlers." As he recalls the incident, the yeshiva students, who Miriam Levinger acknowledges were soldiers as well as students, had come from Kiryat Arba to pray at the tomb of the patriarchs. After prayers, says Nasser, the soldier-students "passed by Beit Hadassah to encourage the women and were singing and dancing in the streets." So, in what he admits was "a well-planned assassination . . . they were attacked by four Palestinians. Six were killed and about eighteen were injured."

The death of the students brought a terrible burden of guilt on Miriam

Levinger. Without her activities, everyone knew, the boys would not have been there; the heat of their mothers' anger burned through her. "After they were killed, I had to do a lot of thinking," she confesses. "I imagine that in their parents' hearts they felt that if perhaps their sons weren't in Hebron, then it wouldn't have happened." But then again, she says, "Being a Jew and being in Israel, if you're not attacked here, then you're attacked there. And if you're not attacked in Israel, then you're attacked in Brussels or in Istanbul." Even as she speaks, the squawking sounds of a walkie-talkie can be heard coming from her kitchen, a reminder that she and her neighbors live in constant fear of attack. From the little black box, she is always in communication with Hebronites in the settlements, in the local yeshivas, and in their cars, ready to reach for their guns and call in the army should a problem arise.

After the murder of the yeshiva students, the settlers raged with anger, furious not only at the Arabs but at the Israeli government and the army for not fully protecting them. Several years earlier, in 1974, in the aftermath of the Yom Kippur War and the first Israeli disengagement from the Sinai, some Israelis, including Rabbi Levinger, felt bitter about the withdrawal. In response, they had formed a group called Gush Emunim ("Bloc of the Faithful"), a fundamentalist religious organization whose purpose was to pursue with a vengeance the establishment of Israeli towns and villages in the occupied territories. After the Camp David Accords in 1978, members of the Gush Emunim felt its efforts had been thwarted and that they had been betrayed by the Begin government because it was willing to make peace with Egypt and to compromise the plan for settlement expansion. The Gush formed an underground group, which then masterminded a plot to destroy the holiest Moslem site in Jerusalem, the Dome of the Rock. Over the course of several years they developed a plan for twenty-four Israeli terrorists to use a mass of precision bombs, guns, and gas to blow up the mosque, leaving the surrounding site undamaged.

It was during the planning stages of this event that the yeshiva students were killed on their way to Beit Hadassah. The Gush Emunim members felt that the government had let them down and even abetted the Arab murderers, whom they believed to be members of a front organization for the PLO called the Palestinian National Guidance Committee. The committee of twenty-one members had been formed in order to stop any Palestinian segment from accepting the Camp David Accords. The very fact that the Israeli government allowed the committee to exist was seen by the Gush Emunim as a kind of complicity.

Three members of the Gush, young men who had grown up with the Levingers and had been nursed on the blood of Hebron and raised on the fodder of fanaticism, decided to take matters into their own hands. After two meetings in their homes, which were also attended by the rabbis, they drew up a scheme to bomb the cars of three Arab mayors, all of whom were active in the Palestinian National Guidance Committee. Their plan was not to kill the mayors, but to maim them, creating crippled symbols of Israeli revenge. In fact, two of the mayors lost their legs; the third escaped unharmed.

Over the course of the next few years tensions mounted and the air became more charged. Miriam Levinger recalls, "The situation was very, very tense. In Hebron the atmosphere was just like before a pogrom." This time, in broad daylight, a yeshiva student named Aaron Gross was murdered, his body chopped into pieces and left just outside the marketplace. At first the boy was mistaken for an Arab, and when Miriam Levinger, who had been trained as a nurse, was asked to help the bleeding victim, she refused.

The Gush Emunim group would not allow this murder to go unavenged. In July 1983 the same three fanatical Hebronites approached the Islamic college in Hebron and, just as classes were ending at lunchtime, threw hand grenades and fired guns at the students, killing three people and wounding thirty-three others.

As the violence continued, Arab terrorists killed more Israelis, and the Gush planned its last act of revenge. In 1984, with the endorsement of Hebron rabbis and almost certainly, though it remains unproven, with a nod from Moshe Levinger, the group plotted to blow up five buses filled with Arab passengers. Once again they meticulously laid out every detail of the action and carefully wired the buses under their fuel tanks so that the explosions would be devastating. But the Israeli secret police had discovered their activities, and moments after the wiring, the group were arrested. Later, when they were put on trial, the plot to destroy the Dome of the Rock was revealed. Three of the Jewish terrorists were sentenced to life imprisonment: one of them, Shaul Nir, lived next door to the Levingers and had helped to build their house; another, Menahamen Levni, had worked closely with Moshe Levinger and was in charge of developing the Jewish section of Hebron; the third was Uzi Sharbaf, the son-in-law of Moshe and Miriam Levinger.

"I had to think it out," she says now, as the wail of the muezzin in the background calls Moslems to noontime prayers. "What I think is that the government has to be firm and do what it should in order to protect the lives of the citizens." To her the Israeli government had not been firm enough with the Arabs and had not recognized their real intent. "We have to realize that what the Arabs write and what they proclaim and what they say, they really mean. If they have the Palestinian charter, that means they want to erase Israel physically and kill the Jews."

Miriam Levinger was born in Brooklyn and moved to the Bronx when she was five. Her parents had come to America in 1927, and for many of the Jews who escaped the persecutions in the ghettos of Germany and the pogroms in the *shtetls* of Eastern Europe, the Bronx was paradise. Home was in one of the dozens of apartment houses that lined the Grand Concourse or in the brownstones and tenements along the side streets. Jobs were readily available, just a subway ride away in Manhattan or, in the case of Miriam's father, in a nearby synagogue, where he was a cantor. Little Miriam lived with her family on Southern Boulevard and 163d Street and went to PS 75, only a few blocks away. But it wasn't recollections of the classroom that so vividly stayed with her. "I grew up with this memory of World War Two," she says, "my mother sitting by the window and crying. It's a childhood memory that forever goes with me. I'll never forget it when the people came to tell her how her parents were taken to Auschwitz and how they were killed." Miriam's eyes fill with tears and her voice tightens as she says, "Eighty percent of my family went up the chimney, and I grew up with that. That is what makes me tick. I am fulfilling a mission for all those who died." With those words the sound of revenge fills the air. Silently, perhaps even unconsciously, she sends a message that the Arabs who dare to live here will pay the price for the Jews who have died.

Miriam was a good student and her teachers recommended she attend Hunter High School in Manhattan, where students were screened and only the brighter ones were accepted. At Hunter the world unfolded, exposing her to a life that reached way beyond the ghettos of the Bronx. Like so many children of immigrant families, the girls she knew were anxious to be accepted into this new culture, eager to cast aside the weight of their Jewish past and to be assimilated into American society. Says Miriam, "They had an identity crisis. They didn't know if they were coming or going." But she had no such problem. "I had my priorities. I took my Jewish background seriously."

In addition to her high school classes, Miriam attended the Teachers Institute, where she took courses in the evening. With great fear, she would take the subway home from school every night, scared of the drunks and the weirdos who rode with her on the train. When she got off at her stop, her walk home was an obstacle course. "We had two bars on our street, and you always had drunks roaming the sidewalks and the gutters," she recalls. "I always had the feeling that any cuckoo would come along and kill me."

Now, she says, all you have to do is open a *New York Post* to see how many people are pointlessly murdered there every day. "For what sake do the Jews who live in New York risk their lives? For the sake of the Diaspora?"

• • •

Miriam Levinger says she is comfortable in this city of Moslem fundamentalists, comfortable in the streets, comfortable in the shops, comfortable with the people. "It's a very honest relationship," she says "much more honest than I had in America. We both know where the other stands."

Although the dialogue in Hebron between the Jews and Arabs is most often correct and to the point, once in a while there is room for a smile. The opponents even look to each other for answers to their seemingly insoluble problems. Not long ago, when her husband went to the Israeli bank where he does business, one of the Arab tellers stopped him. "How long till there will be peace, Rabbi?" the teller asked. "It will take at least one hundred years," Levinger replied. The Arab was taken aback: "You mean, I won't live to see it, and not even my son will live to see it?" Levinger laughed, and feeling generous he replied, "For you, fifty years."

The interaction here between the Jews and the Arabs is basically mercantile: the Jews need the Arabs for their goods and services, and the Arabs need the Jews for their business. But more than that, in some ways they have learned to live with one another, to understand each other's faith, even to speak each other's words.

Miriam is careful not to let the understandings move too far, and she keeps her conversations to a minimum. She has no Arab friends, and when she was invited to an Arab home, she refused. "I'll be very frank with you," she says. "The reason I don't encourage too close a relationship is because I saw in America that close relationships lead to assimilation." Besides, she adds, "The Arabs in Hebron, they also wouldn't like seeing intermarriages, and we don't like seeing intermarriages."

In this Moslem city where religion is as fundamental as food and water, where there are no hotels, and where movie theaters, liquor stores, and even a drop of beer is forbidden, no one begrudges another's religious needs "They respect religion," Miriam explains. "They're religious in Hebron and we're religious also. So on that we understand each other very well. When it comes to young girls or attitudes toward women, we understand each other very well."

They know each other's holidays and even respect the smaller rituals. They know the name of each special day, what it is for, and how it is celebrated. Just before one Purim, an early spring celebration when children dress up like kings and queens and use noisemakers to scare off the ancient Haman, (evil adviser to the Persian king Ahasuerus) Miriam went to a local Arab shop to buy some makeup. When she asked for the cosmetics, the sales clerk showed her some high-priced products. But the owner quickly realized that she needed the makeup for her children. "It's for *id el mashara*," he knowingly told the clerk, using the Arab name for Purim. "Their holiday is coming. Show her something cheap. She needs it for her daughters."

Routine chores, like going to the drugstore or shopping for food, fill her days. "I have five children at home," she explains. "I have laundry, and I have to cook, and I have to shop, and I have to clean. I'm busy the whole day just with housework."

But there are also moments of sheer joy, times spent once a week with a dozen or so other women who gather at the tombs of the patriarchs. There, in the center of Hebron, vestiges of earlier occupations still stand. On top of the steps and rounded stone walls built under the Roman King Herod, a large mosque stands from the seventh century A.D. Inside the Islamic building that encases the tombs, mosaic patterns decorate the stone floors, stained-glass panels grace the windows, and intricate paintings in blue and gold cover the ceilings. Elaborate pillars and minarets protect each tomb and set it off for the worshipers. On Fridays the mosque is open only to Moslems; at sundown, only the Jews are allowed to pray. Most of the time the system works, but the tension lately has been electric and fights have broken out.

Those who work here know that every Monday morning a group of Jewish women from Hebron come and set a circle of wooden folding chairs next to the tomb of Abraham and Sarah. Most of the women are young mothers in their twenties and thirties, dressed in skirts and blouses with large kerchiefs on their heads. Two of the women are Miriam's daughters; one is the wife of Uzi Sharbaf, the terrorist in prison. They come with their diapered infants in strollers, their older babies toddling along. On this June morning, the children wander around the circle, sometimes playing with their Fisher Price telephones and rattles, other times sharing their bottles and their teething rings. Across the hall from the women, three or four Moslems kneel on the ground and pray. The women, led by Miriam Levinger, take turns reading aloud psalms of David, Solomon, and Asaph and then say the ancient prayers by themselves. All of the group quietly say special prayers for women who are childless, for those who are sick, and for those who should marry. When one woman shed tears with her prayers, Miriam looked at her said, "She had something on her heart. She's crying bitterly to her mother, Sarah."

For Miriam the thousands of years since the days of Abraham have almost disappeared. "For us," she says, "four thousand years is like yesterday." She has skipped the space between generations and shortened the umbilical cord. She lives in the time of the Bible, walks in the steps of the patriarchs, and speaks to her ancestors as though they were her parents and she is their child. "With our forefathers the relationship is direct," she says. "We feel toward them as if we are their first children. And they feel toward us as if we are their first children."

Miriam's own children, raised to walk alone among the Arabs, are imbued with that same sense of history, that same closeness to their kin. When her oldest son, Ephraim, named for her grandfather who died in the Holocaust, reached the age of thirteen and was ready for his bar mitzvah, there was no question of where the ceremony would be. It took place in the courtyard of the cave of the Machpelah. Because of that, she says, her children continue their biblical lineage, even softening in their way some of the horror of the concentration camps and the Holocaust. "The victims didn't die, do you understand? Because we are continuing them, continuing them better than where they were."

The question of Who am I?, the searches for one's roots, the doubts of the Diaspora have no part in her children's lives. "They have a very strong sense of identity." she says. "I have highly motivated children who know why they were born and what they are alive for."

Miriam Levinger knows why she was born and where she will die. "I'm very happy to be part of this generation where the return has begun, the reawakening and the stirring as a Jew in my own land," she says. "All over the world, Jewish communities started with a few families coming in—look at Frankfurt or Baghdad—and the Jews settled down and eventually the population grew until it became a great Jewish community. This happened all over the world throughout history, and it can happen in Israel also. I think that eventually it's an evolutionary process; as time goes on, if the Jews are secure in themselves and secure in their sovereignty over Eretz Yisrael, then the Arabs themselves will receive the idea of Jewish sovereignty. And those who don't, well, they have somewhere to go. Those Arabs who accept the situation will remain, and those who don't accept it, won't." As for the possibility of giving up Judea and Samaria, she adds, "I don't contemplate it, because I believe in truth." For the Arabs who live there, the truth may look a little different. But for Miriam Levinger, the truth is in the past, and the past is in the future.

John Wallach and Janet Wallach, eds., *Still Small Voices* (San Diego: Harcourt Brace Jovanovich, 1989), 22–34, 36–40.

PART III

REFLECTING

Chapter 9

Ideas for Exploration

The complexity of the Arab-Israeli conflict and the unresolved dimensions of the peace process suggest several ideas for further reflection and exploration. These could be carried out as projects jointly by several students or prepared as individual, thoughtful responses to the dilemmas presented. An effective way to convey the differences among Israeli Jews, Israeli Arabs, and Palestinians is to set up projects where these different roles are assigned in debates, discussions, or performances. The suggested ideas are grouped loosely into themes that are covered in the volume. Many of the questions do not have "obvious" or "correct" answers. They are listed as ideas or thoughts for reflection and investigation. Additional information and insights can be found in the books that have been included as suggested readings in the bibliography.

DIVERSITY

What are the major sources of diversity among Jews and among Arabs? Do Israeli Jews who originate from Muslim countries have greater insight into the Israeli-Arab community than Israeli Jews from European countries?

In what contexts might Israeli Arabs identify as Israelis and when might they identify themselves as Palestinians?

What are the constructive ways that ethnic cultural continuities can be transmitted to the native-born second and third generations?

Does the Israeli government's policy of facilitating the process by which Jewish immigrants become Israelis conflict with the policy of multiculturalism where the original rich cultural traditions of each community is reinforced and retained? How can you balance assimilation and cultural distinctiveness among immigrants and their children?

How might the Israeli government institute a policy of incorporation of Israeli Arabs into Israeli society while retaining Arab cultural distinctiveness?

ETHNIC AND MINORITY STATUS

Jews and Arabs are often defined as ethnic/national groups, religious groups, or minority groups. What are the main features that make Jews or Arabs an ethnic, religious, or minority group? What are the implications of classifying Arabs and Jews in one way or the other?

Compare the minority status of Israeli Arabs with minorities in other countries. Explain how the situation of Israeli Arabs resembles the situation of African Americans or Americans of Hispanic origins? What might be the best parallels among American ethnic groups for Jews who have immigrated to Israel from Middle Eastern countries?

Are Jews from different countries assimilating in Israel society? Which countries of origin among Jews would have the easiest and most rapid assimilation in Israel? What characteristics of the Israeli born of foreign-born parents would make them feel more Israeli?

How does the fact that Jews who immigrated to Israel come from countries where they were considered a minority influence how they treat the Arab minorities who are their neighbors?

HOMELAND

Compare the notions of "homeland" or "coming home" or feeling at home among Palestinians who are able to visit their family's home in the State of Israel but cannot move back. How does the Palestinian notion of homeland compare to the notion of homeland among immigrants who are Jewish returning home after many generations and 2,000 years?

Arab Palestinians often view themselves in "exile" from their homeland. Jews living in Israel often view Jews living in countries outside of Israel as in "exile." Compare the "exile" imagery of these two communities, their similarities and differences.

FAMILIES AND GENDER

One indicator of whether a group "assimilates" is the extent of marriage between groups of different origins. What might be the barriers to intermarriages between Israeli Jews and Israeli Arabs? Think about a family where the father is Muslim and the mother is Jewish. What issues do you foresee as problems for them, their children, and the members of their extended families?

How might the school experiences of young Jews and Arabs differ among women and men? Do you think that young girls would have greater or fewer difficulties than young boys in identifying with the Palestinian desire for a state?

THE MILITARY AND EDUCATION

How might the army experience of most Jewish young men and women influence their views of the Arab-Israeli conflict?

Could there be a parallel experience for Arab Israelis that would generate their national loyalty to the State of Israel in place of the military experience of young adult Israeli Jews?

How might the required military service among young Israeli Jews influence the way in which they view their national loyalties? How might experience in the military affect the ways in which they view the ethnic diversity among Jews?

If you were writing a text for use in the Israeli public school system, how might you portray the Arab-Israeli conflict? Could you use the same textbook for both Jewish and Arab schools?

Most Arabs and Jews live in segregated communities. Would a policy of residential integration result in greater understanding between these communities? Are there precedents elsewhere that would help you make the case for residential integration stronger?

Israel is one of the countries in which church and state are not separated. Government offices regulate religious activities of various communities. Religion influences family life in Israel directly. Would there be any benefits for the government to adopt a doctrine of separation of Church and State? What would be the negative consequences of such a policy?

POLITICS AND POLICIES

How might you reorganize the celebration of Israel's national independence in such a way that it would incorporate the Arab-Israeli minority?

What policies might you suggest to reduce the clashes between Palestinians and Jews on the West Bank?

What might be the place of Jews in an Arab State of Palestine if it were established? How would it parallel the place of the Arabs in the State of Israel? How would you organize the position of both minorities to result in greater equalities?

POPULAR CULTURE

How might television be used to reduce the conflicts between Jews and Arabs in Israel? How might television be used to reduce the differences between Palestinian Arabs and Israeli Arabs, and between Israeli Jews and Jews in other countries?

Design a video to portray the daily life of a Russian immigrant family in Israel, an Israeli-Arab family, a Palestinian family in Gaza, and a Jewish settler family on the West Bank. What features would you select to display their similarities and differences?

Appendix: Official Documents

Five official documents are included in this appendix, plus a letter. Each of these documents represents a formal statement about the goals and background of the participants in the Arab-Israeli conflict or international agencies that have tried to curtail the conflict. More detailed documents can be found in the volumes listed in the bibliography at the end of this volume. For the early period, see the policy details in the two volumes of the Esco Foundation for Palestine. On the legal aspects of the conflict itself, see the three volumes edited by John Norton Moore on *The Arab-Israeli Conflict*. On the more recent period, see Yehuda Lukacs, *The Israeli-Palestinian Conflict*. Some other documents can be generated from the Web sites of the Israeli government or the Arab and Palestinian Web sites listed in the bibliography.

THE DECLARATION OF THE ESTABLISHMENT OF THE STATE OF ISRAEL
MAY 14, 1948

This document was prepared on May 14, 1948, on the day on which the British mandate over Palestine expired. The Jewish People's council gathered in Tel Aviv and approved the proclamation declaring the establishment of the State of Israel. The United States recognized the new state within a few hours. Three days later, the State of Israel was officially recognized by the Soviet Union.

There are several points to notice in this document. First, note the use of the traditional historical name of Palestine, the Land of Israel, and the anchoring of the new state in the context of the previous history of the Jewish people and their long exile. Second, note the description of the early pioneers and their goals. The legal rights of the Jewish people are reviewed, as is the importance of the Holocaust and the Jews who want to immigrate to the new country. As part of the background, the document calls attention to the recognition by the United Nations of the rights of Jews, like other nations, to their own sovereign state.

This preamble is followed by the declaration itself. The first item focuses on immigration and "Ingathering of Exiles" with a strong statement about the continuity of the Jewish people from the Prophets of Israel as a guide to a peaceful and just nation. At the same time, the reference to the Prophets of the Hebrew Bible points to the ancient claims on the Land of Israel by the Jewish people. Freedom is guaranteed for the people in the new country. There is also an appeal to the Arab inhabitants of the State of Israel to participate in the building of the state on the basis of full and equal citizenship. There is an implicit appeal for peace with the Arab states in the region. There is an appeal as well to the Jewish communities around the world to share in the "redemption" of Israel. David Ben-Gurion and thirty-six officials representing the Jewish community signed the document.

ERETZ-ISRAEL [(Hebrew)—the Land of Israel, Palestine] was the birthplace of the Jewish people. Here their spiritual, religious and political identity was shaped. Here they first attained to statehood, created cultural values of national and universal significance and gave to the world the eternal Book of Books.

After being forcibly exiled from their land, the people kept faith with it throughout their Dispersion and never ceased to pray and hope for their return to it and for the restoration in it of their political freedom.

Impelled by this historic and traditional attachment, Jews strove in every successive generation to re-establish themselves in their ancient homeland. In recent decades they returned in their masses. Pioneers, ma'pilim [(Hebrew)—immigrants coming to Eretz-Israel in defiance of restrictive legislation] and defenders, they made deserts bloom, revived the Hebrew language, built villages and towns, and created a thriving community controlling its own economy and culture, loving peace but knowing how to defend itself, bringing the blessings of progress to all the country's inhabitants, and aspiring towards independent nationhood.

In the year 5657 (1897), at the summons of the spiritual father of the Jewish State, Theodore Herzl, the First Zionist Congress convened and proclaimed the right of the Jewish people to national rebirth in its own country.

This right was recognized in the Balfour Declaration of the 2nd November, 1917, and re-affirmed in the Mandate of the League of Nations which, in particular, gave international sanction to the historic connection between the Jewish people and Eretz-Israel and to the right of the Jewish people to rebuild its National Home.

The catastrophe which recently befell the Jewish people—the massacre of millions of Jews in Europe—was another clear demonstration of the urgency of solving the problem of its homelessness by re-establishing in Eretz-Israel the Jewish State, which would open the gates of the homeland wide to every Jew and confer upon the Jewish people the status of a fully privileged member of the community of nations.

Survivors of the Nazi holocaust in Europe, as well as Jews from other parts of the world, continued to migrate to Eretz-Israel, undaunted by difficulties, restrictions and dangers, and never ceased to assert their right to a life of dignity, freedom and honest toil in their national homeland.

In the Second World War, the Jewish community of this country contributed its full share to the struggle of the freedom- and peace-loving nations against the forces of Nazi wickedness and, by the blood of its soldiers and its war effort, gained the right to be reckoned among the peoples who founded the United Nations.

On the 29th November, 1947, the United Nations General Assembly passed a resolution calling for the establishment of a Jewish State in Eretz-Israel; the General Assembly required the inhabitants of Eretz-Israel to take such steps as were necessary on their part for the implementation of that resolution. This recognition by the United Nations of the right of the Jewish people to establish their State is irrevocable.

This right is the natural right of the Jewish people to be masters of their own fate, like all other nations, in their own sovereign State.

ACCORDINGLY WE, MEMBERS OF THE PEOPLE'S COUNCIL, REPRESENTATIVES OF THE JEWISH COMMUNITY OF ERETZ-ISRAEL AND OF THE ZIONIST MOVEMENT, ARE HERE ASSEMBLED ON THE DAY OF THE TERMINATION OF THE BRITISH MANDATE OVER ERETZ-ISRAEL AND, BY VIRTUE OF OUR NATURAL AND HISTORIC RIGHT AND ON THE STRENGTH OF THE RESOLUTION OF THE UNITED NATIONS GENERAL ASSEMBLY,

HEREBY DECLARE THE ESTABLISHMENT OF A JEWISH STATE IN ERETZ-ISRAEL, TO BE KNOWN AS THE STATE OF ISRAEL.

WE DECLARE that, with effect from the moment of the termination of the Mandate being tonight, the eve of Sabbath, the 6th Iyar, 5708 (15th May, 1948), until the establishment of the elected, regular authorities of the State in accordance with the Constitution which shall be adopted by the Elected Constituent Assembly not later than the 1st October 1948, the People's Council shall act as a Provisional Council of State, and its executive organ, the People's Administration, shall be the Provisional Government of the Jewish State, to be called "Israel."

THE STATE OF ISRAEL will be open for Jewish immigration and for the Ingathering of the Exiles; it will foster the development of the country for the benefit of all its inhabitants; it will be based on freedom, justice and peace as envisaged by the prophets of Israel; it will ensure complete equality of social and political rights to all its inhabitants irrespective of religion, race or sex; it will guarantee freedom of religion, conscience, language, education and culture; it will safeguard the Holy Places of all religions; and it will be faithful to the principles of the Charter of the United Nations.

THE STATE OF ISRAEL is prepared to cooperate with the agencies and representatives of the United Nations in implementing the resolution of the General Assembly of the 29th November, 1947, and will take steps to bring about the economic union of the whole of Eretz-Israel.

WE APPEAL to the United Nations to assist the Jewish people in the building-up of its State and to receive the State of Israel into the comity of nations.

WE APPEAL—in the very midst of the onslaught launched against us now for months—to the Arab inhabitants of the State of Israel to preserve peace and participate in the upbuilding of the State on the basis of full and equal citizenship and due representation in all its provisional and permanent institutions.

WE EXTEND our hand to all neighbouring states and their peoples in an offer of peace and good neighbourlines, and appeal to them to establish bonds of cooperation and mutual help with the sovereign Jewish people settled in its own land. The State of Israel is prepared to do its share in a common effort for the advancement of the entire Middle East.

WE APPEAL to the Jewish people throughout the Diaspora to rally round the Jews of Eretz-Israel in the tasks of immigration and upbuilding and to stand by them in the great struggle for the realization of the age-old dream—the redemption of Israel.

PLACING OUR TRUST IN THE ALMIGHTY, WE AFFIX OUR SIGNATURES TO THIS PROCLAMATION AT THIS SESSION OF THE PROVISIONAL COUNCIL OF STATE, ON THE SOIL OF THE

HOMELAND, IN THE CITY OF TEL-AVIV, ON THIS SABBATH EVE, THE 5TH DAY OF IYAR, 5708 (14TH MAY, 1948).

Published in the Official Gazette, No. 1 of the 5th Iyar, 5708 (14th May, 1948).

THE PALESTINE NATIONAL CHARTER: RESOLUTIONS OF THE PALESTINE NATIONAL COUNCIL JULY 1968

This is the officially translated document by the Palestine Liberation Organization (PLO) based on earlier text adopted in 1964.

This document contains thirty-three articles. The articles demonstrate the fundamental goals of the PLO with regard to the armed struggle against Israel to liberate their land and establish their own state of Palestine. Included at the end of the document is a letter written in September 1993, by Yassar Arafat, the recognized leader of the Palestinians, to Yitzhak Rabin, then prime minister of the State of Israel, stating that those articles that deny Israel's right to exit are no longer valid. These articles of the charter are inconsistent with the PLO's new commitment to Israel following their mutual recognition. (The articles that are no longer valid include Articles 7, 8, 9, 10, 11, 15, 19, 20, 21, 22, and 23.) This letter refers to United Nations documents (discussed below), the renunciation of terror and violence, and the dawning of a new era in the relationship of the PLO to the State of Israel.

The charter begins with the historic role of Palestine as the homeland of the Arab Palestinians and refers back to Palestine of the British period. Palestinians are clearly defined in Article 6, and Jews who had lived in Palestine before the beginning of the Zionist immigration (the end of the nineteenth century) are also Palestinians. Other Jews living in Israel, the overwhelming majority of the Jewish population of the state, would not be included in the Palestinian state. In their struggle for independence, Zionism is associated with imperialism. While rejecting this article subsequently, the original formulation noted the centrality of armed struggle as an overall strategy, with the goal of national self-determination and sovereignty. The links between the Arab nation and the Palestinians are also emphasized. The connections between the struggle for independence and religious ideology is clear as well from the document. The previous international recognition of the State of Israel is rejected. Note the definition of Jews as a religion (and not a nation or people); hence Jews are only citizens of the country in which they reside. Jews in this view are not a "people" nor do they have a national identity.

An interesting exercise is to compare this document, particularly the striking parallels (as well as some obvious differences), to the document prepared to declare statehood of Israel.

> The following is the complete and unabridged text of the Palestinian National Covenant, as published officially in English by the PLO,* based largely on the text adopted earlier in 1964.
>
> In his letter of September 9, 1993, to Prime Minister Rabin, Yassar Arafat stated that those articles that deny Israel's right to exist or are inconsistent with the PLO's new commitments to Israel following their mutual recognition, are no longer valid. Several of the key articles to be amended are highlighted.

Text of the Chapter:
Article 1: Palestine is the homeland of the Arab Palestinian people; it is an indivisible part of the Arab homeland, and the Palestinian people are an integral part of the Arab nation.

Article 2: Palestine, with the boundaries it had during the British Mandate, is an indivisible territorial unit.

Article 3: The Palestinian Arab people possess the legal right to their homeland and have the right to determine their destiny after achieving the liberation of their country in accordance with their wishes and entirely of their own accord and will.

Article 4: The Palestinian identity is a genuine, essential, and inherent characteristic; it is transmitted from parents to children. The Zionist occupation and the dispersal of the Palestinian Arab people, through the disasters which befell them, do not make them lose their Palestinian identity and their membership in the Palestinian community, nor do they negate them.

Article 5: The Palestinians are those Arab nationals who, until 1947, normally resided in Palestine regardless of whether they were evicted from it or have stayed there. Anyone born, after that date, of a Palestinian father—whether inside Palestine or outside it—is also a Palestinian.

Article 6: The Jews who had normally resided in Palestine until the beginning of the Zionist invasion will be considered Palestinians.

Article 7: That there is a Palestinian community and that it has material,

---

*English rendition as published in *Basic Political Documents of the Armed Palestinian Resistance Movement*, Leila S. Kadi (Beirut: Palestine Research Center, December 1969), 137–41.

spiritual, and historical connection with Palestine are indisputable facts. It is a national duty to bring up individual Palestinians in an Arab revolutionary manner. All means of information and education must be adopted in order to acquaint the Palestinian with his country in the most profound manner, both spiritual and material, that is possible. He must be prepared for the armed struggle and ready to sacrifice his wealth and his life in order to win back his homeland and bring about its liberation.

Article 8: The phase in their history, through which the Palestinian people are now living, is that of national (*watani*) struggle for the liberation of Palestine. Thus the conflicts among the Palestinian national forces are secondary, and should be ended for the sake of the basic conflict that exists between the forces of Zionism and of imperialism on the one hand, and the Palestinian Arab people on the other. On this basis the Palestinian masses, regardless of whether they are residing in the national homeland or in diaspora (*mahajir*) constitute—both their organizations and the individuals—one national front working for the retrieval of Palestine and its liberation through armed struggle.

Article 9: Armed struggle is the only way to liberate Palestine. This is the overall strategy, not merely a tactical phase. The Palestinian Arab people assert their absolute determination and firm resolution to continue their armed struggle and to work for an armed popular revolution for the liberation of their country and their return to it. They also assert their right to normal life in Palestine and to exercise their right to self-determination and sovereignty over it.

Article 10: Commando action constitutes the nucleus of the Palestinian popular liberation war. This requires its escalation, comprehensiveness, and the mobilization of all the Palestinian popular and educational efforts and their organization and involvement in the armed Palestinian revolution. It also requires the achieving of unity for the national (*watani*) struggle among the different groupings of the Palestinian people, and between the Palestinian people and the Arab masses, so as to secure the continuation of the revolution, its escalation, and victory.

Article 11: The Palestinians will have three mottoes: national (*wataniyya*) unity, national (*qawmiyya*) mobilization, and liberation.

Article 12: The Palestinian people believe in Arab unity. In order to contribute their share toward the attainment of that objective, however, they must, at the present stage of their struggle, safeguard their Palestinian identity and develop their consciousness of that identity, and oppose any plan that may dissolve or impair it.

Article 13: Arab unity and the liberation of Palestine are two complementary objectives, the attainment of either of which facilitates the attainment of the other. Thus, Arab unity leads to the liberation of Palestine, the liberation of Palestine leads to Arab unity; and work toward the realization of one objective proceeds side by side with work toward the realization of the other.

Article 14: The destiny of the Arab nation, and indeed Arab existence itself, depend upon the destiny of the Palestine cause. From this interdependence springs the Arab nation's pursuit of, and striving for, the liberation of Palestine. The people of Palestine play the role of the vanguard in the realization of this sacred (*qawmi*) goal.

Article 15: The liberation of Palestine, from an Arab viewpoint, is a national (*qawmi*) duty and it attempts to repel the Zionist and imperialist aggression against the Arab homeland, and aims at the elimination of Zionism in Palestine. Absolute responsibility for this falls upon the Arab nation—peoples and governments—with the Arab people of Palestine in the vanguard. Accordingly, the Arab nation must mobilize all its military, human, moral, and spiritual capabilities to participate actively with the Palestinian people in the liberation of Palestine. It must, particularly in the phase of the armed Palestinian revolution, offer and furnish the Palestinian people with all possible help, and material and human support, and make available to them the means and opportunities that will enable them to continue to carry out their leading role in the armed revolution, until they liberate their homeland.

Article 16: The liberation of Palestine, from a spiritual point of view, will provide the Holy Land with an atmosphere of safety and tranquility, which in turn will safeguard the country's religious sanctuaries and guarantee freedom of worship and of visit to all, without discrimination of race, color, language, or religion. Accordingly, the people of Palestine look to all spiritual forces in the world for support.

Article 17: The liberation of Palestine, from a human point of view, will restore to the Palestinian individual his dignity, pride, and freedom. Accordingly the Palestinian Arab people look forward to the support of all those who believe in the dignity of man and his freedom in the world.

Article 18: The liberation of Palestine, from an international point of view, is a defensive action necessitated by the demands of self-defense. Accordingly the Palestinian people, desirous as they are of the friendship of all people, look to freedom-loving, and peace-loving states for support in order to restore their legitimate rights in Palestine, to re-establish peace and security in the country, and to enable its people to exercise national sovereignty and freedom.

Article 19: The partition of Palestine in 1947 and the establishment of the state of Israel are entirely illegal, regardless of the passage of time, because they were contrary to the will of the Palestinian people and to their natural right in their homeland, and inconsistent with the principles embodied in the Charter of the United Nations, particularly the right to self-determination.

Article 20: The Balfour Declaration, the Mandate for Palestine, and everything that has been based upon them, are deemed null and void. Claims of historical or religious ties of Jews with Palestine are incompatible with the facts of history and the true conception of what constitutes statehood. Judaism, being a religion, is not an independent nationality. Nor do Jews constitute a single nation with an identity of its own; they are citizens of the states to which they belong.

Article 21: The Arab Palestinian people, expressing themselves by the armed Palestinian revolution, reject all solutions which are substitutes for the total liberation of Palestine and reject all proposals aiming at the liquidation of the Palestinian problem, or its internationalization.

Article 22: Zionism is a political movement organically associated with international imperialism and antagonistic to all action for liberation and to progressive movements in the world. It is racist and fanatic in its nature, aggressive, expansionist, and colonial in its aims, and fascist in its methods. Israel is the instrument of the Zionist movement, and geographical base for world imperialism placed strategically in the midst of the Arab homeland to combat the hopes of the Arab nation for liberation, unity, and progress. Israel is a constant source of threat vis-a-vis peace in the Middle East and the whole world. Since the liberation of Palestine will destroy the Zionist and imperialist presence and will contribute to the establishment of peace in the Middle East, the Palestinian people look for the support of all the progressive and peaceful forces and urge them all, irrespective of their affiliations and beliefs, to offer the Palestinian people all aid and support in their just struggle for the liberation of their homeland.

Article 23: The demand of security and peace, as well as the demand of right and justice, require all states to consider Zionism an illegitimate movement, to outlaw its existence, and to ban its operations, in order that friendly relations among peoples may be preserved, and the loyalty of citizens to their respective homelands safeguarded.

Article 24: The Palestinian people believe in the principles of justice, freedom, sovereignty, self-determination, human dignity, and in the right of all peoples to exercise them.

Article 25: For the realization of the goals of this Charter and its principles, the Palestine Liberation Organization will perform its role in the liberation of Palestine in accordance with the Constitution of this Organization.

Article 26: The Palestine Liberation Organization, representative of the Palestinian revolutionary forces, is responsible for the Palestinian Arab people's movement in its struggle—to retrieve its homeland, liberate and return to it and exercise the right to self-determination in it—in all military, political, and financial fields and also for whatever may be required by the Palestine case on the inter-Arab and international levels.

Article 27: The Palestine Liberation Organization shall cooperate with all Arab states, each according to its potentialities; and will adopt a neutral policy among them in the light of the requirements of the war of liberation; and on this basis it shall not interfere in the internal affairs of any Arab state.

Article 28: The Palestinian Arab people assert the genuineness and independence of their national (*wataniyya*) revolution and reject all forms of intervention, trusteeship, and subordination.

Article 29: The Palestinian people possess the fundamental and genuine legal right to liberate and retrieve their homeland. The Palestinian people determine their attitude toward all states and forces on the basis of the stands they adopt vis-a-vis to the Palestinian revolution to fulfill the aims of the Palestinian people.

Article 30: Fighters and carriers of arms in the war of liberation are the nucleus of the popular army which will be the protective force for the gains of the Palestinian Arab people.

Article 31: The Organization shall have a flag, an oath of allegiance, and an anthem. All this shall be decided upon in accordance with a special regulation.

Article 32: Regulations, which shall be known as the Constitution of the Palestinian Liberation Organization, shall be annexed to this Charter. It will lay down the manner in which the Organization, and its organs and institutions, shall be constituted; the respective competence of each; and the requirements of its obligation under the Charter.

Article 33: This Charter shall not be amended save by [vote of] a majority of two-thirds of the total membership of the National Congress of the Palestine Liberation Organization [taken] at a special session convened for that purpose.

UN SECURITY COUNCIL RESOLUTION 242, NOVEMBER 1967

Following the Six-Day War in 1967 and the Israeli occupation of territories previously under the control of Egypt, Jordan, and Syria, the Security Council of the United Nations adopted Resolution 242. This document became the foundation of almost all diplomatic efforts to solve the Palestinian-Israeli question.

The resolution emphasizes the issue of acquiring territory by war and the need for peaceful resolution of the issues. In article 1, there is a statement about the withdrawal of Israeli armed forces from the territories acquired in the conflict. The translation of this United Nations document into various languages inserts the article "the" before the word territories, implying that withdrawal should be from *all* the territories. Israel interprets the document without the article "the," implying withdrawal from territories but not necessarily all the territories. There is also an emphasis on the sovereignty of all the states in the area. The guarantee of free navigation through international waterways and the settlement of the refugee problem were also included in the resolution.

The Security Council,

Expressing its continuing concern with the grave situation in the Middle East,

Emphasizing the inadmissibility of the acquisition of territory by war and the need to work for a just and lasting peace in which every State in the area can live in security,

Emphasizing further that all Member States in their acceptance of the Charter of the United Nations have undertaken a commitment to act in accordance with Article 2 of the Charter,

1. Affirms that the fulfillment of Charter principles requires the establishment of a just and lasting peace in the Middle East which should include the application of both the following principles:

Withdrawal of Israeli armed forces from territories occupied in the recent conflict;

Termination of all claims or states of belligerency and respect for and acknowledgement of the sovereignty, territorial integrity and political independence of every State in the area and their right to live in peace within secure and recognized boundaries free from threats or acts of force;

2. Affirms further the necessity

For guaranteeing freedom of navigation through international waterways in the area;

For achieving a just settlement of the refugee problem;

For guaranteeing the territorial inviolability and political independence of every State in the area, through measures including the establishment of demilitarized zones;

3. Requests the Secretary General to designate a Special Representative to proceed to the Middle East to establish and maintain contacts with the States concerned in order to promote agreement and assist efforts to achieve a peaceful and accepted settlement in accordance with the provisions and principles in this resolution;

UN SECURITY COUNCIL RESOLUTION 338, OCTOBER 1973

This document has often been combined with UN Security Council Resolution 242 as an international statement about the processes of a peaceful resolution of the Arab-Israeli conflict. It was passed during the 1973 war between Israel and Egypt and Syria in an attempt to stop the fighting.

The Security Council,
1. Calls upon all parties to present fighting to cease all firing and terminate all military activity immediately, no later than 12 hours after the moment of the adoption of this decision, in the positions after the moment of the adoption of this decision, in the positions they now occupy;
2. Calls upon all parties concerned to start immediately after the cease-fire the implementation of Security Council Resolution 242 (1967) in all of its parts;
3. Decides that, immediately and concurrently with the cease-fire, negotiations start between the parties concerned under appropriate auspices aimed at establishing a just and durable peace in the Middle East.

LETTER FROM YASSAR ARAFAT TO PRIME MINISTER RABIN

In 1993 Yassar Arafat, Chairman of the Palestine Liberation Organization (PLO) wrote a formal letter to Yitzhak Rabin, then the Prime Minister of Israel. The letter emphasizes several key themes. The first theme is the PLO recognition of the legitimacy of the State of Israel and "the right of the State of Israel to exist in peace and security." Second, the PLO was committing itself to a peaceful resolution of the conflict, where negotiations rather than an armed struggle was to become the basis of the relationship. The period is therefore defined as a "a new epoch" where the PLO renounces terrorism. Third, the letter clearly emphasizes that the PLO was the political unit of responsibility to implement the new relationship between Palestinians and the State of Israel. Finally, the letter points to the end of those parts of the Palestinian Covenant that were incon-

4. Requests the Secretary-General to report to the Security Council on the progress of the efforts of the Special Representative as soon as possible.

Appendix: Official Documents 211

sistent with the spirit of the letter. Through this formal document, Arafat was publicly establishing a new basis of relationships between the political representatives of the Palestinians and the State of Israel. The foundation of which were negotiations to solve disputes, a formal rejection of the formal policy, ideology of armed struggle, and violence against the State.

September 9, 1993
Yitzhak Rabin
Prime Minister of Israel

Mr. Prime Minister,
The signing of the Declaration of Principles marks a new era in the history of the Middle East. In firm conviction thereof, I would like to confirm the following PLO commitments:

The PLO recognizes the right of the State of Israel to exist in peace and security.

The PLO accepts United Nations Security Council Resolutions 242 and 338.

The PLO commits itself to the Middle East peace process, and to a peaceful resolution of the conflict between the two sides and declares that all outstanding issues relating to permanent status will be resolved through negotiations.

The PLO considers that the signing of the Declaration of Principles constitutes a historic event, inaugurating a new epoch of peaceful coexistence, free from violence and all other acts which endanger peace and stability. Accordingly, the PLO renounces the use of terrorism and other acts of violence and will assume responsibility over all PLO elements and personnel in order to assure their compliance, prevent violations and discipline violators.

In view of the promise of a new era and the signing of the Declaration of Principles and based on Palestinian acceptance of Security Council Resolutions 242 and 338, the PLO affirms that those articles of the Palestinian Covenant which deny Israel's right to exist, and the provisions of the Covenant which are inconsistent with the commitments of this letter are now inoperative and no longer valid. Consequently, the PLO undertakes to submit to the Palestinian National Council for formal approval the necessary changes in regard to the Palestinian Covenant.

Sincerely,
Yassar Arafat
Chairman
The Palestine Liberation Organization

CAMP DAVID ACCORDS, SEPTEMBER 1978

The Camp David accords was signed by Egyptian President Anwar Sadat and Menachem Begin, the prime minister of Israel, under the auspices of U.S. President Jimmy Carter. Most of the document deals with the future of Sinai, which was then occupied by Israel. The other important part was the granting of "autonomy" for those on the West Bank and Gaza. While the agreement was between Egypt and Israel, the key to the importance of the document rests with the interpretation of the future of the West Bank and Gaza. The implementation of these accords has not been completed for the West Bank.

This document refers to the visit by Sadat to Jerusalem in 1977 and the opportunities that the visit created for establishing peace in the Middle East. The emphasis in this document, as in United Nations Resolutions 242 and 338, is for the territorial integrity of all states in the region. This was a de facto recognition of the State of Israel as a state with rights and political sovereignty. In one interpretation, the formulation of this statement implies directly that the Palestinians had not yet achieved this "state" form of political recognition.

Muhammad Anwar al-Sadat, President of the Arab Republic of Egypt, and Menachem Begin, Prime Minister of Israel, met with Jimmy Carter, President of the United States of America, at Camp David from September 5 to September 17, 1978, and have agreed on the following framework for peace in the Middle East. They invite other parties to the Arab-Israel conflict to adhere to it.

Preamble

The search for peace in the Middle East must be guided by the following:
The agreed basis for a peaceful settlement of the conflict between Israel and its neighbors is United Nations Security Council Resolution 242, in all its parts.
After four wars during 30 years, despite intensive human efforts, the Middle East, which is the cradle of civilization and the birthplace of three great religions, does not enjoy the blessings of peace. The people of the Middle East yearn for peace so that the vast human and natural resources of the region can be turned to the pursuits of peace and so that this area can become a model for coexistence and cooperation among nations.
The historic initiative of President Sadat in visiting Jerusalem and the

reception accorded to him by the parliament, government and people of Israel, and the reciprocal visit of Prime Minister Begin to Ismailia, the peace proposals made by both leaders, as well as the warm reception of these missions by the peoples of both countries, have created an unprecedented opportunity for peace which must not be lost if this generation and future generations are to be spared the tragedies of war.

The provisions of the Charter of the United Nations and the other accepted norms of international law and legitimacy now provide accepted standards for the conduct of relations among all states.

To achieve a relationship of peace, in the spirit of Article 2 of the United Nations Charter, future negotiations between Israel and any neighbor prepared to negotiate peace and security with it are necessary for the purpose of carrying out all the provisions and principles of Resolutions 242 and 338.

Peace requires respect for the sovereignty, territorial integrity and political independence of every state in the area and their right to live in peace within secure and recognized boundaries free from threats or acts of force.

Progress toward that goal can accelerate movement toward a new era of reconciliation in the Middle East marked by cooperation in promoting economic development, in maintaining stability and in assuring security.

Security is enhanced by a relationship of peace and by cooperation between nations which enjoy normal relations. In addition, under the terms of peace treaties, the parties can, on the basis of reciprocity, agree to special security arrangements such as demilitarized zones, limited armaments areas, early warning stations, the presence of international forces, liaison, agreed measures for monitoring and other arrangements that they agree are useful.

Framework

Taking these factors into account, the parties are determined to reach a just, comprehensive, and durable settlement of the Middle East conflict through the conclusion of peace treaties based on Security Council resolutions 242 and 338 in all their parts. Their purpose is to achieve peace and good neighborly relations. They recognize that for peace to endure, it must involve all those who have been most deeply affected by the conflict. They therefore agree that this framework, as appropriate, is intended by them to constitute a basis for peace not only between Egypt and Israel, but also between Israel and each of its other neighbors which is prepared to negotiate peace with Israel on this basis. With that objective in mind, they have agreed to proceed as follows:

A. *West Bank and Gaza*

1. Egypt, Israel, Jordan and the representatives of the Palestinian people should participate in negotiations on the resolution of the Palestinian prob-

lem in all its aspects. To achieve that objective, negotiations relating to the West Bank and Gaza should proceed in three stages:

   a. Egypt and Israel agree that, in order to ensure a peaceful and orderly transfer of authority, and taking into account the security concerns of all the parties, there should be transitional arrangements for the West Bank and Gaza for a period not exceeding five years. In order to provide full autonomy to the inhabitants, under these arrangements the Israeli military government and its civilian administration will be withdrawn as soon as a self-governing authority has been freely elected by the inhabitants of these areas to replace the existing military government. To negotiate the details of a transitional arrangement, Jordan will be invited to join the negotiations on the basis of this framework. These new arrangements should give due consideration both to the principle of self-government by the inhabitants of these territories and to the legitimate security concerns of the parties involved.

   b. Egypt, Israel, and Jordan will agree on the modalities for establishing elected self-governing authority in the West Bank and Gaza. The delegations of Egypt and Jordan may include Palestinians from the West Bank and Gaza or other Palestinians as mutually agreed. The parties will negotiate an agreement which will define the powers and responsibilities of the self-governing authority to be exercised in the West Bank and Gaza. A withdrawal of Israeli armed forces will take place and there will be a redeployment of the remaining Israeli forces into specified security locations. The agreement will also include arrangements for assuring internal and external security and public order. A strong local police force will be established, which may include Jordanian citizens. In addition, Israeli and Jordanian forces will participate in joint patrols and in the manning of control posts to assure the security of the borders.

   c. When the self-governing authority (administrative council) in the West Bank and Gaza is established and inaugurated, the transitional period of five years will begin. As soon as possible, but not later than the third year after the beginning of the transitional period, negotiations will take place to determine the final status of the West Bank and Gaza and its relationship with its neighbors and to conclude a peace treaty between Israel and Jordan by the end of the transitional period. These negotiations will be conducted among Egypt, Israel, Jordan and the elected representatives of the inhabitants of the West Bank and Gaza. Two separate but related committees will be convened, one committee, consisting of representatives of the four parties which will negotiate and agree on the final status of the West Bank and Gaza, and its relationship with its neighbors, and the second committee, consisting of representatives of Israel and representatives of Jordan to be joined by the elected representatives of the inhabitants of the West Bank and Gaza, to negotiate the peace treaty between Israel and Jordan, taking into account the agreement reached in the final status of the West Bank and Gaza. The negotiations shall be based on all the provisions and principles of UN Security Council Resolution 242. The negotiations will resolve, among other matters, the location of the boundaries and the nature of the security arrangements. The solution from the negotiations must also recognize the legitimate right of the Palestinian peoples and their just requirements. In this way, the Palestinians will participate in the determination of their own future through:

i. The negotiations among Egypt, Israel, Jordan and the representatives of the inhabitants of the West Bank and Gaza to agree on the final status of the West Bank and Gaza and other outstanding issues by the end of the transitional period.

ii. Submitting their agreements to a vote by the elected representatives of the inhabitants of the West Bank and Gaza.

iii. Providing for the elected representatives of the inhabitants of the West Bank and Gaza to decide how they shall govern themselves consistent with the provisions of their agreement.

iv. Participating as stated above in the work of the committee negotiating the peace treaty between Israel and Jordan.

d. All necessary measures will be taken and provisions made to assure the security of Israel and its neighbors during the transitional period and beyond. To assist in providing such security, a strong local police force will be constituted by the self-governing authority. It will be composed of inhabitants of the West Bank and Gaza. The police will maintain liaison on internal security matters with the designated Israeli, Jordanian, and Egyptian officers.

e. During the transitional period, representatives of Egypt, Israel, Jordan, and the self-governing authority will constitute a continuing committee to decide by agreement on the modalities of admission of persons displaced from the West Bank and Gaza in 1967, together with necessary measures to prevent disruption and disorder. Other matters of common concern may also be dealt with by this committee.

f. Egypt and Israel will work with each other and with other interested parties to establish agreed procedures for a prompt, just and permanent implementation of the resolution of the refugee problem.

B. *Egypt-Israel*

1. Egypt-Israel undertake not to resort to the threat or the use of force to settle disputes. Any disputes shall be settled by peaceful means in accordance with the provisions of Article 33 of the U.N. Charter.

2. In order to achieve peace between them, the parties agree to negotiate in good faith with a goal of concluding within three months from the signing of the Framework a peace treaty between them while inviting the other parties to the conflict to proceed simultaneously to negotiate and conclude similar peace treaties with a view [of] the achieving a comprehensive peace in the area. The Framework for the Conclusion of a Peace Treaty between Egypt and Israel will govern the peace negotiations between them. The parties will agree on the modalities and the timetable for the implementation of their obligations under the treaty.

C. *Associated Principles*

1. Egypt and Israel state that the principles and provisions described below should apply to peace treaties between Israel and each of its neighbors—Egypt, Jordan, Syria and Lebanon.

2. Signatories shall establish among themselves relationships normal to states at peace with one another. To this end, they should undertake to abide by all the provisions of the U.N. Charter. Steps to be taken in this respect include:

    a. full recognition;
    b. abolishing economic boycotts;
    c. guaranteeing that under their jurisdiction the citizens of the other parties shall enjoy the protection of the due process of law.

3. Signatories should explore possibilities for economic development in the context of final peace treaties, with the objective of contributing to the atmosphere of peace, cooperation and friendship which is their common goal.

4. Claims commissions may be established for the mutual settlement of all financial claims.

5. The United States shall be invited to participate in the talks on matters related to the modalities of the implementation of the agreements and working out the timetable for the carrying out of the obligations of the parties.

6. The United Nations Security Council shall be requested to endorse the peace treaties and ensure that their provisions shall not be violated. The permanent members of the Security Council shall be requested to underwrite the peace treaties and ensure respect for the provisions. They shall be requested to conform their policies and actions with the undertaking contained in this Framework.

For the Government of Israel:
Menachem Begin

For the Government of
the Arab Republic of Egypt

Muhammed Anwar al-Sadat
Witnessed by
Jimmy Carter,
President of the United States of America

Framework for the Conclusion of a Peace Treaty between Egypt and Israel

In order to achieve peace between them, Israel and Egypt agree to negotiate in good faith with a goal of concluding within three months of the signing of this framework a peace treaty between them:

It is agreed that:

The site of the negotiations will be under a United Nations flag at a location or locations to be mutually agreed.

All of the principles of U.N. Resolution 242 will apply in this resolution of the dispute between Israel and Egypt.

Unless otherwise mutually agreed, terms of the peace treaty will be implemented between two and three years after the peace treaty is signed.

The following matters are agreed between the parties:

1. the full exercise of Egyptian sovereignty up to the internationally recognized border between Egypt and mandated Palestine;

2. the withdrawal of Israeli armed forces from the Sinai;

3. the use of airfields left by the Israelis near al-Arish, Rafah, Ras en-Naqb, and Sharm el-Sheikh for civilian purposes only, including possible commercial use only by all nations;

4. the right of free passage by ships of Israel through the Gulf of Suez and the Suez Canal on the basis of the Constantinople Convention of 1888 applying to all nations; the Strait of Tiran and Gulf of Aqaba are international waterways to be open to all nations for unimpeded and nonsuspendable freedom of navigation and overflight;

5. the construction of a highway between the Sinai and Jordan near Eilat with guaranteed free and peaceful passage by Egypt and Jordan; and

6. the stationing of military forces listed below.

Stationing of Forces

No more than one division (mechanized or infantry) of Egyptian armed forces will be stationed within an area lying approximately 50 km. (30 miles) east of the Gulf of Suez and the Suez Canal.

Only United Nations forces and civil police equipped with light weapons to perform normal police functions will be stationed within an area lying west of the international border and the Gulf of Aqaba, varying in width from 20 km. (12 miles) to 40 km. (24 miles).

In the area within 3 km. (1.8 miles) east of the international border there will be Israeli limited military forces not to exceed four infantry battalions and United Nations observers.

Border patrol units not to exceed three battalions will supplement the civil police in maintaining order in the area not included above.

The exact demarcation of the above areas will be as decided during the peace negotiations.

Early warning stations may exist to insure compliance with the terms of the agreement.

United Nations forces will be stationed:

1. in part of the area in the Sinai lying within about 20 km. of the Mediterranean Sea and adjacent to the international border, and

2. in the Sharm el-Sheikh area to insure freedom of passage through the Strait of Tiran; and these forces will not be removed unless such removal is approved by the Security Council of the United Nations with a unanimous vote of the five permanent members.

After a peace treaty is signed, and after the interim withdrawal is complete, normal relations will be established between Egypt and Israel, including full recognition, including diplomatic, economic and cultural relations; termination of economic boycotts and barriers to the free movement of goods and people; and mutual protection of citizens by the due process of law.

Interim Withdrawal

Between three months and nine months after the signing of the peace treaty, all Israeli forces will withdraw east of a line extending from a point east of El-Arish to Ras Muhammad, the exact location of this line to be determined by mutual agreement.

For the Government of
the Arab Republic of Egypt:
Muhammed Anwar al-Sadat

For the Government of Israel:
Menachem Begin

Witnessed by:
Jimmy Carter,
President of the United States of America

Annotated Bibliography

Many books have been written about the Arab-Israeli conflict and the emergence of the State of Israel. Below is a list of the books that have been most helpful in the preparation of this volume. These books contain detailed documentation of the patterns that have been described. An increasing number of Web sites, which, in turn, have a large number of links, could be useful for conducting additional research and for obtaining documentation of different perspectives on the current and historical patterns. These Web sites are listed at the end of this bibliography.

BOOKS

Aburish, Said K. *Cry Palestine: Inside the West Bank.* Boulder: Westview Press, 1993. This book contains a set of semi-journalistic accounts of the Palestinians on the West Bank during some of the more violent clashes between Palestinians and Israelis. These profiles convey the depths of feelings and the views of the people (and leaders) about the prospects of peace.

Alcalay, Ammiel. *Keys to the Garden: New Israeli Writing.* San Francisco: City Lights Books, 1996. This fascinating collection of twentieth-century Israeli literature focuses on writers born in, or whose origins are from, Middle Eastern countries, primarily Turkey, Iran, India, and the Arab world. Two dozen writers are presented whose short stories, essays, and poetry deal with the concerns of cultural and personal identity, gender, and political allegiances. The collection reveals the reflections of continuing but changing ethnic orientations among second-generation Israelis.

Al-Haj, Majid. *Education, Empowerment and Control: The Case of the Arabs in Israel.* Albany: State University of New York Press, 1995. This volume contains the best and most thorough examination of Arab-Israeli educational issues. Although it concentrates on core educational issues, it is grounded in a scholarly acquaintance with the general social science literature and with a sensitive understanding of the Arab-Israeli case. The critical but sensible view comes from one of the leading social scientists in Israel.

Azar, George Baramki. *Palestine: A Photographic Journey*. Berkeley: University of California Press, 1991. This impressive collection of photographs of Palestine and Palestinians illustrates some painful and vivid confrontations between Palestinians and Israelis. The photographs of the *intifada* are extraordinary.

Azmon Yael, and Dana Israeli, eds. *Women in Israel*. New Brunswick, N.J.: Transaction Press, 1993. This systematic collection of social scientific analyses of the role of women in Israeli society covers the fundamental issues of gender differences and gender inequalities in all the major spheres of social life.

Benvinisti, Meron. *City of Stone: The Hidden History of Jerusalem*. Berkeley: University of California Press, 1999. One of the most comprehensive books about Jerusalem, written by a former deputy mayor, *City of Stone* details the expansion of Jerusalem since 1967, with comparisons to the 1948 period. Some of the fundamental difficulties that involve the separation of Jews and Arabs in a united city are outlined. Jerusalem remains "holy" to Palestinians and Jews, and it is one of the core arenas of political debate about the role of Jerusalem in the future of a Palestinian state and in Israel.

Esco Foundation for Palestine. *Palestine: A Study of Jewish, Arab and British Policies*, 2 vols. New Haven, Conn.: Yale University Press, 1947. This comprehensive, two-volume source on the complexities of policies articulated during the British mandate period provides extraordinarily rich detail on the views of the various participants to the processes that led up to the establishment of the State of Israel. The focus is on policies, but the details illustrate the arguments that remain at the center of the Arab-Israeli conflict over a half a century later.

Gluck, Sherna Berger. *An American Feminist in Palestine: The Intifada Years*. Philadelphia: Temple University Press, 1994. This volume is the personal odyssey of an American feminist who visited Gaza, the West Bank, and Jerusalem. The perspective is an important balance to the male-dominated accounts of the *intifada*. The author conveys some of the frustrations and pains of the Israeli occupation through the eyes of women organizers and peace activists. A strong sense of Israeli injustice is conveyed, and a romanticized view of the women who have been active in supporting the Palestinian uprising is presented. It is not a balanced presentation on its own, but it does offer an interesting portrayal of a perspective often absent in other journalistic accounts.

Goldscheider, Calvin. *Israel's Changing Society: Population, Ethnicity and Development*. Boulder, Colo.: Westview Press, 1996. This basic sociological and demographic view of the emergence of Israeli society and its patterns of family, social class, and ethnic transformations emphasizes population and ethnic issues among the Israeli-Jewish population and the Israeli-Arab communities. It focuses on local communities, women, and inequality over the first fifty years of Israel's development.

Grossman, David. *Sleeping on a Wire: Conversations with Palestinians in Israel*. New York: Farrar, Straus and Giroux, 1993. Grossman, a writer and a journalist, presents an insightful set of portraits of Israeli Arabs and the issues of their relationship to the State of Israel and to nonresident Palestinians. This volume is well written with passion and insight.

Herzog, Hanna. *Gendering Politics: Women in Israel.* Ann Arbor: University of Michigan Press, 1999. This book is the most up-to-date analysis of the role of women in politics in Israel. This thorough and scholarly examination brings to bear the latest in political and social analysis with a focus on the gender issue. It reveals much about the ideology and the political issues in Israel.

Kimmerling, Baruch, and Joel Migdal. *Palestinians: The Making of a People.* New York: Free Press, 1993. The most authoritative political and social history of the Palestinians, *Palestinians* anchors the analysis in rich historical detail starting with the Arab revolt in the middle of the nineteenth century against Ottoman control of Palestine through the emergence of Zionism in Europe and its impact on Palestine. The volume brings together and organizes in a balanced way the issues through the dispersal of Palestinians in the 1948 war and in the more recent period. Scholarly and thoughtful, it is a classic in the understanding of the Palestinian issue.

Lesch, Ann, and Dan Tschirgi. *Origins and Development of the Arab-Israeli Conflict.* Westport, Conn.: Greenwood Press, 1998. This volume, which appears in the Greenwood Press Guides to Historic Events in the Twentieth Century, focuses on the historic origin of the Arab-Israeli conflict with particular attention given to political issues and the role of the United States in the conflict.

Lukacs, Yehuda. *The Israeli-Palestinian Conflict: A Documentary Record, 1967–1990.* Cambridge, England: Cambridge University Press, 1992. The basic documents of the Arab-Israeli conflict are presented with an emphasis on formal documents and political issues. It represents a good set of reference materials.

Mandel, Neville. *The Arabs and Zionism before World War I.* Berkeley: University of California Press, 1976. This book remains one of the most engaging and authoritative historical research accounts of the Arabs and Zionism before World War I. It argues for the Arab awareness of the threats of Zionism and the political measures taken by them to counteract Zionism early in Palestine.

Moore, John Norton, ed. *The Arab-Israeli Conflict,* 3 vols. Princeton, N.J.: Princeton University Press, 1974. These volumes include an extensive and rich collection of materials, readings, and documents on the Arab-Israeli conflict. There is a particular focus on international legal issues and alternatives for a peaceful settlement. This is the authoritative treatment on the history and development of the legal aspects of the conflict. Interesting in large part for documenting the earlier proposed solutions to the conflict, it can serve as a basis for comparisons with the more recent period.

Pappé, Ilan, ed. *The Israel/Palestine Question.* London: Routledge, 1999. This collection of historical essays focuses on the "new" history of the Palestinians, placing them in the broader context of the history of the Ottoman and British periods. The essays reconsider the origins of Zionism, the details of the 1948 war and the exodus of Palestinians, and the *intifada*. The critical historical essays are based on new and thorough scholarship and debates in Israel. This is a challenging and provocative set of readings.

Peretz, Don. *Intifada: The Palestinian Uprising.* Boulder, Colo.: Westview Press,

1990. This book presents a detailed coverage of the Palestinian uprising, the *intifada*, in its multidimensional forms. The author outlines the origins and the role of Israeli policies and shows their impact on the territories as well as on Israeli society and the international repercussions.

Ramras-Rauch, Gila. *The Arab in Israeli Literature*. Bloomington: Indiana University Press, 1989. The interrelationship of Arabs and Jews within Palestine and in the State of Israel is reflected in their literary expressions, novels, and short stories. In this interesting and scholarly presentation, over a dozen Israeli writers are examined in their cultural contexts. The changing and diverse views of Arabs in this literature are also examined. The image of the Arab in the eyes of Hebrew and Israeli writers is reviewed from the turn of the century until the 1980s. The author shows the growing importance of this image in Israeli fiction.

Slapikoof, Saul. *Consider and Hear Me: Voices from Palestine and Israel*. Philadelphia: Temple University Press, 1993. This volume presents profiles of people and their perspectives in Israel and Palestine. The voices represent a selective exposure to Palestinians and Israelis with a strong bias toward those involved in the peace movement. The volume is interesting and provocative for the presentation of some of the voices critical of government efforts, focusing on some of the leadership of Palestinians and those on the margins of Israeli society.

Smooha, Sammy. *Arabs and Jews in Israel*, vols. 1 and 2. Boulder, Colo.: Westview Press, 1989, 1991. These two volumes present the rich details of several surveys of Israeli Arabs on a wide range of political, social, and economic issues. These opinion polls present for the first time the basis for understanding Israeli Arabs from their own point of view. Questions about their relationship to political and cultural identity and to the Palestinian issues form the core of these excellent reference volumes. Rich statistical details are placed in a helpful set of alternative theories and descriptions. It is accessible and fundamental for understanding Israeli Arabs.

Wallach, John, and Janet Wallach. *Still Small Voices*. San Diego: Harcourt Brace Jovanovich, 1989. This collection of portraits of persons living on the West Bank and in Gaza is written by two journalists. Concerned mostly with the elite and leaders, the volume conveys some of the political, cultural, and religious differences between Palestinians and Jewish settlers. Helpful notes appear throughout. Most of the reportage is through the voices of the journalists rather than directly through the participants themselves.

WEB SITES

http://www.cbs.gov.il/engindex.htm. The Web site of the Central Bureau of Statistics of Israel contains a rich array of systematic statistics on Israel. Check further under their *Statistical Abstract* for detailed statistical information as well as their monthly *Bulletin of Statistics* for up-to-date information.

http://www.israel-mfa.gov.il/mfa/go.asp?MFAH00pq0. This site contains detailed political documents starting with the Balfour Declaration up to the most recent documents associated with the peace process. Related to this site is *http://www.israel-mfa.gov.il/mfa/home.asp*, the Web site of the Ministry of Foreign Affairs of Israel. Formal documents and detailed government information are included.

http://www.knesset.gov.il/knesset/engframe.htm. This is a major source of information on the Israeli Knesset, its history and current political makeup. A variety of Israeli government links are connected to this site.

http://www.assr.org/vlibrary/source.html. This is the Web site for Arab Social Science Research. There are interesting links to journals, governments, libraries, courses, and universities.

http://www.arab.net/palestine/palestine_contents.html. This is an important Web site for Palestine-related materials. There are links to history, government, and geography and other Palestine-related Web sites.

http://www.palestine-net.com/. This is a major Web site for a wide range of current and historical links with Palestinian-oriented materials.

Index

Administered territories, 83–84, 88–89, 97–99; and Arab Israelis, 83, 84, 88–89; and settlers, 97–101
Aging, 26–28
Akko, 70, 163
Algeria, 115
al-Nakba, 17, 147
American Jews, 105, 107–111
Arab Israelis: and administered territories, 83, 84, 88–89; and agriculture, 74, 76–77; and Balfour Declaration, 60–61; birth rates, 23, 68; and British, 6–9, 61–63; Christian, 65; defined, 21, 57, 59, 65; and democracy, 83; demography of, 20–25, 59, 63–68; and dependency, 65, 75–76, 79, 96; discrimination, 65; economy of, 75–79; education of, 80–83; and ethnicity 112; family, 72–76; fertility of, 23, 64, 68, 71–76; and gender, 72–76; and immigration, 6–9. 15–17, 18, 37, 38, 49, 50, 56–57, 95; and inequality, 64; internal migration of, 61–62, 71–76; mortality of, 68, 71, 74; national identity of, 82–85; and Palestinians, 59, 71, 84, 87, 96–97, 110–111; and policies, 82–85; population growth of, 59–62; refugees, 9, 24; regional variation, 70; religion, 65; residential concentration, 10, 76–80; urbanization, 76–80; voices of, 66–68, 164–165, 175–179; women, 72–76; work, 66–68, 78–79
Ashkenasim, 10, 23, 56, 124. *See also* Ethnicity

Balfour Declaration, 6–7, 57, 60–61
Barak, Ehud, 48, 117
Ben Gurion, 117
Birth rates, 23–24, 91–92, 112–113; and Arab Israelis, 23, 68, 71–76; and Palestinians, 91–92. *See also* Fertility
British mandate, 3, 6–9, 19, 49, 61–63

Colonialism, 4, 15
Cyprus, 8–9

Daroushe, Mohammed, 81–82
Death rates. *See* Mortality
Democracy, 83
Demography, 20–28; age and sex, 26–28; of Arab Israelis, 59–62, 63–68; and colonialism, 15; comparative, 25–27; and economic development, 21–31, 37–39; and economic dependency, 36–37; and economic measures, 31–34; and educational change, 34–36; and ethnicity, 39–40, 112; and immigration, 20–21, 23–24, 38–41; and inequalities, 26; and nation building, 14–18, 20–25; and Palestinians, 88–91; pyramids, 26–28; and residential concentration, 21; and standard of living, 36; unique, 25–29; and Zionism, 27–28, 37–39, 100–101. *See also* Birth rates; Fertility; Immigration; Migration; Mortality
Diaspora, Jewish, 87–88, 101–106; Palestinian, 87–97
Discrimination, 65, 113
Druze, 23, 65

Eastern Europe, 4
Economic dependency, 36–37
Economic development, 19–20, 29–37, 91–94
Education, 32, 34–35, 45; and Arab Israelis, 35, 75–79; and employment, 34–36
Efrat, 142–145
Egypt, 11, 45, 127
Employment and education, 34–36
Ethiopia, 46
Ethnic democracy, 83

Ethnicity, 111–116, 123–137; and Arab Israelis, 112; definition, 56; and demography, 39–40, 112; and discrimination, 113; and economic development, 21–31, 37–39; and education, 113; and family formation, 28; and fertility, 112–113; and health, 112–113; and immigration, 39–43, 46–47, 50–53; and migration, 112; and mortality, 112–113; and nationalism, 111–116; and residential concentration, 112–114; and urbanization, 112; and Zionism, 114–115

Family, 25, 27–28, 72–76
Fertility, and Arab Israelis, 23, 64, 68, 71–76; changes in, 23–24; and ethnicity, 112–113; and immigration, 23–24; and Palestinians, 91–92
Foreign workers, 93
Fundamentalist, 180

Gaza, 11, 21, 46, 50, 87, 88. *See also* Administered territories
Gender, 72–76
Germany, 37
Golah 87–88, 101–106. *See also* Diaspora, Jewish
Golan Heights, 11, 46, 117
Gush Emunim, 98

Haifa, 23, 26, 163
Health, 91–92, 112–113
Hebrew, 44–45
Hebron, 3, 180–191
Herzl, Theodor, 5
Hitler, Adolf, 7
Holocaust, 9, 37, 40, 44, 45, 108, 114
Homeland, 163

Immigration, 39–49; American, 45–47, 102; and Arab Israelis, 6–9, 15–18, 37–38, 49–50; and British Mandate, 6–9, 19, 49; and colonialism, 4, 15; consequences of, 49–53; and economic growth, 29–30; Ethiopian, 46–47; and ethnicity, 39–43, 46–47, 50–53; and fertility, 23–24; and geographic distribution, 26; illegal, 8; mass, 41, 44–45; and nation-building, 10–11, 39–43; North African, 44–46; official view of, 14–15, 55–56; and Ottoman government, 4–6; to Palestine, 3–9; and Palestinians, 95–96; and population growth, 3–9, 49–50; post-1967, 45–47; Russian, 6, 11, 46–49, 54–55, 102, 103, 106, 117; western, 45–47; and Zionism, 4–6, 39–43, 48

Independence Day, 114
Indian Jewish, 127–137
Industry, 33–34
Intifada, 11, 93, 116, 163
Iran, 45
Iraq, 45, 52, 102
Italy, 32

Japan, 32
Jericho, 11, 21, 87, 88
Jerusalem, 3, 23, 26, 89, 100, 101
Jewish Agency, 61–62
Jordan, 11
Judaism, 105–110
Judea and Samaria, 21, 89, 99, 100. *See also* Administered territories

Kibbutz(im), 6, 98–99
King Solomon, 118
Klita (immigrant absorption), 55
Korea, 33

Labor Party, 11
Land Day, 16, 163
Law of Return, 53, 106
Lebanon, 11
Libya, 45
Life expectancy. *See* Mortality
Likud, 11, 89
Lod, 163

Marriage, 28
Meir, Golda, 139
Migration (internal): and Arab Israelis, 61–62, 71–76; and ethnicity, 112
Mishna, 118
Morocco, 45, 52, 127
Mortality, 23, 25; and Arab Israelis, 68, 71, 74; and ethnicity, 112–113; and Palestinians, 91–92
Moshav(im), 99

Nationalism, Arab, 6–9, 82–85
Nationalism, Jewish, 6–9, 111–116. *See also* Zionism
Nation building, 13–18; Arab perspectives, 15–17; and demography, 14, 18, 20–25; and economic development, 19–20; and immigration, 10–11, 39–43; Jewish perspectives, 14–18; and politics, 15, 18–19
Nazism, 7
Netanyahu, Benjamin, 48, 117
North Africa, 44–46

Occupation, 33–34, 93–95
Ottoman Empire, 4–6

Palestinians: and administered territories, 88–89, 97–98; and Arab Israelis, 59, 71, 84, 87, 96–97, 110–111; birth rates of, 91–92; defined, 21; demography of, 88–

91; dependency of, 96; and Diaspora, 87–97; economy of, 91–94; education of, 95; fertility of, 91–92; health of, 91–92; identity of, 87, 96; and immigration, 95–96; and inequality, 94; mortality of, 91–92; national identity of, 96–97, and natural increase, 90–91; and occupation, 93–95; population growth of, 90; residential segregation of, 99–100; voices of, 147–162, 166–175
Passover, 16, 114
Peel Commission, 62–63
Pogrom, 123
Poland, 7, 115
Population. *See* Demography

Refugees, Jewish, 8–9, 40, 44
Refugees, Palestinian, 9, 24, 119
Religion, 105–107, 109–110
Residential concentration, 25; of Arab Israelis, 10, 77–78, 80; and ethnicity, 112–114; and Palestinians, 99–100
Romania, 40, 45, 115
Russia, 6, 11, 46–49, 54–55, 102–103, 106, 117

Safed, 3
Sephardim, 10, 23, 45, 56, 124
Settlers, Jewish, 11–12, 89, 97–101, 119, 142–145, 180–191; and population growth, 100–101; and Zionism, 98, 100
Social class, 112–114
Standard of living, 36
Syria, 11

Taiwan, 33
Tel Aviv, 23, 26, 70, 100

Tiberias, 3
Tunisia, 45, 52, 115

United Nations, 9
United States, 4, 7; Jews in, 105, 107–111
Urbanization, 25; and Arab Israelis, 76–80; and ethnicity, 112; and Zionism, 114–115

Voices: of Arab Israelis, 66–68, 164–165, 175–179; of Eastern European Jews, 141–142; of Ethnic Jews, 123–127; of German origin Jews, 139–141; of Indian Jews, 127–137; of Jewish Israelis, 127–137, 139–146; of Jewish Settlers, 142–145, 180–191; of Palestinians, 147–162, 166–175; of Russian Jews, 54–55

War, of Independence, 9; Six Day (1967), 11, 45–46, 103; World I, 6; World II, 9; Yom Kippur (1973), 11
Weizmann, Chaim, 85
West Bank. *See* Administered territories
Work, 66–68

Yemen, 52, 102
Yiddish, 44, 108–109
Yishuv, 4–9, 38

Zichron Yaakov, 163
Zionism, 37–38; and demography, 27–28, 37–39, 100–101; and ethnicity, 114–115; and immigration, 4–6, 39–43, 48; and settlers, 98, 100; and urbanization, 114–115

About the Author

CALVIN GOLDSCHEIDER holds a joint appointment as Professor of Sociology and Ungerleider Professor of Judaic Studies at Brown University.